Ethical and Legal
Issues
for Mental Health
Professionals

Ethical and Legal Issues for Mental Health Professionals
in Forensic Settings

Steven F. Bucky
Joanne E. Callan
George Stricker
Editors

Sylvie P. Marques, Assistant Editor

Routledge
Taylor & Francis Group
New York   London

Routledge
Taylor & Francis Group
270 Madison Avenue
New York, NY 10016

Routledge
Taylor & Francis Group
2 Park Square
Milton Park, Abingdon
Oxon OX14 4RN

© 2009 by Taylor & Francis Group, LLC
Routledge is an imprint of Taylor & Francis Group, an Informa business

Printed in the United States of America on acid-free paper
10 9 8 7 6 5 4 3 2 1

International Standard Book Number-13: 978-0-7890-3816-6 (Hardcover) 978-0-7890-3817-3 (Softcover)

Library of Congress Cataloging-in-Publication Data

Ethical and legal issues for mental health professionals : in forensic settings / Steven
      F. Bucky, Joanne E. Callan, George Stricker, editors ; Sylvie P. Marques, assistant
      editor.
        p. ; cm.
      Includes bibliographical references and index.
      ISBN 978-0-7890-3816-6 (hardback : alk. paper) -- ISBN 978-0-7890-3817-3 (pbk. :
      alk. paper)
        1. Mental health personnel--Professional ethics--United States. 2. Mental health
      services--Legal status, laws, etc.--United States. 3. Forensic psychiatry--United States.
      I. Bucky, Steven F.
        [DNLM: 1. Mental Health Services--ethics--United States. 2. Mental
      Health Services--legislation & jurisprudence--United States. 3. Forensic
      Psychiatry--ethics--United States. 4. Forensic Psychiatry--legislation &
      jurisprudence--United States. WM 62 E822 2009]

RC455.2.E8E823 2009
174.2--dc22   2008041602

Visit the Taylor & Francis Web site at
http://www.taylorandfrancis.com

and the Routledge Web site at
http://www.routledge.com

Contents

Contents

Acknowledgments

I would like to take this opportunity to express my sincere appreciation and thank the coeditors, Dr. Joanne Callan and Dr. George Stricker, who were involved in the development, organization, writing, and editing of the manuscript; and to thank our exceptional editing assistants: Sylvie Marques, PhD, and Jennifer Zellner, PhD, who worked hard with professionalism, enthusiasm, and competence.

I would also like to thank my family, including my sons Scott, Keith, and Rob; my daughters-in-law Marvelynn, Jennifer, and Candice; my grandchildren Brooklynn, Madison, Joshua, Braden, and "peanut" (who at the time of this printing was not born). I give special thanks to my loving wife and best friend of 39 years, Marilyn, who has been unconditionally accepting and supportive of my professional responsibilities and whose guidance, love, and support have been invaluable in my life.

Editors

Steven Bucky, PhD, received his doctorate in clinical psychology at the University of Cincinnati in 1970. Since 1972, he has been at the California School of Professional Psychology at Alliant International University in San Diego as a full professor, the director of professional training, and chair of the Ethics Committee and has taught the advanced ethics course. Dr. Bucky is also in private practice that focuses on children, adolescents, and families; substance abuse; forensics; and the assessment and treatment of professional and college athletes.

Joanne E. Callan, PhD, received her doctorate in 1970 from the University of Texas at Austin. She is a distinguished professor in clinical psychology at the California School of Professional Psychology, Alliant International University as well as associate clinical professor in the Department of Psychiatry, University of California San Diego, and a training and supervising analyst at the San Diego Psychoanalytic Society and Institute. Formerly executive director of the American Psychological Association's Education Directorate, she has a private practice in psychology and psychoanalysis.

George Stricker, PhD, is professor of psychology at Argosy University, Washington, D.C. campus. He received the American Psychological Association award for Distinguished Contribution to Applied Psychology in 1990 and for Distinguished Career Contributions to Education and Training in Psychology in 1995. Dr. Stricker is the author or editor of approximately 20 books, 30 book chapters, and more than 100 journal articles.

Assistant Editor

Sylvie P. Marques, PhD, holds a doctorate in clinical psychology. She has served as a therapist at San Diego State University, University of San Diego (UCSD), and the Preuss School at UCSD. She has worked with autistic children, in an inpatient setting for adults in psychiatric crisis, and at a specialized school setting for children and adolescents. Dr. Marques is an adjunct professor teaching college-level course work within the psychology discipline. Dr. Marques's family immigrated to the United States from Portugal, and Portuguese is her first language.

1

Introduction

Steven F. Bucky

This is a companion volume to the editors' earlier handbook, focusing as did its predecessor on the integration of ethical, legal, and clinical issues for mental health professionals (MHPs). It was written for practicing clinicians who increasingly find themselves in processes that involve the legal system. The goal of this volume is to help the clinician integrate ethical, legal, and clinical material as it relates to forensic settings and processes.

It is worth noting that forensic issues are of increasing interest to new students committed to becoming licensed MHPs. For example, incoming students at the first editor's institution, the California School of Professional Psychology at Alliant International University, frequently ask for special training practica, internships, and supervision on forensic issues. These issues are also clearly of interest to students at Alliant's other campuses, where a relatively new Forensic Center has been established.

MHPs are generally held to a very high standard when involved in the legal process; thus, skill in courtroom processes is required, and attention to relevant ethical issues is of particular importance for MHPs who are associated with the forensic arena. There is also increased vulnerability to ethics and licensing board complaints and civil lawsuits. For example, the fastest-growing type of licensing board complaint is against MHPs who are professionally involved in child custody evaluations (see Gold, chapter 6 in this volume).

The goal of this book is to keep current with legal and ethical guidelines and principles, especially in light of recent revisions to ethics codes and changes to statutes and legal precedents (e.g., the extension of the Tarasoff ruling as a result of *Ewing v. Goldstein*, an appeals case decided in 2004). The reader should bear in mind that a code of ethics applies to all members of a particular professional organization (e.g., American Psychological Association, American Association for Marriage and Family Therapy, National Association of Social Workers), and that laws and forensic practices are specific to geographic locations. To function competently, the MHP must integrate rules, regulations, laws, and guidelines and apply them in cautious, justifiable, and legally and ethically sound ways in the courtroom. The quality of professional judgments and professional practices and the perception of objectivity, fairness, and balance are high priorities in clinical practice in general and are of even greater importance in the MHP's forensic activities. Additional principles worth noting include such issues as basing decisions on the scientific foundations of the profession and arriving at judgments and recommendations that are clearly described and supported by the evidence and research.

The Organization of This Volume

This volume is organized in three parts. Part I addresses issues that are specific to court situations. In chapter 2, Donald Bersoff describes the nature and purpose of depositions. Depositions are seen as part of the discovery process that helps to determine the outcome of the action that has been brought. Oral depositions are described, and specific advice is given as to how best to approach a deposition. In chapter 3, David Stein addresses the role of psychologists involved in personal injury litigation. Issues related to assessment, interpretation, and report writing are discussed, and trial preparation, testimony, and posttrial considerations are outlined. Pamela Thatcher then discusses specific aspects of preparation and testimony for psychologists who are called to testify as a percipient witness or an expert witness (see chapter 4).

Part II of the book addresses issues that are related to forensic assessments and techniques. In chapter 5, Arthur Wiens and Reed Mueller describe how to complete and use a psychological evaluation in an ethical and socially responsible manner and suggest strategies for minimizing the probability of ethical violations. In chapter 6, already touched on, Russ Gold addresses issues commonly at the center of lawsuits and formal complaints arising out of child custody work. The evaluation process in child custody cases is discussed, with special attention placed on the need to maintain objectivity throughout the evaluation process by asserting appropriate boundaries. Margaret Lee then discusses acting as a special master in high-conflict postdivorce child custody cases (see chapter 7). In chapter 8, Richard Romanoff describes conducting criminal forensic evaluations and the ethical considerations in performing these assessments.

Part III of the book addresses issues that are specific to mental health professionals and litigation. In chapter 9, O. Brandt Caudill discusses the various forms of litigation that mental health professionals may find themselves facing and how these different types of litigation can be quantified. Margaret Bogie and Eric Marine describe the life cycle of a professional liability claim, historical claims data, and future trends in professional liability litigation and their expected impact on claims (see chapter 10). In chapter 11, Constance Dalenberg, Eve Carlson, and O. Brandt Caudill discuss the acceptance or lack of acceptance regarding the existence of recovered memories and the recovered memory experience and accuracy, emphasizing the importance of an unbiased assessment. Finally, Julia Ramos Grenier and Muriel Golub discuss the ethics complaint procedure for the American Psychological Association and the structure and functioning of a state ethics committee (see chapter 12).

Reference

Ewing v. Goldstein, 120 Cal. App. 4th 807 (2004).

Section I

The Mental Health Professional and the Legal System: Court Situations

The first part of this book takes up a variety of issues related to the mental health professional's interactions with the legal system, concluding with the various court situations that can occur for the practitioner. More specifically, depositions, personal injury cases, and preparation for court testimony are described in detail. Although depositions can take many forms, only oral depositions are discussed. Specific advice is given regarding how best to approach a deposition. In personal injury cases, psychologists may be called as consultants, experts, or percipient witnesses, the last because of an ongoing relationship with the client. Examples are given of appropriate behavior in each of those roles. A mental health professional called to testify may function as a percipient witness or as an expert witness. Differences between depositions and trial testimony are described. Consultation with the attorney is an important part of preparation for testimony, and specific aspects of preparation and testimony are described.

2

Depositions
Discovery, Procedures, and Practice Pointers

Donald N. Bersoff

Introduction

Litigation and trials are not synonymous. It is unlikely that a civil case filed in a federal or state court will be heard in a trial setting.[1] The case may be dismissed early on for technical legal reasons (e.g., the case was brought in the wrong jurisdiction) or because the plaintiff made a claim the law does not recognize. If the case survives such early challenges, the judge can still render a decision without a trial (i.e., summary judgment) if the court concludes that both sides agree to the central facts and the case can be decided as a matter of law. And, of course, a case may be ended before trial if the opposing parties decide that a settlement is in their best interests.

The vehicle that helps determine whether a civil case should go to trial or be terminated sooner is the process of "discovery."[2] Every state government and the federal government have developed rules for engaging in, controlling, and enforcing discovery in civil litigation.[3]

Nature and Purposes of Depositions

Civil trials are specifically designed to avoid surprise. Before trial, each side is entitled to know almost everything about the other side's case, both its strengths and its weaknesses. That knowledge is gleaned through discovery. There are at least seven methods for obtaining discovery: (a) oral depositions; (b) written depositions; (c) written interrogatories (i.e., questions propounded by the other side that must be answered in writing by the parties to whom they are addressed); (d) requests for the production of documents or things; (e) requests for permission to enter on land or property; (f) requests for a physical or mental examination of parties; and (g) request for admissions. This chapter is limited to a discussion of oral depositions, a process in which attorneys for one of the parties interrogates under oath potential witnesses, including expert witnesses, who may testify for the opposing parties.

The overarching purposes of an oral deposition can perhaps be best characterized as defensive and offensive (Suplee & Donaldson, 1988). From a defensive perspective, the opposition uses the deposition to fully educate itself about the other side's case, asking more and more detailed questions "to squeeze the witness dry of all relevant information" (Suplee, 1982, p. 266). In this way, the experienced interrogator learns all the opposing witnesses know and, in the case of experts, what their opinions will be and what facts they have relied on to arrive at those opinions. This legitimate search for evidence permits the attorney to evaluate\the strengths and weaknesses of the respective positions of the parties, seek a settlement if that appears warranted from the deposition testimony, or be better able to confront and counter the deponents' testimony should the case ever come to trial. In addition, should one or more of the witnesses whose depositions have been taken become unavailable through death, illness, or unavoidable scheduling conflicts, the deponents' testimony is preserved, and relevant portions of the deposition may be read at trial.

From an offensive perspective, the opposition seeks to use deposition testimony against the witness at trial. Because depositions are taken under oath, they can be powerful weapons for attacking the credibility and reliability of witnesses, particularly when statements they make during the deposition are at odds with statements made during trial. Witnesses can then be confronted during cross-examination by this conflicting testimony. Similarly, opposing attorneys can use depositions to create conflicts at trial between deponents' testimony and that of other experts or witnesses. Finally, the deposition may be used to support a motion for summary judgment if all the testimony discloses that there are no material factual issues in dispute.

The Scope of Discovery

The scope of discovery, including depositions, is very broad. Most of the rules of evidence that control the introduction of evidence in a courtroom do not pertain during a deposition. In trial, only relevant evidence testified to by a competent witness and otherwise comporting with the rules of evidence is admissible. Evidence is relevant if a logical connection exists between the evidence and the proposition for which it is offered, that is, if it has the tendency to make the existence of a material fact more probable or less probable than it would be without the evidence.

Under the *Federal Rules of Civil Procedure* (1996), information may be acquired during discovery that does not necessarily conform to the rules of evidence that control at trial:

> Parties may obtain discovery regarding any nonpriviledged matter that is relevant to the claim or defense of any party–including the existence, description, nature, custody, condition, and location of any books, documents, or other tangible things and the identity and location of persons having knowledge of any discoverable matter. For good cause, the court may order discovery of any matter relevant to the subject matter involved in the action. *Relevant information need not be admissible at trial if the discovery appears reasonably calculated to lead to the discovery of admissible evidence.* Rule 26(b), pp. 144–145. (emphasis added)

Because of the breadth of discovery, interrogators can ask deponents questions in a deposition they could not in a courtroom. Such questions can include inquiries about personal matters or about statements that would fall within the proscription of the hearsay rule in court.[4] Although some of these questions may be objected to and forbidden if asked at trial, it may be perfectly permissible to ask them in a deposition and to require the deponent to respond.

Deposition Procedures

Although they are legal proceedings and conducted in conformity with formal rules of procedure, depositions do not take place in courtrooms. They are almost always held in the offices of the opposing lawyer,[5] although some state courts require that depositions be held at the local courthouse. Those who attend depositions include the person whose deposition is being taken (e.g., an expert witness or one of the parties to the suit) and the attorney who is conducting the deposition, as well as lawyers for all the parties in the lawsuit, the parties themselves if they so wish, a notary public, and a court reporter who records the entire deposition verbatim, although the last two roles are usually filled by the same person.

Depositions are scheduled by serving notice on the intended deponent [*Federal Rules*, 1996, Rule 30(b)(1), pp. 72–73]. Such notice must include not only the name and address of the deponent but also the date, time, and place of the deposition as well as the method by which the testimony will be recorded [Rule 30(b)(2), p. 73]. If the deponent is a party to the litigation, serving the notice is enough to require compliance. If the deponent is not a party but, for example, an expert, the notice is accompanied by a subpoena ordering the deponent's presence. The notice may be attached to a *subpoena duces tecum,* which is essentially a request that certain documents designated in the subpoena be produced at the deposition. For example, an expert who will be deposed may be asked to bring a copy of his or her curriculum vitae, the test protocols completed by the party/patient, and notes taken during the patient's psychological assessment or therapy.

In the typical deposition, the attendees sit around a conference table. The deponent and his or her attorney sit on one side of the long edge of the table and the opposing attorney on the other side, with the court reporter in the middle, at the short end of the table. The parties, if they attend, sit with their respective representatives. Neither the judge who may ultimately hear the case nor a jury is at the deposition.

The atmosphere at a deposition is deceptively informal. The law firm at whose offices the deposition is taken will supply coffee and soft drinks, and the lawyers may engage in what looks like collegial banter. Everything that the deponent says, however, even in a light moment, in the restroom, or during a break may find itself eventually recorded in the transcript of the deposition, to the horror and chagrin of the unwary deponent. Take the following example: An expert witness who is being deposed finds himself in the men's room with the opposing attorney. At the wash basin, the expert offhandedly remarks that he wishes he was as positive about his opinion as he was told to sound during his deposition testimony. The attorney makes some jocular rejoinder, but when he gets back to the conference table and the deposition proper is resumed, the lawyer asks the expert to repeat for the stenographic, sworn record what he said in the men's room about the strength of his opinion. Thus, it is often a crucial mistake for the deponent to treat the deposition frivolously. Depositions are often of consequential, if not vital, significance. They are considered the most important of all the pretrial discovery mechanisms, and despite the apparent demeanor of the actors, depositions should be accorded the utmost solemnity.

The first formal event that occurs at a deposition is the taking of the oath, administered by the notary public/court reporter. This ritual serves to solemnize the proceeding. The examination by opposing counsel then begins. Depositions are most usually recorded stenographically by a court reporter, but at the instigation of the party taking the deposition, it may be recorded by audiotape or videotape. In those cases, however, the federal rules warn that the appearance or demeanor of the deponents or attorneys cannot be distorted through audio or videotaping (*Federal Rules*, 1996, Rule 30[b][4], p. 73).

Deponents are required to answer all questions, even those they may consider objectionable or intrusive. The lawyer representing the deponent may have a legitimate cause to object if a particular question were asked at trial, but given the broad scope of discovery and the different evidentiary rules that govern it, there are many fewer bases for objecting to the opponent's questions. The attorney representing the deponent may lodge objections for the record and at times may be compelled to object if he or she wishes to preclude the use of inadmissible testimony at trial. Nevertheless, the deponent must answer the question during the deposition.

There are times when the lawyer representing the deponent will instruct the deponent not to answer, but that occurs infrequently. Certain testimony may be protected by one of the recognized privileges (e.g., attorney-client or psychotherapist-patient), and such testimony is not admissible even at depositions. The deponent in that situation should follow the lawyer's advice and not answer. On very rare occasions, on motion of the deponent's representative and on a court order, a deposition may be terminated if the court finds that the deposition is being conducted in bad faith or in such a manner as to annoy, embarrass, or oppress the deponent or the party (*Federal Rules*, 1996, Rule 30[d][3]).[6]

After the deposition is complete, the court reporter usually has up to 30 days to complete the transcription, although with more computerized technology being used to record depositions, they can be transcribed overnight and, with increasing frequency, recorded and transcribed simultaneously. If requested by the deponent or a party prior to the completion of the deposition, the transcript can then be reviewed by the deponent and the attorney representing the deponent.

There is a form allowing the deponent to correct errors in the transcription. After review, the deponent is required to sign the transcript.[7] Deponents should read these transcripts carefully because once they are signed they become official court documents that can be relied on at trial. It is not unusual for a court reporter to leave out a simple but crucial word like "not" from a statement. For example, a deponent may have said, "It is my opinion that the defendant is not fit to be the custodial parent," but it was recorded as "the defendant is fit to be the custodial parent." The need to make a correction in this case is obvious.

A deponent also has the discretion to make substantive changes in the transcript as well as correct typographical errors. In that case, however, there is a risk that the examining attorney will reopen the deposition and question the deponent further about the substantive amendments.

Practice Pointers

Psychologists who are notified that they will become deponents, whether as fact witnesses, parties, or expert witnesses, will be entering an arena with which, in the majority of cases, they are unfamiliar and uncomfortable. Just as an attorney is expected to be naïve and unknowledgeable about taking a projective test or being a patient in therapy, the psychologist is similarly untutored as a participant in litigation. It is a given that any litigator conducting a deposition will know the applicable rules, and experienced lawyers will have developed a whole bag of tricks for increasing the probability that they remain in control of the deposition and are able to take advantage of the ignorance of those whom they depose.

Given this imbalance, it is of utmost importance that all potential witnesses undergo thorough briefing and review of all the elements of the deposition before they take a seat at the deposition table. The preparation of the deponent should include information about the nature of the litigation, the claims and defenses of the parties as then presently known, the reasons for taking the deposition, and some techniques and strategies for responding to the attorney's interrogation. It is also a time to carefully review the documents that may be discussed during the deposition and submitted during trial. If a lawyer refuses to spend whatever time is reasonably necessary to prepare the deponent, the psychologist, if at all able, should refrain from participating in the case. The deponent may expect the interrogator to ask in a somewhat accusatory tone whether he or she has conferred with an attorney in preparation for the deposition. The deponent should have, however, no fear of answering the question affirmatively. It is only a foolhardy witness and an incompetent attorney who do not prepare fully for a deposition.

After the social niceties, the oath, and introductions are out of the way, the attorney taking the deposition will almost always begin with some version of instructions to the deponent. It is essential that the deponent pay attention to these instructions, which go something like this:

> I'm going to ask you some questions to find out what you know with regard to this lawsuit. If you do not hear a question, I will be glad to repeat it. If you do not understand a question, I will be glad to repeat or rephrase it. If you need to use the bathroom, take a break, have some coffee, or drink some water, I will be glad to recess the deposition for as long as you need, although not while a question of mine is pending. If you find yourself getting tired, disconcerted, or rattled and need to stop for the day, please let me know. If you are not sure of an answer, you are not compelled to answer; simply tell me that you do not remember or know the information needed to answer the question. If you do answer a question, however, I will assume you have heard and understood it. If some answer you gave earlier later appears incorrect to you or was incomplete, I have no problem with you correcting or adding to your initial answer. Please tell me if you understand all the instructions I have just given you.

All of this friendliness and concern for deponents' well-being and comprehension should not lull them into a false sense of security. This solicitude is designed solely to bind deponents to their testimony. Suppose the psychologist expert testifies during the deposition that it is his or her opinion that the relevant party is not at risk for acting out violently toward others. At trial, however, the psychologist offers somewhat conflicting testimony. The cross examiner then confronts the psychologist with the contradiction. If the psychologist attempts to rationalize the contradiction by asserting that he or she did not understand the nature of the question at the deposition and was tired at the point the question was asked, the cross-examiner will almost assuredly remind the psychologist of the instructions the attorney gave, and the psychologist said he or she understood, at the deposition.

After the deponent is given some form of the instructions paraphrased here, the deposition proper starts. With an expert who is being deposed, it is very common to begin with a review of the expert's credentials, based on the curriculum vitae submitted at the time of, or prior to, the deposition. Some attorneys may go for the jugular and leap directly into the substance of the expert's testimony, hoping to catch the witness off guard, but the vast majority of expert witness depositions begin with questions concerning the expert's credentials.[8]

The vita review itself may take several hours. There is very likely to be extensive questioning about the deponent's educational training and professional experience, the subject matter of all publications, and some aspects of the deponent's personal life. In cases involving custody disputes, for example, interrogating attorneys may ask psychologist experts about their own marital history and whether they have been involved in custody disputes. An affirmative admission may then be used at trial in an attempt to establish the expert's bias.

It is a given, but worth making explicit, that the deponent must always tell the truth. To fulfill the psychologist's ethical and legal obligations (Bersoff, 2008), the deponent's testimony should be objective, fair, and accurate. Regardless of who may be paying the deponent's fees, if any, the psychologist whose deposition is being taken should testify as an objective scientist, not as an advocate for a particular position.[9]

Honoring the view that the witness's primary duty is to enable the legal system to render a just decision based on an honest presentation of the evidence does not mean that the witness has an obligation to make the other side's case. Deponents are universally advised not to give any more information than that which is strictly necessary to answer the question. The rationale for the proscription against volunteering information is based on the offensive purposes of the deposition. Anything the witness says during the deposition can be used against the witness or the party for whom the witness is testifying. Thus, the consensus advice is to answer all questions with a simple "yes" or "no," if possible. There is no need to memorize answers, educate the examiner, or supply information that is not requested. For example, suppose a neuropsychologist who has conducted an evaluation of a plaintiff claiming eligibility for workers' compensation maintains two offices: one at a professional place of business, shared by other mental health providers, and one at home. Suppose further that the neuropsychologist maintains all files in the home office, thinking them more secure there. At the deposition, the psychologist is asked if he or she has kept a copy of the test protocols in the files at his or her professional office. The correct answer under the "no volunteer" rule is "No," not "No, but I do have copies in my home office." It is expected that the competent attorney will follow up with a question inquiring whether the files are kept somewhere else, and the ethical psychologist must then answer in the affirmative. A deponent has no obligation to anticipate questions that have not been asked or to make the examining attorney's job easier. Ironically, these rules may be particularly difficult for psychologists to follow given their training as members of the helping professions. But a deposition, according to the vast majority of litigators, is no time to be helpful. A deponent's testimony is supposed to be fair and accurate, but not helpful.

Although in the majority of cases the no volunteer rule is eminently sensible, I have been in a few depositions at which the witness I have represented has used an alternative approach, which on occasion can be effective. I call it the "bore 'em to death" strategy. Using this technique, the deponent gives a very long-winded answer to what the attorney expected to be a short answer to a quick question. For example, the examiner may ask, "When did you begin seeing this patient?" The expected reply would be the date on which therapy began. The psychologist could give, however, a long, rambling, but relevant answer about the referral history, the number of attempts to set a date, a discourse on the technical meaning of "patient," and so forth. Enough of these monotonously extensive answers can lead even the most conscientious attorney to shorten the deposition. And, if the attorney tries to interrupt and berate the witness, it could be viewed as badgering and offered as the basis to discontinue the deposition as oppressive. Although some deponents can use the bore 'em approach effectively, there is always the danger of saying too much, of appearing to dissemble, and of acting hostile. It hardly ever pays for deponents to lose their temper or act contemptuously. Thus, unless the alternative is fully considered, the better rule in most cases is to answer truthfully but succinctly.

Because psychologists love to help, teach, and interpret, they may also break another cardinal rule of testifying at a deposition: Deponents should not answer questions they do not comprehend. In depositions, there is no obligation to instruct attorneys how to make questions more understandable. Deponents should simply tell interrogators they do not understand the questions. It is the attorneys' responsibility to repeat or rephrase them.

Even if the deponent understands the question, it is important for the deponent to wait until the entire question is framed, to listen to the question carefully, to think about and formulate an appropriate answer, and then to verbalize a response.[10] Depositions are not TV quiz shows with a premium on fast reaction times. And, unlike many standardized tests, there is no advantage to guessing. The deponent is not there to exhibit his or her intelligence but to apprise the opposition of the strength and weaknesses of both sides' case. It is quite appropriate, even preferred, that if the deponent is not sure of the correct answer, to respond, "I don't know." The examiner has the right to press for an answer or to ask for estimates but cannot force deponents to state something under oath of which they are not sure. For example, assume that the case in which an expert witness deponent is being deposed involves the allegation that the defendant's negligent driving and subsequent crash injured the adult plaintiff and led to the development of agoraphobia. The attorney may ask the witness, who evaluated the plaintiff, how many times he has testified for plaintiffs as opposed to defendants. Unless the witness has kept a precise record and is sure of the answer, the right response is some variant of "I have no idea." It is perfectly permissible for the attorney to press further and ask for an estimate (e.g., "Would you say more than 10 times?"). If the deponent can answer that in yes-or-no fashion, that is fine, but if it is impossible to do so, the proper answer remains, "I don't know."

One common deposition ploy is to ask questions in such a way that they commit a deponent to language and ideas favorable to the examiner's case. For example, after extended testimony on a particular subject, like the underlying personality structure of the person the psychologist examined, the attorney may say, "So, would it be fair to say that your client has basically a sociopathic personality?" If that description coincides precisely with the deponent's prior testimony, a short "Yes" may suffice. But in the majority of cases, this is a characterization the attorney wants the witness to adopt and to commit to under oath. It is not a good idea to let the attorney control characterizations, descriptions, or opinions. When faced with a leading question that encompasses an answer the attorney wishes to have, it is recommended practice for deponents to restate the response in his or her own words or to merely say that they have already responded to the question and stand by that answer.

Besides interrogating witnesses, examining attorneys may ask deponents to authenticate documents[11] and discuss their contents. As with questions, it is essential that deponents look over the documents carefully, including noting the author, the addressee, and those to whom photocopies might have been sent, and to read the entire document slowly and carefully, even if presumably written by the deponent. If the deponent was the signatory, the deponent may be asked who actually drafted the document, from whom the information in the document was obtained, to whom were copies sent, if the deponent received a reply, and whether the recipient agreed or disagreed with its contents.

If the deponent was the addressee, the deponent may be asked what response was made; when a response, if any, was drafted; who drafted the response; who else was consulted regarding the contents; and what action the deponent took in response to the document, beyond answering it. As with questions, however, there is no obligation to remember all the documents or letters a deponent has written or received. Thus, it is quite appropriate, if truthful, to respond, "I don't know," when asked these questions.

The right of examiners to ask questions about documents extends to documents that deponents bring with them. That is why it is almost always recommended that the witness leave all documents at the office or at home, save perhaps the deponent's curriculum vitae, unless otherwise instructed by the witness's representative.

If the deponent is a crucial witness, a deposition may go on for several days. If there are multiple parties in the litigation on the other side, each of the parties' attorneys may take turns asking the deponent questions, although one attorney will almost always take the lead. As noted, it is unusual for the deponent's counsel to ask any questions during the deposition. Only when some serious rehabilitation of the deponent is required will the deponent's attorney initiate inquiries. But questioning one's own witness is risky during a deposition and can often prolong it, as once the witness's attorney finishes asking questions, all the opposing attorneys can begin another round of questions.

There is an exception to the recommendation that retaining attorneys not question their own experts. In some states, a written or videotaped deposition of an expert witness may be used at trial, whether or not the witness is available to testify. The federal rules also allow this to be done but only if the parties agree. Such depositions are more like trial testimony. In those instances, the retaining lawyer will question the witness, and the opposing lawyer will then cross-examine. Thus, the retaining lawyer will want the expert to prepare extensively and testify fully.

There is one final (and, perhaps, the only pleasant) recommendation. If the deponent is serving as an expert witness, the party taking the deposition must, in almost all cases, pay the opposing expert a reasonable fee for the time expended not only in the deposition but also for the time used to prepare for the deposition and to travel to it (*Federal Rules*, 1996, Rule 26[b][4][C], p. 65). Therefore, such deponents should submit a bill for their time in an expedient fashion.

Conclusion

Although depositions have a lot in common with a psychologist's initial interview of a potential patient (both want to discover as much information as possible), unlike a clinical interview, all discovery, but particularly depositions, are adversary proceedings. Because of their fundamental significance in litigation, they are usually conducted by experienced litigators who have developed a whole series of trick questions and ploys, refined through the years. Psychologists who become deponents must realize that they are operating in a hostile environment. They have not been called to appear to teach, instruct, empathize, help, or treat. They are there to provide offensive and defensive weapons for the opposition. Nevertheless, deponents—whether as witnesses of fact or expert witnesses—have an obligation to be truthful, accurate, and fair. They should carry out these obligations by being polite, succinct, patient, and cautious.

Notes

1. Similarly, very few criminal prosecutions get to trial. The vast majority are resolved with the state offering, and the defendant accepting, a plea bargain, the equivalent of a settlement in civil litigation.
2. There is very circumscribed discovery in criminal litigation, and it is almost unheard of for attorneys to take depositions prior to criminal trials. Thus, I restrict this chapter to a discussion of discovery in the context of civil litigation, such as personal injury suits, custody disputes, or malpractice actions against psychologists.
3. It would be unwieldy to describe the discovery rules for every jurisdiction in the United States; thus, this chapter uses the federal rules of civil procedure as the model. It is likely that the states in which readers practice will have rules that closely follow the federal model, but caution and prudence dictate that psychologists who may be called to attend depositions be familiar with the rules in their jurisdiction.
4. *Hearsay* is an out-of-court statement made by a declarant, offered for its truth, and not falling within one of the accepted hearsay rule exceptions. For example, suppose a witness is asked whether she knows if the father, who is seeking custody of his child, abuses drugs. Suppose that the witness attempts to testify at trial that she heard the mother, who is also seeking custody of her child, state that the father is a drug addict. If such testimony is offered to prove that the father is an addict, it would be objected to and would be inadmissible in civil and criminal cases. However, such a question and such a response would not be objectionable as hearsay if made during a deposition.
5. Lawyers who retain experts or represent psychologists ordinarily will not conduct a deposition of their own experts or clients. It is the opposing attorneys who want to have the benefit of discovery. Presumably, the retaining lawyer will have full knowledge of the facts or opinions relevant to the case

long before a deposition is conducted. Nevertheless, as discussed in this chapter, there are times when retaining lawyers will conduct depositions of their experts or their clients.

6. Under the federal rules, the only other time that a deponent does not have to answer a question is to enforce a previous limitation on evidence directed by the court (*Federal Rules*, Rule 30[d][1], 1996, p. 74).

7. There are conflicting views on whether the deponent should review and sign the transcript, but I always recommended that the clients I represent at deposition carefully read and correct errors in the transcript before signing. It does bind the deponent to the testimony, but it helps ensure that embarrassing contradictions do not have to be explained at trial.

8. Some examiners will even go back further than the data on the vita. One psychologist whose deposition I attended—serving not as an expert but as a defendant in an antitrust suit—was asked about his elementary and high school education. The time was not wasted; I learned that he and I had attended Stuyvesant High School in New York City at about the same time.

9. Because every question should be answered honestly, it is not good practice to begin the answer to a particular question with the response, "To be candid [or frank, etc.]. . . ." The interrogator may ask if the witness was not being candid all other times.

10. Because depositions are recorded, deponents should always answer in words, not by a nod of the head, a shrug of the shoulders, or some other nonverbal response.

11. At trial, each party may want to introduce documents as evidence. To do so, there must be some assurance of the relevance and authenticity of each of the documents. During a deposition, therefore, the attorney will ask the witness to testify whether he or she was the author of the document, whether the signature is that of the author, and perhaps whether the document was made in the ordinary course of the deponent's professional work. These are factors that are involved in authentication and that help the judge decide whether the evidence is admissible.

References

Bersoff, D. N. (2008). *Ethical conflicts in psychology* (4th ed.). Washington, DC: American Psychological Association.

Federal Rules of Civil Procedure. (2008). St Paul, MN: Thompson West.

Suplee, D. R. (1982). Depositions: Objectives, strategies, tactics, mechanics, and problems. *The Review of Litigation, 2,* 255–328.

Suplee, D. R., & Donaldson, D. S. (1988). *The deposition handbook: Strategies, tactics, and mechanics.* Eau Claire, WI: Professional Educational Systems.

3

Personal Injury
Consultation, Evaluation, and the Expert Witness
David D. Stein

Introduction

The role of psychologists in personal injury (PI) litigation dates back to the 1960s, when a landmark decision (*Jenkins v. United States*, 1962) allowed psychologists to testify as expert witnesses. Facilitating legislation followed in most states, thereby codifying this role in statutes. At about the same time, legislatures were enacting licensing laws that recognized psychology as an independent profession. Prior to that time, psychologists had been involved in the diagnosis and treatment of individuals who had suffered injuries in such cases. It was not until the 1960s and 1970s that they were given legal recognition in most, if not all, states to serve as experts and thus render opinions to attorneys and the courts in the context of a particular legal case. Today, increasing numbers of psychologists, variously trained as forensic psychologists, evaluate and consult in a variety of PI cases along with their psychiatrist colleagues.

Legal Considerations

Since the late 1980s, psychologists have sharpened their understanding of the legal system's expectations and requirements of the services they perform. In particular, they have come to realize that a standard clinical evaluation, which might be appropriate in a clinic or hospital setting, is insufficient in the legal arena. Specifically, there are legal questions that must be addressed, and the psychologist's clinical opinions must bear on these legal issues. In the area of PI, psychologists have had to become quite familiar with tort law.

In most PI cases, a plaintiff (allegedly injured) sues a defendant for negligence. *Negligence* is defined as either doing something that a reasonably prudent person would not do or as the failure to do something that a reasonably prudent person would do under circumstances similar to those in the admitted evidence (Hastings College of Law, 1996). Negligence is also the failure to exercise ordinary or reasonable care that would be expected to avoid injury to oneself or others under circumstances similar to those in the admitted evidence. Thus, if a party violates laws or duty to another as a proximate cause of injury, then that violation constitutes negligence. *Proximate* means that there is a connection between the conduct of the defendant and the injury, and that the accident was a foreseeable result of such conduct. In comparative negligence jurisdictions, if both plaintiff and defendant demonstrate negligence, then the amount of damages to which the plaintiff would otherwise be entitled would be reduced in proportion to the amount of negligence attributable to the plaintiff. In contributory negligence jurisdictions, the plaintiff's damages are eliminated entirely.

The plaintiff has the burden of proof by the preponderance (greater than 50%) of the evidence (the lowest legal threshold) to show that the plaintiff was in fact injured, that the defendant was negligent, and that such negligence was a proximate cause of the injury. The elements of damage that might occur include physical pain and suffering, mental anguish, the denial of social pleasure and enjoyment, the loss of earning capacity, and in relevant cases, the cost of medical/psychological care for the injury. One can collect an award for the aggravation of any preexisting condition proximately resulting from the injury, but the preexisting condition per se is not compensable. This bears often on the "cracked vase" notion in PI: A psychologically vulnerable person is predisposed to experience considerable aggravation, but the law says one "must take the person as they [sic] are." Thus, psychologically vulnerable plaintiffs may win awards because of the ease with which their preexisting condition can be aggravated and sustained.

A tort is a wrong that has mental sequelae from physical harm or is a psychological injury due to psychological trauma, pain, stress, and the like (Weissman, 1985). Such mental sequelae may be caused by toxic substances, drugs, workplace accidents, natural disasters, communicable diseases, and discrimination. There are general and specific damages, the latter often involving wage loss. Negligence or intentional torts in a work setting are usually covered under PI and not workers' compensation. Many accidents do not have to involve a physical impact (Prosser, 1939). The proximity in time or space or a plaintiff's relationship to the one injured are important factors in helping determine the foreseeability of an event and whether the defendant owed a duty to care to the plaintiff (*Dillon v. Legg*, 1968; *Molien v. Kaiser Foundation Hospitals*, 1980; *Palsgraf v. Long Island R.R.*, 1928) and therefore has possible liability for the negligent infliction of emotional distress. The ultimate legal question (e.g., did the auto accident cause the posttraumatic stress disorder?), which the trier of fact (judge or jury) must address, can be given as an opinion by an expert witness during the proceedings in a civil case but not in a criminal case. An expert's opinion must be of reasonable certainty but does not have to be of absolute certainty.

Typical Roles for Psychologists

Essential core skills in psychologists' training that differentiate them from related professional experts include psychodiagnostic and neuropsychological assessment, test theory and construction, and statistics (American Psychological Association, Education Directorate, 1996). Psychologists' ability to bring a scientific basis to many aspects of their opinions has enhanced their status and credibility with attorneys and judges (Stromberg, Lindberg, & Schneider, 1995). This credibility may be related to the fact that tests are standardized and validated for thousands of people, whereas findings generated by a clinical interview alone can give the appearance of the evaluator's idiosyncratic perspective. As psychologists' testimony has proven to be valuable to the legal system, psychologists have expanded their more traditional role of simply interpreting psychological tests in legal cases to performing in-depth clinical interviews, consulting, and rendering opinions on various aspects of mental status and capacity, treatment recommendations, and prognoses relative to the injury in question. Historically, psychologists typically had their test findings incorporated into a psychiatrist's evaluation, and the latter gave depositions and court testimony. Today, psychologists are often the only mental health professionals utilized in some PI cases.

Psychologists are often asked to serve as consultants to legal professionals rather than disclose themselves as experts. As experts, their work and opinions can be ascertained through normal discovery procedures. As consultants, they may assist an attorney in formulating the mental health components of a case, such as reviewing scenarios that would favor either side. The psychologist might review records and deposition transcripts and assess their strengths and weaknesses. On some occasions, the psychologist might review and summarize some literature that would assist an attorney in learning about the current scientific status of a particular issue. Sometimes, the psychologist can advise regarding who in the community might be a helpful expert in the case. This is particularly true when there may be a head injury or insult to the body that could cause brain damage. Here, the psychologist can explain the relative contributions of a psychiatrist, neurologist, neuropsychologist, or endocrinologist, for example, as well as the contributions of various neurological tests such as brain scans and the like. And, in general, the psychologist can advise on the relative complexity of the evaluation needed to make one's case, balancing what might be very expensive "overkill" against an insufficient evaluation. Also, the psychologist can help an attorney think through jury selection and the likely biases and prejudices that might be relevant.

Sometimes, the attorney wishes to convert the consultant into an expert. In those cases, it is often better to have that psychologist opine on theoretical or research issues, his or her own professional experience, or another expert's evaluation of the client rather than to evaluate the plaintiff personally. The reason is that the psychologist's work as a consultant was oriented to helping the attorney, so there is an appearance of bias when the psychologist "objectively" evaluates the client in the framework of what should be "neutral" interest in the outcome. That is, when a psychologist evaluates someone, it is presumed that there is no a priori expectation of what the findings will be. Sometimes, a psychologist's results will not be helpful to the attorney's case, and the findings will not be utilized. If the psychologist has been consultant to an attorney on the case and then performs an evaluation, there can be an appearance of bias in that the psychologist might be subtly influenced to shape the findings to support the attorney's theory of the case.

The most typical role for a psychologist retained by plaintiff's attorney in PI cases is to evaluate the plaintiff. Usually, the plaintiff is evaluated by the plaintiff's expert first, and the results are made available to the defendant's attorney. Sometimes, the latter will have his or her own expert repeat the evaluation or use the findings from the plaintiff's expert as well as some contact with the plaintiff to form opinions. In these contexts, it is not uncommon for a plaintiff to go through two extensive psychological or neuropsychological test batteries within a few days as well as evaluations by psychiatrists or other medical experts. Validity issues have been raised regarding the meaning of such repeated testing because of practice effects, fatigue (Lezak, 1983), or opportunities to look up answers or be coached between testings. In many cases, however, attorneys believe, perhaps rightly, that they want their own expert to perform a full evaluation to feel more secure that results were not biased in the direction of the original examiner.

Some states allow attorneys to request audiotaping or videotaping of the evaluation. The rationale for doing this in a clinical interview is the possible inappropriateness of a clinician's questions regarding some legal aspect of the case when no attorney is present to object. However, the taping of the examination when performing psychological testing can produce multiple and unknown effects on the process and invalidate many of the findings. For this reason, the examining psychologist probably should not allow such taping. The law has been inconsistent on the rights of attorneys to allow such taping during testing and varies from state to state.

Due to rising costs in litigation generally, attorneys must make choices regarding how much work each of their experts should do. It is important to help the attorney clarify the referral questions as precisely as possible to circumscribe the amount of work that the various professionals involved need to do. It is not unreasonable, for example, to have a psychiatrist do an in-depth psychiatric interview, share the findings with the psychologist on the same side, and have the psychologist interview in a much more selective and complementary manner. The psychologist would then perform whichever psychological or neuropsychological tests were deemed necessary and integrate the information from all sources into his or her opinions. What has often been a practice historically, but is now considered inappropriate, is having a psychiatrist "represent" the psychologist's test findings in a deposition or court hearing. A good cross-examination on test findings can dramatically reduce the credibility of almost any psychiatrist, but more importantly can vitiate the importance of those findings, because in that situation there is usually no other avenue for those data to be entered as evidence.

Over the years, the emergence of neuropsychological testing has greatly enhanced the contributions psychologists can make in cases involving organic impairment. Some court cases have challenged whether psychologists, who are not physicians, can make direct causal statements about brain damage (*Kriewitz v. Savoy Heating and Air Conditioning Co.*, 1981). On balance, the careful wording of one's neuropsychological findings as "known correlates of impairment" seems to be an effective way to present data. In addition, in the absence of any other compelling cause for the demonstrated impairment, positive neuropsychological findings may be the only data that show the deficits. Time after time, a clinical interview, a neurological office exam, lab tests, and various neurological scans fail to show any impairment because the findings are too subtle and may only show up on the highly sensitive neuropsychological tests (Reitan & Davison, 1974).

A final major role for psychologists in PI cases is as the treating doctor or psychotherapist. When undertaking this role, the psychologist is brought into the case by the legal system because he or she happens to be treating or did treat the patient who is bringing the lawsuit. The patient is injured and sues as a plaintiff. At some point, the patient is asked to disclose all doctors who have been seen, and the psychologist is identified. By filing a suit in which his or her mental health has been put at issue, the patient waives the psychotherapist-patient privilege and forces the psychologist to reveal any and all aspects of the treatment if the defense so wishes. In this context, the psychologist does not also act as the evaluating psychologist but instead offers opinions only about the treatment context. In many cases, patients have not been fully informed by their attorneys of the ramifications of the therapist's revealing such personal and sensitive material. Or the patient may have a distorted view of what the therapist will say and is dismayed when the testimony is at variance with what was expected. Surprisingly often, the attorney will not talk to the psychologist before filing the suit and thus is blind to the potentially devastating impact such testimony might have on the case. Many therapists find that being compelled into the legal arena is an anxiety-provoking experience and are often not prepared to testify in the way a forensic psychologist does. Moreover, they are concerned that their involvement will jeopardize the therapeutic relationship.

Typically, the therapist, as treating doctor, has been defined as a percipient or fact witness and is not deposed as an expert. A *percipient witness* is someone who has observed or been involved in an event and can speak to his or her observations and experience of it. An *expert witness* has particular education, training, and experience that can be drawn on to explain to the trier of fact matters that go beyond the average knowledge of a layperson. Controversy has arisen, however, over whether a therapist can talk intelligently about the patient's diagnosis and treatment without utilizing expertise. This issue has been played out over which fees will be paid to the psychologist for his or her time. At times, an attorney will define the treating doctor as a percipient witness and request just the facts about what has happened in psychotherapy, such as number and dates of sessions, diagnosis, treatment plan, and so on, without asking for a psychological explanation of the patient's problems. Technically, a percipient witness is usually paid less than $50 per day.[1]

When a psychologist is the treating doctor, it is important to have good records (American Psychological Association, 1993) and to openly and honestly answer questions. There can be a strong tendency to try to "protect" the patient by not revealing too much. But, the reality is that the treating psychologist often does not know what would be helpful or harmful in these situations. It is advisable for the treating psychologist to consult with a forensic psychologist about the specifics of depositions (see Bersoff, chapter 2, this volume) and court testimony (see Thatcher, chapter 4, this volume) and possibly to retain one's own attorney, especially if the case is complicated.

The treating psychologist should never agree to evaluate the patient in the same context as an expert because of the role conflict (American Psychological Association, 2002; Committee on Ethical Guidelines for Forensic Psychologists, 1991). The treating psychologist's opinions are based on the special therapeutic relationship that has been established. Consequently, he or she cannot conduct the more objective type of evaluation that an expert can perform since the latter has access to different data sources and contacts and develops opinions in a psycholegal context. It is also possible that the therapeutic relationship could be compromised because the psychologist would be obtaining data that did not emerge from the psychotherapy sessions and thus would not be in a position to discuss the nature of the evaluation or the related legal issues in the therapeutic sessions. Likewise, one's testimony may contribute substantially to an award for the plaintiff, who might later, in gratitude, seek out the evaluating psychologist for treatment. Again, this mixing of evaluating and treating functions is considered inappropriate because, should the psychologist treat the patient at that point, it would jeopardize the evaluative role in the future in the event that the same psychologist is called on to wear a forensic hat again (e.g., in an appeal). Also, the kind of contact one has had with the plaintiff during the legal case can readily cause problems that are not easily analyzed in the transference and countertransference aspects of therapy. It is almost always better to refer clients whom one has evaluated to colleagues for psychotherapy if that is requested.

Issues in Performing an Evaluation

As mentioned, the typical role for a psychologist in PI is to perform an evaluation. When one is contacted, usually by the attorney, it is important to establish contractual arrangements that can be embodied in a letter of understanding, typically produced by the attorney but actively contributed to by the psychologist. If possible, this is a good time to clarify the referral questions and have them promulgated in the letter of understanding. If one is going to be doing the evaluation for the plaintiff, one should stipulate a retainer to be received, roughly based on the number of hours of work anticipated. Most psychologists would include time for records review, travel, consultation with the attorney and possible family members or collaterals, test administration, scoring, analysis, and a written report (the last only if specified by the attorney). Many attorneys prefer not to have the psychologist's findings in written form to make depositions and cross-examination more difficult for the opposing side. Also, a written report can legally force disclosure of information that in some cases the attorney may wish to preclude. If a written report is authorized, it is expected that the plaintiff or defendant will see the report. Unlike psychologists' reports in a clinical context, one cannot stipulate that it is inadvisable for the client to see the report because it might be damaging to his or her mental health. In a legal context, clients and their attorneys determine that issue.

Likewise, there is no absolute obligation to give the client a report face to face on the results, as one might in a therapeutic context. The purpose here is to evaluate, although one can make recommendations in the report of what might be therapeutically beneficial. It is often helpful to tell the attorney on the phone, after clarifying which tasks one will be asked to perform, the estimated number of hours of work expected prior to deposition and to request a retainer for that amount. One's actual billing will be at one's forensic hourly rate, and in some cases one may need to refund money to the attorney if the evaluation took less time. It is important to receive a retainer because when one is deposed or appears in court and has not been paid, one can be made to look as though one's findings are biased to ensure being paid. Many times, payment will be made by the plaintiff directly. In this situation, one also needs a retainer, not only for the reasons mentioned, but also because a verdict for the defense can sometimes stimulate a plaintiff not to pay. If one testifies in court, the attorney who retained the psychologist pays for all aspects of preparation and time in court. Many professionals have half-day and full-day fees for court appearances, a practice designed to protect the psychologist, who may have to cancel therapy sessions with patients to be available or to deal with delays in court that prevent one from actually testifying at the time the attorney would like.

Some psychologists just bill at the hourly rate and try to accommodate the attorney so that their bill does not run up too high. As long as psychologists can do this without sacrificing their own income, attorneys are usually quite appreciative. There is no right or wrong way to bill, but these issues should be thought out ahead of time and specified in writing in the original agreement to render services. It should be noted that there are no clear guidelines on how to set a fee for forensic services. Typically, such a fee is set at anywhere from one and one-half to three times as much as one's hourly psychotherapy fee. The rationale for the higher rate is that one's expertise, training, and experience in forensic psychology as well as the extra stress and strain justify such a fee. Supply and demand as well as what is usual and customary in a community are also major factors in determining what is acceptable. In some states, an attorney who believes the psychologist's fee is too high can protest to the judge, who will then render a ruling; or, one may be asked to show that he or she has asked for and received such a fee in prior cases. For psychologists who do not hold themselves out as forensic psychologists and are asked to testify because they are the treating psychotherapist, it is probably a good idea to charge a fee not much higher than one's psychotherapy fee.

If one is hired by the defense to either evaluate the plaintiff directly or review records, one is usually paid by or through an insurance company, and it is unlikely that one can receive a retainer. It is therefore important to have a written letter of understanding that specifies that the attorney will be responsible for the bill if the insurance company fails to pay or limits the amount paid.

Most PI evaluations performed by a psychologist involve a clinical interview and psychodiagnostic testing. As mentioned, a more limited clinical interview can take place if a mental health colleague is doing the more extensive interview. It is important to discuss with the attorney which records one needs to see, because in some cases there can be thousands of pages of medical records, and many will not be relevant. The attorney needs to understand that if conclusions are reached in the absence of key information, the cross-examination might be very embarrassing. It is better, then, to err on the side of seeing as many substantive records as is economically feasible.

It is important to administer a full test battery for a variety of reasons. As is true in most clinical testing, one wants to assess the full range of cognitive, emotional, and behavioral functioning, and one never knows beforehand which combination of tests will be the most useful in any particular case. Sometimes, for example, a faked Minnesota Multiphasic Personality Inventory (MMPI) or Millon Clinical Multiaxial Inventory (MCMI) can invalidate its clinical yield, so that other personality measures, such as the Rorschach inkblot test or the Thematic Apperception Test, would need to be used. It is best to use standard tests with the best reliability and validity data and administered in standard fashion. Whenever possible, the tests should be standardized for the plaintiff's population or there should be research evidence that the test has adequate validity with populations not part of the original standardization sample. Idiosyncratic administration of tests or the use of methodologically weak tests or scales can be seriously criticized during cross-examination. Extra effort needs to be devoted to careful and accurate scoring. In some cases, if the psychologist is knowledgeable, the administration and interpretation of interest and aptitude tests should be part of the battery to determine future occupational options following injury when a patients' return to his regular occupation is precluded. These tests can also be administered by career specialists, but it is probably less costly to have the psychologist do it if properly trained.

It should be mentioned that computer scoring and interpretation are still problematic today. Many tests can be accurately and speedily scored by computers, but the computer narrative interpretations still leave much to be desired. As good as only a few are, they cannot analyze the data to produce a highly individualized, precise, and accurate interpretation of the client for the following reasons.

Programmed algorithms suggest possibilities, so the narrative includes different options for interpretations. The psychologist's job, however, is to provide a highly individualized interpretation in which alternative possibilities have been essentially ruled out through analytical reasoning utilizing all the data points available. In addition, the psychologist's understanding of test construction and statistics as well as sophisticated theory puts him or her in a better position to assess the relative weighting of the points made in the computer narrative. Also for these reasons, the psychologist, unlike the psychiatrist, is in a better position to discuss the strengths and weaknesses of a computer interpretation if it was relied on in reaching the interpreter's opinions. In this context, the individualized interpretation by the psychologist can integrate theory (e.g., defenses, character structure, adaptive resources, etc.) in a way that has not yet been matched by computer interpretation. The latter can be a helpful guide, but the statements generated cannot necessarily be relied on.

In many PI cases, testing the client once is not enough. The time elapsed from the date of injury to the first deposition of a mental health professional can encompass months or even years. For example, if the plaintiff is evaluated 3 to 5 months after a closed head injury, the findings might be quite different from an evaluation that took place 2 years after the injury. Plaintiff and defense positions can be favored differently depending on when the examination takes place. Therefore, multiple evaluations are often done to see if there is a recovery pattern and to determine whether the plaintiff's condition is permanent. The plaintiff's life choices, motivation, and attitude toward recovery during this time period become part and parcel of the expert's opinions.

When an evaluation takes place, it is advisable to conduct it over at least 2 days to observe the person on different occasions. Often, this is not possible for logistical reasons, and an evaluation must be completed in a single day with occasional breaks.

Interpretations of Findings Within a Psycholegal Framework

After the psychologist has analyzed all the data, whether the data are transferred into a written report or merely conceptualized, data must be related to the relevant psycholegal concepts in PI litigation. In most PI cases, there is great concern regarding which factors are proximate, coexisting, or preexisting because final decisions hinge on the compelling nature of these factors as they are elucidated in court or in settlement conferences. At present, we are more reliant on information from interviews, observation, collateral contacts, and records to sort out these factors than we are on test data, yet there are some helpful test formulas and ratios, as I argued in an unpublished presentation (Stein, 1994), that can help differentiate among preexisting, coexisting, and proximate causes. It is the job of the psychologist to look for all of these possible factors and to weigh them accordingly because he or she will be asked about them in deposition or in court. For example, it is to the advantage of the defense to find coexisting and preexisting factors dominating the picture to lessen the effect of a proximate cause for which they might be negligent. The opposite would be true for the plaintiff's position. An example would be to discover whether emotional trauma from an injury or accident comes primarily from a precipitating event or from coexisting or preexisting factors such as marital or financial problems, job stresses, or severely pathological relationships within one's family. Making a timeline of the plaintiff's functioning prior to and after the event and specifying which factors might have influenced the plaintiff's mental state can be quite helpful in analyzing these points.

Is the extant condition an exacerbation of a preexisting condition or disability? If so, this is often referred to as the cracked vase or "thin skull" personality. A plaintiff who has a precariously integrated or fragmented personality, perhaps functioning at a marginal level of personal and social adaptation, gets worse as a result of the injury or accident. One often observes phobic or agoraphobic reactions, significantly increased anxiety, depression, reality distortions, the inability to improve from treatment, and much poorer functioning in occupational or personal spheres. Law requires that "you take the person as they are," and therefore an exacerbation of a preexisting condition can render the plaintiff immobilized for long periods of time. If a preexisting condition or disability is so aggravated, the damages of such a condition or disability are limited to the additional injury caused by the aggravation. Practically, this can amount to long-term compensation should the exacerbated condition fail to improve sufficiently to allow the person to resume relatively adequate occupational or social functioning. In such instances, it is crucial for the defense to attempt to rule in coexisting factors as the basis for the "exacerbated" condition again to limit its client's negligence. Likewise, emotional distress or disabilities that would have emerged anyway, absent the proximate cause, are factors that the defense looks for to limit its client's liability; therefore, very close scrutiny of the person's life before and after the accident or injury is required to adequately consider nonproximate factors.

The area of pain evaluation certainly bears on the degree to which physical pain and suffering occurred, specifically whether any doctor can determine an organic basis for the damage. In fact, when that question cannot be reliably answered, legitimately felt pain, as measured by many of the typical tests used, can support a claim for damages (e.g., Sternbach, 1974).

"Mental anguish" and "denial of social pleasure and enjoyment" can be demonstrated by test levels or indicators of anxiety or depression, phobic and agoraphobic responses to injuries, and the preoccupation and nonadaptability evident in some people after injury.

Treatment recommendations and likely outcomes are almost always asked of an expert in PI cases, and the modality, length of treatment, and likely costs are specifically requested. This is one area in which consider-able work has been done since the 1990s (Maruish, 2004), stimulated in large part by the reduction of exclusively psychodiagnostic testing oppor-tunities in the managed care climate. Efforts are being made, for example, in the nationally based Society for Personality Assessment to show that it is worth the initial expenditure in psychological testing to specify which kind of treatment, under what conditions, and for what length of time will be the most cost-efficient combination. The Weiner and Exner (1991) article on the Rorschach variables that change differentially in short- and long-term treatment has already become a landmark study in guiding treatment decisions.

Resistance to change, often driven by unconscious forces that might prevent the person from getting better (e.g., secondary gain from the attention of others or respite from life's difficulties), can be identified on a number of standard clinical psychological tests and can therefore help predict when a typical psychotherapy referral might fail. Depending on the clinical picture, specific recommendations should be made for either regular outpatient psychotherapy, sociotherapy or group psychotherapy, medication consultation, residential treatment, support groups, or par-ticular rehabilitation training.

The issue of "malingering" or "exaggeration" must be addressed in PI cases because there is a vested interest in the plaintiff's receiving a finan-cial award. This area has been well researched over the years, especially so during the 1980s and 1990s (Rogers, 1997). In addition to using spe-cially designed tests and scales for those purposes, therapists should avail themselves of the many indicators in the standard test battery that can help yield an opinion that is more probable than not. Careful interview-ing that can elicit inconsistencies between statements, or between emo-tions or gestures and words, can also help uncover dissimulation (Adams & Rankin, 1996).

Loss of earning capacity is often explored in a PI case. There are now sophisticated companies that can analyze a person's pre- and postin-jury earnings, work life, and fringe benefits to reach a value for future earnings loss in fairly precise figures.[2] Many soft tissue injuries are often not perceived by a jury as having significant work-related effects, so a vocational and economic analysis is frequently quite helpful. This type of analysis, in conjunction with career tests and the overall evaluation, can more comprehensively address realistic vocational options for the injured person.

Further Consultation Prior to Trial

After the psychologist completes the evaluation, a phone call or visit with the attorney follows. Here, one often finalizes whether there will be a written report if this decision has not already been made. This is also the time when the attorney decides whether the psychologist's findings will be helpful and whether to declare the psychologist an expert. If the findings are not favorable for the attorney, the psychologist's work will have been done under the attorney-work product privilege, and the findings will not be available to the other side. If one is declared an expert, the other side will probably arrange a deposition under the discovery laws. Prior to the deposition, it is often a good idea to see the plaintiff for at least an hour, especially if one has not seen the plaintiff for many months or years. This allows one to assess any further degree of recovery, adaptation, or their absence since one last saw the plaintiff and to explore some aspects of what are considered weak points in the case, in the hopes of finding new information that might strengthen one's position. If given the choice, it is more comfortable to have the deposition in one's own office rather than in the attorney's office. Sometimes, however, books or articles lying around the office can give the attorney ideas about what to ask.

It is important to realize that all one's notes, scribblings, data, billing records, and so on can legally be procured by the other side. Usually, this happens at the deposition. It is important to organize one's file into relevant categories so one can have quick access to the information needed to answer a question. This is particularly important in court, where one does not want to be fumbling around with papers in front of a judge or jury. Since there are many ethical issues regarding the dissemination of raw test data (Committee on Legal Issues, 1995), it is recommended that the psychologist request that the opposing attorney sign a stipulated protective order (see California Psychological Association, 2004) that ensures the limited use and appropriate exposure of the raw data and test records to a properly trained psychologist. If the attorney refuses, he or she may then file a motion to compel, which may seek monetary sanctions against the psychologist. The psychologist will need to make written opposition to the motion, and legal counsel should be consulted.

By the time one is deposed, and especially if one has been asked by the attorney not to prepare a written report, one should have a clear conceptual understanding of how one sees the case and be able to explain one's findings and opinions. Alternative explanations that the other side would favor should have been anticipated, and when given the chance, one should explain why they are not valid or have limited acceptability.

Trial Preparation and Testimony

Fewer than 10% of PI cases actually go to trial (Trubek, Sarat, Felstiner, Kritzer, & Grossman, 1983). Most are settled beforehand,[3] and the psychologist's evaluation is part of the information used to reach a settlement. But, for those cases that do go to trial, the psychologist should keep a few points in mind. Do not bring psychological tests, books, or manuals into court unless you are required to do so by opposing counsel. Spend considerable time with the attorney who retained you so that your direct examination can be as strong as possible. Unlike the deposition, where opposing counsel asks questions he or she is interested in, the trial allows one to clearly and coherently express one's findings in the case. A good direct examination features all the psychologist's strengths and assets as an expert and gives one the opportunity to provide a convincing and compelling case. Often, it is formatted so that one can explicate an interesting narrative about the findings that engages the judge or jury. It is equally important to anticipate the vulnerable points that opposing counsel will try to emphasize on cross-examination and deal with them on direct examination. The attorney who retained the psychologist and who has a total picture of the case can guide the choice of what is strategically or tactically beneficial to raise on direct examination.

Some courts have limited the nature and scope of testimony that a psychologist can give (e.g., *Kriewitz v. Savoy Heating and Air Conditioning Co.*, 1981). In a Florida appellate case (*GIW Southern Valve Co. v. Smith*, 1985), the court stated that a psychologist could testify regarding an existing mental condition and existing organic brain damage but could not speak to a patient's prognosis for future brain condition. In this regard, a discussion with the attorney about what might be appropriately limited testimony can be quite helpful so that one is not taken by surprise while on the stand. One never knows which way a judge will decide concerning what testimony or evidence is admissible. Since a psychologist must be as objective as possible and since one's work will almost assuredly be scrutinized by a psychologist on the other side, one must admit to some findings that may not support one's position. Credibility to the judge or jury is highly dependent on appearing honest and straightforward. If caught in an obvious distortion, the judge or jury can disregard one's entire testimony.

Know the testimony areas of other experts on the same legal side. You will not see them testify, but you might well wish to refer to what they have said or will say in court.

After the Trial

Typically, after you testify, there may not be an opportunity to discuss anything with the attorney who retained you until the next day or later. Be sure to arrange beforehand a phone conversation or meeting to go over your work on the case and ask for honest criticism on your strengths and weaknesses. If you have any transcripts of your depositions available, go over them carefully and critique them so that in future depositions or court appearances, you can improve your responses to typical questions. Take notes on the strengths and weaknesses of other experts' reports and depositions to refine your own professional work.

Although a psychologist's involvement in PI work can be taxing and require the utmost care and scrutiny of one's efforts, it can also be rewarding, not only because of the intellectual challenge of figuring out a complex case, but also because of the invaluable service that is provided to relevant participants in the case. It is one of the arenas in a psychologist's world where the scientific basis of the field melds with the practitioner's role in a truly integrated manner.

Notes

1. In California, a law (Cal. Assembly 1204) was passed in 1995 that requires professionals in these roles to be paid as experts.
2. See, for example, Mulhern and Dansker (1995), which deals with such estimates in soft tissue injury cases.
3. The settlement-versus-trial disposition model for litigation outcomes is, to be sure, a simplification of the civil judicial process. There are all sorts of alternative dispositions, including abandonment by the plaintiff and adjudications such as dismissals and default judgments. See, for example, the working paper by Hadfield (2004), written from a law and economics perspective.

References

Adams, R. L., & Rankin, E. J. (1996). A practical guide to forensic neuropsychological evaluations and testimony. In R. L. Adams, O. A. Parsons, J. L. Culbertson, & S. J. Nixon (Eds.), *Neuropsychology for clinical practice* (pp. 455–487). Washington, DC: American Psychological Association.

American Psychological Association. (1993). *Record keeping guidelines.* Washington, DC: Author.

American Psychological Association. (2002). Ethical principles of psychologists and code of conduct. *American Psychologist, 57,* 1060–1073.

American Psychological Association, Education Directorate. (1996). *Guidelines and principles for accreditation of programs in professional psychology.* Washington, DC: Author.

Cal. Assembly 1204, 1995–1996 Reg. Sess. (1995).

California Psychological Association. (2004). *Responding to requests for raw test data* (Expertise Series). Sacramento, CA: Author.

Committee on Ethical Guidelines for Forensic Psychologists. (1991). Specialty guidelines for forensic psychologists. *Law and Human Behavior, 15*(6), 655–665.

Committee on Legal Issues. (1995). *Strategies for coping with subpoenas or compelled testimony for test data.* Washington, DC: American Psychological Association.

Dillon v. Legg, 68 Cal. 2d 728, 441 P.2d 912 (1968).

GIW Southern Valve Co. v. Smith, 471 So.2d at 82 (1985).

Hadfield, G. (2004). Where have all the trials gone? Berkeley Electronic Press. Retrieved from: http://law.bepress.com/usclwps/lewps/art12.html

Hastings College of the Law. (1996). *Personal injury institute.* San Francisco: Author.

Jenkins v. United States, 307 F.2d 637 (D.C. Cir. 1962).

Kriewitz v. Savoy Heating and Air Conditioning Co., 396 So.2d 49 (Ala. 1981).

Lezak, M. D. (1983). *Neuropsychological assessment* (2nd ed.). New York: Oxford University Press.

Maruish, M. E. (Ed.). (2004). *The use of psychological testing for treatment planning and outcome assessment* (3rd ed.). Mahwah, NJ: Erlbaum.

Molien v. Kaiser Foundation Hospitals, 27 Cal.3d, 916, 167 Cal. Rptr. 831, 616, P.2d. 813 (1980).

Mulhern, J., & Dansker, M. (1995). Assessing economic damages in the soft tissue injury case. *Lawyers World, 1*(1), 16–17.

Palsgraf v. Long Island R.R., 248 N.Y. 339 (1928).

Prosser, W. L. (1939). Intentional infliction of emotional suffering: A new tort. *Michigan Law Review, 37,* 874.

Reitan, R. M., & Davison, L. A. (1974) *Clinical neuropsychology: Current status and applications.* Washington, DC: Winston and Sons.

Rogers, R. (Ed.) (1997). *Clinical assessment of malingering and deception.* New York: Guilford.

Stein, D. D. (1994, April). *For the defense: Diagnostic and forensic questions in personal injury.* Paper presented at the annual Meeting of the Society for Personality Assessment, Chicago.

Sternbach, R. A. (1974). *Pain patients.* New York: Academic Press.

Stromberg, C., Lindberg, D. I., & Schneider, J. (1995). A legal update on forensic psychology. *The psychologist's legal update, no. 6* (pp. 3–16).Washington, DC: The National Register of Health Service Providers in Psychology.

Trubek, D. M., Sarat, A., Felstiner, W. L. F., Kritzer, H. M., & Grossman, J. B. (1983). The costs of ordinary litigation. *UCLA Law Review, 31,* 72–127.

Weiner, I. B., & Exner, J. E. (1991). Rorschach changes in long-term and short-term psychotherapy. *Journal of Personality Assessment, 56*(3), 453–465.

Weissman, H. N. (1985). Psycholegal standards and the role of psychological assessment in personal injury litigation. *Behavioral Sciences and the Law, 3*(2), 135–147.

4

Preparing for Court Testimony

Pamela Thatcher

While the function of deposition testimony is to elicit information, the function of trial testimony is to win the case. A mental health professional may be involved in testifying at trial as a percipient witness, as a retained expert, or as a party.

A *percipient witness* is a mental health professional who has observed facts and circumstances in the case. An example of a percipient witness is a mental health professional who has been the treating psychotherapist to a patient involved in a lawsuit. A *retained expert* is, essentially, a mental health professional specifically retained for purposes of formulating an opinion for a lawsuit. Examples of retained forensic experts are as follows: one who has been asked to formulate an opinion about another professional's conduct (i.e., whether the defendant's mental health professional's conduct met the standard of care in the community); one who has evaluated a plaintiff for purposes of determining if that plaintiff has sustained damage; or one who serves as a court-appointed custody evaluator.

Mental health professionals should not act in a dual capacity—both as a percipient witness and as a retained forensic expert. An example of this would be a mental health professional treating a plaintiff/patient who alleges a sexual assault by a prior practitioner. Many times, mental health professionals are asked to offer testimony regarding the treatment or damages as well as whether the defendant's conduct was below the standard of care.

Trial testimony, whether in the context of a percipient or retained expert, is essential to the success of the case. A mental health professional's knowledge, skill, education, and credibility are all called into question at trial.

The trial is a formal proceeding, unlike a deposition. The mental health professional will have to testify in a courtroom setting. Both parties, together with their respective attorneys, will be present, as well as the judge, the court reporter, court clerk, bailiff, and perhaps a jury. Testimony is given from "the stand." Further, members of the public are usually permitted in most cases.

If possible, mental health professionals should attempt to familiarize themselves with the courtroom surroundings to reduce anxiety. While mental health professionals often find themselves unwilling participants in litigation, there are ethical responsibilities in properly representing one's patient. If one is overly anxious about testifying, then steps should be taken to reduce the anxiety and improve one's performance. For instance, there are consultants who utilize videotape sessions involving mock questions and answers. There are other resources, such as multivolume books that go beyond the scope of such work and include specific question-and-answer formats. The important point to remember is that, personal issues aside, the professional is engaged in the process for the benefit of another. The primary goal of mental health professionals in testifying at trial will be to present themselves as credible by succinctly stating opinions and supporting them with facts developed during the course of the case.

The mental health professional will be subject to questions on direct examination by the party requesting his or her appearance at trial. Opposing counsel is then able to cross-examine the mental health professional. There are also questions on redirect and recross, respectively, by the parties. At all times, the judge is in charge of the trial and all that goes on in the courtroom.

During the course of examination, objections will be made by the attorneys. The judge will rule on all objections, and the mental health professional must wait for the judge's ruling before giving a response. If the judge sustains the objection, no answer is necessary, and the questioning attorney will formulate another question. If the judge overrules the objection, the witness should respond. If the witness no longer remembers the question, he or she should ask the judge directly if the question can be repeated. Thus, objections at trial are handled very differently from objections at a deposition (see Bersoff, chapter 2, this volume, for information pertaining to the nature of depositions).

Another significant difference between deposition and trial testimony is in the information offered during the testimony. At the deposition, the questioning is usually conducted by opposing counsel. Usually, at trial the "friendly" attorney will initiate the questions. Thus, the professional witness should state all opinions and state all supporting facts. Moreover, the focus of communication should be on the judge or, if a jury is present, on the jury directly. The attorney asking the questions is simply assisting in the delivery of information.

There are important points to bear in mind regarding testimony on cross-examination as well. Discussion with friendly counsel prior to trial should have identified areas of cross-examination. Once under cross-examination, an expert should strive to answer every question. While dancing around issues is appropriate to a limited degree, the witness's credibility will be severely prejudiced if the counsel on cross-examination has to move repeatedly to strike the expert's responses and the judge does strike them, perhaps ultimately admonishing the expert to respond.

If damaging facts or weaknesses in the case are being elicited on cross-examination, it is the duty of friendly counsel to rehabilitate the expert or witness on redirect examination. Responses to cross-examination questions should be more limited and succinctly stated unless the information being elicited is helpful to the case. Many times, the success of a case is assisted by counsel's conducting a poor cross-examination. For instance, in questioning the expert about his or her background, the expertise of the witness may be expanded on or reiterated for the jury. On the other hand, a successful cross-examination may also further the opposing side's position. For example, it may be elicited on cross-examination that the expert's opinion is based on facts that have not been established at trial or facts that do not exist.

Since the time of the deposition, there most probably has been intervening discovery. For instance, there are pretrial interrogatories exchanged between the parties, depositions conducted of opposing experts, and possibly an independent medical or mental examination performed of the injured party. Mental health professionals should confirm that they have been given all the relevant information in this regard.

In addition, the mental health professional should also confer with counsel to determine whether the "theme" established for the case is still the same as it was during the discovery phase of the matter. Many times, a case theme or focus will change, or be refined, based on the evidence adduced during the course of discovery. It is essential that the expert be aware of the focus of the case so that the ultimate trial testimony is supportive of this focus. If the expert's testimony will not support this change of focus, then these issues should be discussed prior to the time the expert takes the stand. Moreover, if the additional discovery information changes the mental health professional's testimony in any way, now is the time to discuss the change in opinion. It should be remembered that deposition testimony and discovery responses made by the parties may be changed or updated and therefore should be provided to the mental health professional.

Mental health professionals should also reconfirm what opinions will be elicited from them at trial. Many times, the initial opinion elicited during the consultation stages may need to be refined for trial purposes. In addition, the expert's opinion should be supported by the facts in the case.

Frequently, opposing counsel will file a pretrial motion to limit the expert's testimony to those issues identified by the attorney in the disclosure of expert witnesses. This disclosure of expert witnesses must delineate all issues an expert will offer at the time of trial and must be sent prior to trial. The pretrial motion may also try to limit trial testimony to those opinions that have been offered at the expert's deposition. In civil matters, the disclosure of experts may begin at least 70 days prior to trial. Thus, it is essential that the mental health professional and attorney discuss what opinions the expert is willing to offer at the time of trial. A failure to properly plan may mean that critical expert testimony may be excluded from trial. The strength of any expert's deposition testimony may dictate whether a case will settle prior to trial. The stronger the expert's performance, the better the outcome may be for the retaining party. Thus, a deposition of any expert is critical. The credibility of the expert bolsters the retaining party's credibility as well. For instance, if a well-renowned and well-respected expert is willing to testify that a mental health professional's conduct is within the standard of care, then the party's defense position is very strong. Mental health professionals should also consider the impact of a given case on their reputation. For instance, an expert who offers testimony only on behalf of defendants in every instance is suspect.

It is essential at trial that a mental health professional offering an expert opinion be intimately familiar with the facts of the case. Just because an expert offers an opinion that someone was negligent or damaged does not make it so. A judge or jury will be weighing the testimony of each witness.

A thorough review of all the materials, especially one's prior deposition testimony is essential to success. All materials should be gathered, organized, and reviewed again. Professionals must be able to support their opinions with a recitation of the facts that support them. The better versed one is on the facts, the more convincing one will appear to a trier of fact, whether judge or jury. An expert's job is to educate the jury and convince its members.

There is nothing worse than having an expert testify that he or she received only a portion of the relevant information available in a case.

Juries immediately think that the attorney is trying to hide something from his or her own expert. In one matter, a mental health professional acting as an expert was extremely disorganized and severely prejudiced a case. The mental health professional testified that he had only been provided with the deposition testimony of a few defense witnesses and had not reviewed the plaintiff's deposition testimony. While the expert had been provided with many deposition transcripts, he could not find them at the time of his deposition. This expert presented testimony on liability and damages in a void, which significantly and negatively impacted his credibility.

Another example of furnishing an opinion without an adequate factual foundation was one in which an expert relied on a treating physician's records rather than the physician's deposition testimony. The problem became clear when the expert had to admit that the physician's written notes were sparse and largely illegible. The reasonable inference the jury drew from this testimony was that the expert had no foundation for his opinion. Unfortunately, the deposition testimony of the physician, which was not reviewed by the expert, included testimony of the physician reading his notes into the record together with an explanation. Thus, the expert significantly impaired his party's case by a failure to review available deposition testimony diligently.

The expert's opinion should be soundly based on the evidence. The expert should be familiar enough with the discovery provided to refer to specific testimony, exhibits (discussed in another paragraph), records, and the like that support his or her opinion. For example, an opinion that the plaintiff did not form a meaningful transferential relationship must be supported by specific facts, for instance, that the plaintiff only had a few sessions with the mental health professional (the defendant); that the plaintiff continued to see another mental health professional, consulted over a longer term, concurrently; that the brief therapy was issue specific; or that the modality utilized does not specifically attempt to involve the transference relationship for treatment.

An expert who has not been provided with all the deposition testimony and documents is also subject to attack. If key facts involve dates, times, diagnosis, and the like, these should all be confirmed by a close review of the records. A mental health professional was effectively impeached on cross-examination when it turned out that the basis for the testimony was provided by the employing attorney. Unfortunately, deposition testimony and certain documents did not support the attorney's rendition of facts to the mental health professional. Thus, the entire testimony was suspect.

Sometimes, individuals will misstate the facts in the case as opposed to drawing a reasonable inference from them. If an attorney is misstating facts, the expert will be subject to attack. Do not rely on others. Mental health professionals should not wait for an attorney to contact them regarding these matters. Mental health professionals should take the initiative in confirming that the attorney understands the opinion of the mental health professional and the basis for that opinion. It would be most helpful to counsel if mental health professionals could inform counsel, for instance, that there has been a recent study performed concerning one of the tests utilized by the professional during the independent mental examination. If the mental health professional's role is that of a treating professional or percipient witness, it is essential that the attorney have the most recent session notes or is aware of whether the diagnosis or prognosis had changed regarding the plaintiff/patient.

Another issue that should be addressed prior to the time of trial is whether the mental health professional would like to use any form of demonstrative evidence during the course of testimony. *Demonstrative evidence* is the kind of evidence that is addressed directly to the senses, without intervention of testimony. This evidence may include maps, diagrams, photographs, models, charts, medical illustrations, or x-rays. Both the mental health professional and the attorney should review any exhibits that will be used at trial, especially those that will be enlarged for emphasis. There should be a discussion about the use of the exhibits and what testimony can be offered by the expert to illustrate an important point by reference to the exhibits. The mental health professional should understand the reason that the exhibit is being used by counsel. An example of such an exhibit may be a session note that documents the specifics about alleged abuse. Often, good exhibits at trial are transparent, lay definitions of key technical terms, such as "transference or countertransference," or of criteria for the relevant diagnosis. These can all explain the expert's testimony and educate the jury. If the expert is using terms that the jury does not understand, the expert's testimony will have little impact.

This brings to mind an actual example in which a trial exhibit was referred to ineffectually by a mental health professional. During trial, a mental health professional held up a card from the Rorschach inkblot test. The mental health professional had performed an independent mental examination of the plaintiff for the purpose of determining the level of the plaintiff's alleged damages caused by the defendant's alleged wrongful conduct. In explaining how damaged the plaintiff had been from the conduct, the expert mental health professional held up a Rorschach card for the jury to view. He explained that the plaintiff had seen a black widow with a red belly on the card, which evidenced a high level of damage to the plaintiff. One quick look at the jury was enough to determine that a number of jury members had also seen a black widow spider on the card. It called into question not only the test's validity, but also the expert examiner's conclusions about the plaintiff.

Another example positively illustrates the use of exhibits. In a case involving child abuse, a child's drawing, which documented a depressive feeling, was enlarged and commented on by the treating mental health professional at trial. The large picture, containing mostly figures done in brown, black, and red, made a dramatic impact.

Prior to actually taking the stand during trial to testify, the mental health professional should inquire whether the trial will be a bench trial (one not involving a jury) or will be held before both a judge and jury. These two are completely separate, and testimony should be aimed accordingly.

Good practice dictates that the mental health professional review his or her deposition testimony most carefully. Should the mental health professional testify differently at the time of trial from the testimony given at the time of the deposition, this will be a primary avenue for opposing counsel to attack credibility. If the expert determines that the trial testimony must be different, then this issue should be discussed with counsel prior to trial.

A cautionary note is called for at this time. Mental health professionals should not agree to perform services as expert consultants in a matter if they do not intend to testify at the time of trial. A party could be placed in a very difficult situation should counsel be forced to retain a new consultant, or expert witness, immediately prior to the time of trial. The mental health professional should also confirm that he or she will be available at the time of the scheduled trial. If the mental health professional is not called as the first witness at the time of trial (which is highly unlikely), then the mental health professional should get a status report from the attorney regarding what the testimony has been during the course of trial. If there has been significant testimony that would have an impact on the expert's testimony, it is imperative to know this information before taking the stand.

The attorney should also be able to provide the testifying expert with an impression about the judge as well as information obtained about the jury during voir dire (i.e., the initial questioning process during the selection of a jury). Information is usually obtained about employment, perceptions, prior jury experience, and similar matters. In a complex case involving juror questionnaires, there may be a large amount of information about the jurors. If questionnaires are used in a matter and there has been no order by the court concerning their confidentiality, certain information may be available to the mental health professional.

An expert's demeanor on the witness stand is also important. An example of an expert's condescending attitude occurred during the trial of a mental health professional's malpractice case. The defendant/mental health professional had allegedly been sexually inappropriate with the plaintiff/client during the course of therapy. On direct examination, the expert testifying on behalf of the plaintiff about the issue of the standard of care described the defendant/mental health professional's conduct as "foreplay." During cross-examination, the question was posed to this expert to define the term *foreplay* as he had utilized it during his direct examination. The response was given in a condescending tone, as follows: "Counsel, don't you know what foreplay is?" The expert ultimately testified that *foreplay* is the conduct engaged in immediately preceding intercourse. Based on the fact that the therapeutic relationship lasted for a long period of time (i.e., over 5 years) with no intercourse, the next question focused on whether the defendant/mental health professional had really engaged in foreplay over this extended period of time without consummation. At the conclusion of the trial, several jury members shared the observation that they had been offended by this expert's demeanor. One of the reasons the jury gave was that the expert was male and the examining attorney was female. The expert also severely impugned his credibility by using a rather provocative term that did not match the circumstance. It was not reasonable to the jury that the defendant/mental health professional might really have engaged in foreplay for numerous years without the activity culminating in intercourse.

Another matter that arises at trial is the use of hypotheticals. A hypothetical is a good way to present a case to the jury. The hypothetical should be discussed before trial. The expert can assist counsel in formulating an effective hypothetical. There should also be a discussion about which key facts would change the expert's opinion. There are usually several key facts about which the parties disagree in any case. The expert must be clear on which are the key conflicting facts and be ready to respond to a hypothetical utilizing the unfavorable facts.

When a hypothetical is posed to an expert at trial, the expert should respond accordingly. Most hypothetical questions used at trial have been preapproved by counsel for the parties. If an expert refuses to provide an opinion to an opposing party's hypothetical, that significantly and negatively impacts the expert's credibility. In one matter, a judge actually ordered an expert to respond to an opposing counsel's hypothetical. The expert still refused to do so. It was clear from the ultimate decision that the judge totally rejected the expert's testimony. Thus, it is important to have responses prepared to the adverse party's hypothetical.

Fee arrangements for mental health professionals should always be clarified at the outset. If you are a percipient witness (i.e., a treating mental health professional) and will be asked to testify to your diagnosis and other treatment issues, you should confirm that you will be afforded an expert witness fee unless the jurisdiction does not permit that fee level.[1] Also, clarify whether you will be accepting a lien for services and confirm the lien in writing to the patient and counsel. Never accept a lien that is contingent on a successful verdict. It ruins credibility, apart from the fact that there are adverse ethical considerations as well.

Likewise, if mental health professionals are retained as experts, they should clarify all fee arrangements and confirm these in writing with the attorney. It is good business to require a refundable retainer against which services are billed during the pendency of the case.

If there is a well-recognized work that the mental health professional may be relying on, the mental health professional should notify counsel retaining his or her services. The mental health professional should also review the work to ensure that it supports his or her position. Mental health professionals should also advise the retaining attorney of any adverse lawsuits against them. Further, if the mental health professionals have published any written opinions or made any presentation that conflicts with the position they are currently taking, they should notify the retaining counsel. It is a nightmare at trial to be confronted with an article of one's own that directly contradicts a current opinion. Do not bet on the fact that opposing counsel will not have access to your written word.

An expert should only offer testimony in areas in which he or she is trained and familiar regarding the standard of care. One of the easiest ways to impeach an expert's credibility is when that expert testifies that another professional's conduct fell below the standard of care. It can be shown, however, that the expert does not utilize the modality of therapy employed by the defendant and is not familiar with this modality in that the expert has not taken any courses or read any works in the area. In one case, the opposing expert was critical of a treating mental health professional's use of experimental psychotherapy. However, the opposing expert was totally unfamiliar with this modality: its uses, its function, and its desired effect. How could the expert know if this modality was appropriate for the problem presented to the defendant by the patient? How would the expert know if the therapy was conducted appropriately within a given framework? The jury did not believe that this expert had the appropriate foundation to render an opinion. You cannot be an expert in all areas, and you should recognize your limitations or else sacrifice your credibility.

At trial, the mental health professional should not bring any documents to the stand without clearing them with the counsel who has retained the expert's services. Any document the mental health professional may carry to the stand is subject to disclosure at trial. On the other hand, mental health professionals should familiarize themselves with any exhibits on which counsel will be questioning them once they are on the stand.

In summary, mental health professionals should establish their role at the onset. They should be prepared by knowing the focus of the case and of their own testimony; in addition, they should be familiar with all relevant information.

Note

1. State fee schedules for witnesses differentiate between expert and percipient witnesses. Under some state laws, but not all, percipient witnesses may be entitled to expert witness fees.

Section II

_____

Forensic Assessment and Techniques

The second part of this book discusses several diverse modes of evaluation in a forensic setting: how to complete and use a psychological evaluation in an ethical manner; how to evaluate child custody cases; and how to handle various aspects of juvenile justice and criminal forensic evaluations. Issues commonly at the center of lawsuits and formal complaints arising out of child custody work are addressed, and the evaluation process in child custody cases is discussed. In the discussion of juvenile justice, there is a focus on the roles and functions of mental health professionals involved in dependency cases being adjudicated by juvenile courts. That chapter explicates, for example, the evaluator and therapist roles that mental health professionals may assume, and it also notes ethical as well as practical issues important for mental health professionals to observe. Finally, that discussion is continued in the chapter on criminal forensic evaluations, which emphasizes training, skills, and practice standards that should be observed, despite efforts by retaining attorneys to violate those standards.

5

How to Complete and Use a Psychological Evaluation in an Ethical Manner

Arthur N. Wiens and Reed M. Mueller

Introduction

This chapter will assist both students and experienced clinicians to complete psychological evaluations and use psychological tests in a socially responsible and ethical manner. Such practice will be consistent with various guidelines and standards that have been established by various professional organizations, codes we review briefly here.

At the outset, we call attention to a summary of ethical codes by Cynthia B. Schmeiser (1992), who specializes in large-scale assessment, item and test bias, and applied research. She observed that questions regarding moral duties, obligations, and responsibilities are present in all aspects of our lives. As our values and beliefs change and our society struggles to adapt to the effects of these changes, questions of ethics unfold, raising new issues for us to consider. On that basis, she argued that the professions have distinct ethical obligations to the public, and that these obligations encompass professional competence, integrity, public safety, confidentiality, objectivity, and truthfulness, all of which are intended to preserve and safeguard public confidence. She also observed that, unfortunately, there are almost daily reports in the media of moral dilemmas and unethical behavior by professionals. In her own area of large-scale assessment of students, she noted abuses in regard to the following aspects of testing: preparing students to take tests; the use and interpretation of test results; students' being provided with the actual test questions before a test has been administered; unauthorized extensions of time limits on standardized tests; falsification of answer sheets; and violations of the confidentiality of students' test scores. Her conclusion was that the "measurement profession" should consider developing and adopting a code of professional conduct.

Ethics for Psychologists

The American Psychological Association (APA) has such an ethics code, to be sure. Canter, Bennett, Jones, and Nagy (1994) started their commentary on the APA's Ethics Code (2002) with the following considerations:

> Sound ethical decision-making is based on a process that involves multiple steps, some of which are preventive and taken in advance, and some of which are taken at the time the ethical dilemma presents itself. These steps are as follows: (1) know the Ethics Code, (2) know the applicable state and federal laws and regulations, (3) know the rules and regulations of the institution where you work, (4) engage in continuing education in ethics, (5) identify when there is a potential ethical problem, (6) learn the skills needed to analyze ethical obligations in often complex situations, and (7) consult with senior professionals knowledgeable about ethics. (p. 3)

Regarding the need for up-to-date knowledge about ethics, Canter et al. noted that, in these days of rapidly expanding databases, innovative services, new health care delivery systems, new research interests, novel education and training experiences, ubiquitous lawyers, litigious consumers, and ever-changing ethical rules, there is much opportunity to lose sight of the rules and subtleties of ethics unless one persists with efforts at continuing education. Even so, the psychologist may have blind spots, and it is important to admit and consider that no one practitioner has all the answers and that what might be presumed to be a relatively simple or even routine psychological professional activity could have a harmful effect on a particular consumer.

Each section in the ethics code is relevant to and important for the practicing psychologist. Our present interest, however, is in Section 9, "Assessment" (APA, 2002). The coverage is quite broad and includes such introductory caveats as the prohibition against making statements about individuals whom the psychologist has not personally assessed. Similarly, many types of assessment and intervention activities will require informed consent from the patient-participant.

Section 9.01: Bases for Assessment

When a psychologist writes a report or makes a diagnosis or offers a set of recommendations, the evaluative statements have been appropriately substantiated. It is suggested that a clinical interview is a prudent assessment procedure to verify the observations or conclusions that are being drawn from psychological test data (APA, 2002, Section 9.01). What should the ethical psychologist do in situations when this is not possible? For example, a psychologist may be asked to interpret a Minnesota Multiphasic Personality Inventory (MMPI) profile on a patient someone else has examined and the psychologist has never seen and with whom the psychologist has no professional relationship. A similar situation may also obtain for computerized test interpretations, for which an actuarial report is processed in a fashion that takes very little of the personal history of the patient.

Section 9.02: Use of Assessments

The standard in Section 9.02 (APA, 2002) has to do with the proper use of assessment techniques, interviews, tests, and other instruments, which should not be used to address questions beyond the scope of their purpose or design. Obviously, psychologists should read the test manuals and know whether a test was designed to help with the assessment situation at hand (e.g., a custody evaluation). If tests are used for personnel assessment, the psychologist will also have to be familiar with the provisions of two federal laws—the Americans with Disabilities Act (1990) and the Uniform Guidelines on Employee Selection Procedures (1978).

Section 9.03: Informed Consent in Assessments

The Section 9.03 standard (APA, 2002) describes the necessity of informed consent in assessments and evaluations and, when informed consent is not required (i.e., mandated by law or governmental regulations), the necessity to inform the individual of the nature and purpose of the assessment in understandable language. In addition, a psychologist must obtain informed consent for the use of an interpreter and ensure that confidentiality is maintained.

Section 9.04: Release of Test Data

Section 9.04 (APA, 2002) has to do with not misusing assessment techniques and assessment reports and preventing others from misusing them. The inference to be drawn here is to refrain from releasing test reports or test data to persons (other than the patient) who are not qualified to use such information. There is extended discussion in this section about proper responses when test data are requested by subpoena or other health care providers.

Section 9.05: Test Construction

Section 9.05 states (APA, 2002) that psychologists who develop and conduct research with tests and other assessment techniques should use scientific procedures and current professional knowledge for test design, standardization, validation, reduction or elimination of bias, and recommendations for use. (This standard is discussed further in this chapter.)

Section 9.06: Interpreting Assessment Results

In interpreting test results, the ethical psychologist takes into account possible reservations about the validity of the findings (APA, 2002, Section 9.06). For example, was the patient fluent in English, fatigued, stressed, or poorly motivated to perform on the tests?

Section 9.07: Assessment by Unqualified Persons

Psychologists ensure that persons who use psychological tests are competently trained to do so or, if still in training, that they are properly supervised (APA, 2002, Section 9.07). It should be recognized that supervising psychologists have the ultimate responsibility for the patients and for the professional performance of persons whom they are currently supervising. By way of comparison with medical training, this point has been clearly spelled out in "teaching physician" rules that have been developed by the Health Care Financing Administration (1995). Essentially, the "personal and identifiable direction" given to interns and residents was further explicated in requirements for the physical presence of the supervisor on site and the supervisor's being present in the room with the patient when the key portions of the assessment that led to the diagnosis are being completed.

Section 9.08: Obsolete Tests and Outdated Test Results

The first component of the standard regarding obsolete tests and outdated test results (APA, 2002, Section 9.08) is that the ethical psychologist should not base conclusions on tests that are outdated for the current assessment purpose. Further, the assessment data should be current. A second component of this standard is that psychologists should not use tests that have been superseded by newer versions of a test or by other tests that are better suited for the assessment at hand.

Section 9.09: Test Scoring and Interpretation Services

The standard in Section 9.09 (APA, 2002) has three components. The first one is essentially truth in advertising, namely, that the test vendor accurately describe information about the test's norms, validity, and reliability as well as the intended applications of the procedures. Second, psychologists select scoring and interpretation services on the basis of evidence for their validity. Third, the individual clinician is ultimately accountable for psychological assessment services regardless of the use of automated scoring services.

Section 9.10: Explaining Assessment Results

The language of the standard regarding explanation of assessment results is quite detailed (APA, 2002, Section 9.10), but states in effect that psychologists take reasonable steps to ensure that appropriate explanations of test results be given to those assessed. There will be times when the referring source will have other data to be integrated into a feedback session with the patient, and if this is to be the case, the psychologist should make it clear to the patient at the outset. Most practicing psychologists will want to schedule a face-to-face feedback session with the patient to ensure that additional clarification can be provided so that the patient understands the assessment findings and conclusions (e.g., patients not misunderstand the 50th percentile as a 50, which might be interpreted by them as a failing score).

Canter et al. (1994) were aware that there are some psychologists who, in the interest of securing income and keeping their financial accounting current, refuse to send an assessment report to a referral source or some other party involved in a patient's clinical care until full payment has been made for their services. It is our opinion that assessment information cannot be withheld even if payment for the professional services has not been made. It is the psychologist's responsibility to settle in advance on payment arrangements. Even so, there will be some likely occasions when the psychologist will not receive compensation or will have to wait a long time to receive payment.

Section 9.11: Maintaining Test Security

As stated by Canter et al. (1994), psychologists bear the legal and ethical responsibility of trying to protect test materials. When test materials are requested for review or for teaching purposes, psychologists should determine not only the source of the request but also the intended audience (APA, 2002, Section 9.11). Requests for testing materials are often made by college and high school students who would like to incorporate them into term papers they are preparing. Psychiatry residency program directors often make similar requests.

Standards for Educational and Psychological Testing

The "standards" referred to in this section and published in 1985 reflect the consensus reached by three national organizations: the American Educational Research Association, the APA, and the National Council on Measurement in Education. The standards booklet is the most recent in a series of five publications spanning a period of over 40 years, intended to inform professionals who use tests about the best available technical and ethical recommendations regarding testing practices and procedures. These standards represent a painstaking consensus crafted by a 12-member committee backed by 125 advisers and ratified by 16 ad hoc reviewers. As can be inferred from the multiple publications, there is a constant evolution of thought and practice as related to testing standards.

Standards (American Educational Research Association et al., 1985) is a fairly exhaustive document that has been divided into four major sections: "Technical Standards for Test Construction and Evaluation;" "Professional

Standards for Test Use;" "Standards for Particular Applications;" and "Standards for Administrative Procedures." The first section contains five chapters and 82 standards covering test validity; test reliability; test development and revisions; scaling, norming score comparability, and equating; and test publication, namely, technical manuals and user guides.

The second section on professional standards for test use may be of the most interest to many readers. It contains seven chapters and 62 standards. In the introduction to this section, the authors noted the following:

> In applying standards to test use, as opposed to test development, more flexibility and use of professional judgment are required. The appropriateness of specific test uses cannot be evaluated in the abstract but only in the context of the larger assessment process. The principal questions to be asked in evaluating test use are whether or not the test is appropriate (valid) for its specific role in the larger assessment process and whether or not the test user has accurately described the extent to which the score supports any decision made or administrative action taken. (American Educational Research Association et al., 1985, p. 41)

The seven chapters in this section cover general principles of test use, clinical testing, educational and psychological testing in the schools, test use in counseling, employment testing, professional and occupational licensure and certification, and program evaluation. It is sobering to think that this document can be regarded as essential for psychologists for structuring individual practices in a responsible manner. It should certainly have as prominent a place on the clinician's desk as diagnostic manuals.

The third section of the *Standards* has two chapters and 15 standards covering the testing of linguistic minorities and testing people with handicapping conditions (American Educational Research Association et al., 1985). We are reminded that, for a non-native English speaker and for a speaker of some dialects of English, every test given in English becomes, in part, a language or literacy test. While testing in the language of the test takers may sometimes be appropriate, one cannot assume that translation produces a version of the test that is equivalent in content, difficulty level, reliability, and validity. Psychometric properties cannot be assumed to be comparable across languages. Modification of tests for handicapped test takers has raised the issue that there have been few empirical investigations on the effects of special accommodations on resulting scores or on psychometric properties of the tests. Indeed, there are unresolved issues regarding such modifications. Should test scores obtained in nonstandard conditions be flagged so they neither mislead test users nor harm handicapped test takers whose scores do not accurately reflect their abilities? Would identifying the test takers as handicapped deny them the opportunity to compete on the same terrain as nonhandicapped test takers? One must weigh professional and ethical considerations in arriving at solutions when testing language minorities and handicapped individuals.

The fourth section contains two chapters with 21 standards (American Educational Research Association et al., 1985). This section covers test administration, scoring and reporting, and protecting the rights of test takers. It calls attention to the fact that interpretation of test results is most reliable when the measurements are obtained under standardized or controlled conditions. It also calls attention to the fact that informed consent implies that the test takers or representatives have been made aware, in language that they can understand, of the reasons for testing, the type of tests to be used, the intended use, and the range of material to be released and to whom.

Wagner (1987), in reviewing the *Standards* (American Educational Research Association et al., 1985) and noting how many people contributed to their formulation, still felt that the booklet was quite readable, clear, and instructive. He recommended that anyone who constructs, administers, or interprets tests undertake a thorough initial reading of the *Standards* and, once familiar with the layout, refer to specific sections whenever technical, ethical, or procedural questions arise. He further observed that testing developments are ongoing, and, in a sense *Standards* was outdated the moment it was published. He thought, however, that it should suffice until the next revision came along.

From the Ethics Code to Specific Practice Recommendations

Two neuropsychologists, Binder and Thompson (1995) have given us a good example of how to implement ethical assessment in a specialty practice. Specifically, they generated a set of recommendations for practice regarding the issues of avoiding harm to the patient, ensuring competence of the practitioner, test validity, valid test interpretation, maintenance of records, use and supervision of nondoctoral personnel, release of raw data, documentation of results, multiple relationships, and fees. In general, they urged that clinicians adhere to the ethics code rather than to a personal standard of professional behavior.

Of particular interest in their publication is the formulation of 20 recommendations pertaining to neuropsychological assessment (Binder &

Thompson, 1995). The recommendations represent the authors' interpretation of how to apply the APA ethics code (APA, 2002) to this aspect of psychological practice. Their first recommendation is that "psychologists remain aware of general trends in the relevant neuropsychological literature" (Binder & Thompson, 1995, p. 29). The sixth is that "psychologists use up-to-date neuropsychological tests and norms, and rely on current knowledge" (p. 33). They considered important demographic characteristics of individuals in making interpretations and acknowledged limitations in our current knowledge. Recommendation 20 asserts that "psychologists do not attempt to answer referral questions using methods that are likely to be inadequate because of time or remuneration limitations" (p. 43). The recommendations cited here are representative of their set of 20 recommendations and demonstrate that it is possible to write implementation statements derived from more general ethical guidelines. Binder and Thompson illustrated their recommendations with examples drawn from practice.

Another useful practice formulation was offered by Johnson-Greene, Hardy-Morais, Adams, Hardy, and Bergloff (1997). Johnson-Greene and his coauthors, also clinical neuropsychologists, observed that until the mid-1900s in America true informed consent was nonexistent. However, it has now become well entrenched in the medical community, more recently has been embraced by psychologists, and more recently still by neuropsychologists. Informed consent, as much an ethical as a legal concept, is presented as a conscious effort to promote patient autonomy and self-determination. From their discussion of various issues concerning informed consent, Johnson-Greene et al. derived six recommendations for providing informed consent to patients receiving neuropsychological evaluations. Their first recommendation is: "The patient should be provided with a basic description of the intended purpose of the evaluation from the perspective of the neuropsychologist. Also, provide the name of the person(s) requesting the evaluation, if this is someone other than the patient" (p. 459). Other recommendations cover discussion of the procedures to be used, the limits of confidentiality, records location, and informed consent from guardians where indicated. The sixth recommendation is: "Written documentation of informed consent outlining the aforementioned points should be obtained from the patient or legal representative prior to evaluation" (p. 459).

An Ethical Assessment Strategy

Given the issues discussed in this chapter, we propose that to act ethically the psychologist utilize a focused yet comprehensive assessment strategy to satisfy the values of both nonmaleficence and beneficence. Such an assessment strategy will include issues such as the following: examining and fine-tuning the referral question; defining roles and providing informed consent; selecting measures; interviewing effectively; assimilating multiple sources of information, including reports and measures from family members, significant others, other third-party observers, and available records; integrating psychological test results with other sources of information; examining the internal consistency of this information; and defining impressions, recommendations, and limitations for the assessment.

As a first step toward conducting ethical assessment, one must examine one's assumptive structure regarding psychological assessment. The effective clinician must be willing to eschew faulty assumptions about psychological assessment. In so doing, he or she will be more effective, thus allowing for increased beneficence. The neuropsychologist R. Sbordone (1996) introduced a list of commonly held false assumptions about psychological assessment. An abstract of Sbordone's assumptions is enlightening with regard to psychological assessment in general. In reviewing his list, one can construct several categories of *false assumptions*.

First, it is false that extra-measure sources of information are unimportant. That is to say, it is false to assume that obtaining a detailed clinical history, information from individuals other than the patient, and review of medical or legal records, are unimportant or at least less important than the results from our measures. On the contrary, evaluation of interview and testing behavior are in fact of utmost importance because our measures are influenced by differential levels of effort or motivation given to the task. Because of this, behavioral observation is imperative in order to use psychological measures effectively.

Second, it is a false assumption that our measures have perfect sensitivity and specificity. Thus, many clinicians assume that, if pathology is not indicated by the measures utilized in the assessment, pathology is in fact not present; conversely, if pathology is indicated by the measures used, pathology is in fact present. This overconfidence in the results of psychological measures results in naïve interpretation of results that may falsely identify an individual as having or not having a diagnosable mental disorder.

Finally, it is a false assumption that our measures are *the* essential ingredient to the process of psychological evaluation; while they are an important and effective piece of such evaluation, they are not the essential ingredient. They are only as good as the conditions wherein they are used, and even then they have varying levels of utility in predicting future behavior. The results obtained from these sources of information must be evaluated within the context of the personal history of the individual being evaluated, the behavior of that person throughout the entire assessment, the environment in which the assessment takes place, and the environments in which inferred behaviors of the patient are to be generalized.

Framing the Assessment

In addition to getting themselves unencumbered by false assumptions, clinicians must also pave the way to smooth assessment by fine-tuning referral questions. To do this, it is quite important that they speak directly to the referral source about which questions the referral sources hope to have answered through this process. This is the time when the clinician should identify which questions he or she can answer adequately and confidently and which questions are more difficult or impossible to answer through a psychological assessment. From this discussion, the psychologist will be able to ascertain how best to aid both the patient and the referral source, develop specific goals for the assessment, ready release of information forms for appropriate historical records (e.g., medical records), and consider appropriate psychological measures for the assessment.

Once this is completed, the next task for the psychologist is to define the roles of those connected to the assessment by providing informed consent to the patient. This is a golden opportunity for the clinician not only to meet ethical requirements, but also to effectively frame the assessment experience for the patient because, in our opinion, an effectively described assessment often enhances patient effort and communication during the assessment. Consider the example of an adolescent brought to a mental health clinic for assessment of disruptive behavior. If the assessment is not framed adequately for the adolescent, it is possible, perhaps even probable, that the results of psychological testing will be an inadequate reflection of his or her current status because of impaired effort or frank opposition to the tasks. If, however, adolescents are helped to understand that the assessment will benefit them and will answer questions of concern, psychologists are more likely to obtain valid psychological assessment results.

In addition, the specific pieces of informed consent include discussion of the purpose of the assessment, the roles of those involved, the limitations of confidentiality, the presence of supervision (if any), and who will be privy to the results. Finally, the importance of obtaining appropriate records should be emphasized, with appropriate release of information procedures followed.

The Interview

At this point, the initial portions of the interview should be completed. While we provide a brief overview of interview topics, we are not able, within the confines of this chapter, to provide a comprehensive discussion of interview technique.[1]

In our view, the purpose of the interview with the patient is not primarily to obtain the raw facts of the patient's history; rather, it is to obtain the *patient's* perspective on this history, along with the patient's perception of the presenting problem. In focusing on the presenting problem, the clinician should assess the onset, duration, frequency, intensity, context, and exacerbating conditions or circumstances for the identified problem. In the course of obtaining these pieces of data, the clinician can begin to understand the impact the patient sees the problem having on his or her life. Following this, the global and specific effects of the presenting problem on the patient's social role and interpersonal functioning should be discussed (e.g., "How does this problem affect your relationships with those close to you?" "How does this problem affect you at work or school?").

Next, the clinician should move on to a more specific assessment of the patient's perspective on his or her psychosocial history. In obtaining this history, it is important to assess it globally. Effective clinical psychologists interest themselves in the family, educational, occupational, medical, mental health, and substance use history of the patient. With regard to family history, the importance of obtaining the patient's view of his or her upbringing, sibling relationships, family disciplinary style, parents' marital relationship, and family medical and mental health history are all important. In addition, the assessment of present family relationships (e.g., marital status and relationship; relationships with children) is important.

The patient's educational history is also important not only in obtaining a perspective on the patient's academic prowess, but also assessing how he or she interacted with others (e.g., authority figures such as teachers, as well as peers) in a setting distinct from the family environment.

Obviously, the clinician will also attempt to evaluate patients' intellectual development: Did they have any learning difficulties? Did they repeat any grades? Were there conduct or emotional problems? Did they have concentration deficits? What were their typical grades? What subjects were easiest and most difficult? What was the highest level of education completed? Such questions will assist the psychologist in adequate interpretation of the results of psychological measures by viewing these data from the perspective of the patients' learning history. In addition, the clinician must evaluate patients' occupational history, considering questions of previous employment satisfaction, problems with employers, and frequency of job turnover. Interpersonal relationships with coworkers also can be assessed at this point. The patients' views of changes in work habits, performance, and satisfaction since the onset of the presenting problem also should be assessed at this point.

Medical history is extremely important. Not only should the psychologist raise queries about present and past medical conditions and events, but the psychologist should also obtain the developmental history of the individual. For example, do patients recall hearing about any developmental delays? Did they have any major childhood ailments or diseases? Did they have any neurological conditions, such as seizure disorder, syncopal episodes, cerebral vascular accidents, or significant head injuries? Did they have any significant sensory deficits or losses (e.g., vision, hearing)? Any positive indications of these conditions should give rise to more questions regarding how they may have affected patients' development, personality, and functioning across environments. In addition, should they be likely to influence results of the evaluation, such indications should be discussed in the narrative of the report of the psychological assessment.

In addition, mental health history is crucial. One needs to ascertain the mental health history of the patient prior to the presenting problem. Any present or previous episodes of depression, anxiety, thought disorder, substance use, or other disorders should be discussed. Plus, previous psychotherapy, substance abuse treatment, and hospitalizations, along with respective effects and processes, should be discussed. Finally, current use of psychotropic medications should be discussed along with the patient's perspectives on potential benefits from use of these medications.

Finally, the mental status of the patient should be assessed. The neuropsychologist E. D. Bigler (1984) emphasized important aspects of the mental status exam. He suggested that the orientation (i.e., the accurate awareness of time, place, person, and situation) of the patient should never be assumed and must be assessed, even when the patient appears to be oriented. Next, the examiner should evaluate the patient's dress and grooming, asking the question of whether aspects of the person's personal hygiene are neglected. Moving on to the area of language, the examiner should note "whether conversational speech appears normal or whether there appears to be a paucity of content or loquaciousness" (p. 31). Affect and mood should also be evaluated. The etiology of the mood disturbance, from the patient's perspective, should be frankly discussed. In addition, the congruence of affect with mood should be commented on. Thought content and process should also be considered, including the presence or absence of loose associations, tangentiality, obsessions, compulsions, phobias, and suicidal or homicidal thinking. If either of the last two is present, further assessment is warranted, including evaluation of the presence or absence of intent or plan, frequency of the thoughts, lethality of the means, as well the demographic characteristics of the patient that might increase the probability of successful suicide behavior (Bednar, Bednar, Lambert, & Waite, 1991). Memory, general fund of information, insight, and judgment can be evaluated clinically last, perhaps with the Mini Mental State Examination proposed by a National Institute of Mental Health (NIMH) research group (Crook et al., 1986), if it is not the plan of the clinician to conduct further cognitive assessment. This is quite important, even if the assessment does not concern "cognitive functioning" but rather concerns "personality functioning." The psychologist must still assess basic cognitive functions inasmuch as impairment in areas outlined can heavily influence the accuracy of a patient's verbal self-report, not to mention responses on self-report personality measures.

Measure Selection

Once the initial portion of the clinical interview has been completed, the second phase of the assessment can be initiated: measure selection and use. In the present managed care context, we must utilize every moment of time with a patient effectively. Toward this end, we would do well to refine our measure selection algorithm. We need to be able to answer as many questions as possible with an appropriately succinct and sound interview and records review and then answer any remaining questions and firm up diagnostic impressions with *focused* use of psychological measures. Selection of instruments should follow directly the information obtained from the interview as well as a review of the fundamental questions related to the initial referral. As outlined in the section on psychological test standards, examiners should have a firm understanding of the psychometric strengths and weaknesses of each instrument they use.

When the question concerns cognitive functioning or dysfunction, the psychologist should consider an assessment of the following cognitive domains: verbal and nonverbal abilities (i.e., traditional IQ measures); attention and concentration; language; memory; perception (e.g., visual, tactile, and auditory); and self-regulatory, executive, and problem-solving functions (Bigler, 1984). In addition, personality dynamics, even in a "cognitive assessment," should be assessed with reliable and valid instruments. The reason for this is clear: Emotional status has been linked to associated variation in cognitive test results. As such, the responsible clinician should seek to establish the emotional status of the patient when given either personality or cognitive evaluation questions.

Furthermore, assessing global functioning and emotional status through multiple methods allows the psychologist to produce a report that considers the convergent validity of several sources of the same information. For example, we should endeavor to obtain evaluation of the patient by (a) using appropriate self-report and individually administered instruments and (b) using measures of psychological and cognitive functioning obtained from close observers in the home, care-setting, or educational environment. After receiving appropriate permission to administer and obtain these measures, the clinician should also seek to interview all appropriate parties to gather collateral information about the patient's complaints and history as well as to ascertain a clinical assessment of the validity of the measures completed by collateral sources of information.

One way to ascertain the validity of collateral information is to examine these data along with all other data obtained, including test results, historical records (e.g., medical, legal, academic), and patient interview results, for the internal consistency (or lack thereof) of these informational sources. When the psychologist observes highly consistent results across all sources, he or she can present results more confidently, making appropriate recommendations and inferences from the assessment context to the contexts of the referral questions; however, when this is not the case, the ethically minded psychologist should plainly state the lack of consistency, possible reasons for this, and questions that remain unanswered.

Conclusion

While developing and following an ethical assessment strategy provides some protection for the ethically minded psychologist, further efforts can, and should, be made. Why is this, and what further efforts can be made? Pope and Vetter (1995) reported that psychologists, in a national survey of previously encountered ethical dilemmas, identified two frequent ethical challenges in psychological assessment situations. First, there was concern regarding the "availability of tests (or computerized interpretations) to those 'not' trained in testing" (p. 58). This came to be a problem when psychologists were asked to interpret psychological measures blindly, without ever seeing the client. Of course, conducting an ethical assessment requires patient contact for the many reasons already mentioned. Keeping these considerations in mind, and explaining them adequately to those who pressure psychologists to "interpret" measures blindly, is essential both for ethically consistent behavior and for the further usefulness of our psychological assessment enterprise.

A second main source of concern regarding ethical dilemmas in psychological assessment was "basing conclusions on inadequate data or ignoring important sources of data" (Pope & Vetter, 1995, p. 58). Again, keeping in mind the need for psychologists to examine the internal consistency of their reports is important to avoid such problems. For those assessments in which the internal consistency is low, the psychologist should recognize and report accordingly. This finding is itself an important piece of the overall evaluation.

Additional efforts to reduce the risk of unethical assessment behavior include reviewing the assessment results with the patient as an important follow-up to an assessment. This review (a) greatly aids the patient in understanding and using the assessment and (b) allows the psychologist an opportunity to clear up observed inconsistencies and errors in historical information about the patient. In addition, the development of appropriate quality assurance measures within a psychological assessment practice is also prudent. Such measures include report turnaround time guidelines, checklists of important information to include in a report (e.g., educational history, assessment of suicide potential), and frequent peer review of reports.

Notes

1. The reader might usefully consult other published writings, such as two contributions by the first author (Wiens, 1990, 1991), for a comprehensive discussion of interview purpose and technique.

References

American Educational Research Association, American Psychological Association, & National Council on Measurement in Education. (1985). *Standards for educational and psychological testing.* Washington, DC: American Psychological Association.

American Psychological Association. (2002). Ethical principles of psychologists and code of conduct. *American Psychologist, 57,* 1060–1073.

Americans with Disabilities Act of 1990, 42 U.S.C.A. 12101 et seq. (West 1993).

Bednar, R. L., Bednar, S. C., Lambert, M. J., & Waite, D. R. (1991). *Psychotherapy with high risk clients: Legal and professional standards.* Pacific Grove, CA: Brooks/Cole.

Bigler, E. D. (1984). *Diagnostic clinical neuropsychology.* Austin: University of Texas Press.

Binder, L. M., & Thompson, L. L. (1995). The ethics code and neuropsychological assessment practices. *Archives of Clinical Neuropsychology, 10,* 27–46.

Canter, M. B., Bennett, B. E., Jones, S. E., & Nagy, T. F. (1994). *Ethics for psychologists: A commentary on the APA ethics code.* Washington, DC: American Psychological Association.

Crook, T. H., Bartus, R. T., Ferris, S. H., Whitehouse, P., Cohen, G. D., & Gershon, S. (1986). Age-associated memory impairment: Proposed diagnostic criteria and measures of clinical change: Report of a National Institute of Mental Health Work Group. *Developmental Neuropsychology, 2,* 261–276.

Health Care Financing Administration. Medicare teaching physician rules. 60 Fed. Reg. 236 (Dec. 8, 1995).

Johnson-Greene, D., Hardy-Morais, C., Adams, K. M., Hardy, C., & Bergloff, P. (1997). Informed consent and neuropsychological assessment: Ethical considerations and proposed guidelines. *The Clinical Neuropsychologist, 11,* 454–460.

Pope, K. S., & Vetter, V. A. (1995). Ethical dilemmas encountered by members of the American Psychological Association: A national survey. In D. N. Bersoff (Ed.), *Ethical conflicts in psychology* (pp. 49–64). Washington, DC: American Psychological Association.

Sbordone, R. (1996). Ecological validity: Some critical issues for the neuropsychologist. In R. Sbordone & C. Long (Eds.), *Ecological validity of neuropsychological testing* (pp. 15–42). Delray Beach, FL: St. Lucie Press.

Schmeiser, C. B. (1992, Fall). Ethical codes in the professions. *Educational Measurement: Issues and Practice*, pp. 5–11.

Uniform Guidelines on Employee Selection Procedures, 41 C.F.R. §60, pt. 60-3 (1978).

Wagner, E. E. (1987). A review of the 1985 standards for educational and psychological testing: User responsibility and social justice. *Journal of Counseling and Development, 66*, 202–203.

Wiens, A. N. (1990). Structured clinical interviews for adults. In G. Goldstein & M. Hersen (Eds.), *Handbook of psychological assessment* (2nd ed., pp. 324–341). New York: Pergamon Press.

Wiens, A. N. (1991). Diagnostic interviewing. In M. Hersen, A. E. Kazdin, & A. S. Bellack (Eds.), *The clinical psychology handbook* (2nd ed, pp. 345–361). New York: Pergamon Press.

6

Evaluating Child Custody Cases
Techniques and Maintaining Objectivity

Russell S. Gold

Introduction

Since the 1970s, the involvement of mental health professionals in aspects of child custody disputes has increased many times. In part, this is because our society and the courts have been addressing custody issues in a manner different from that of the past. At the end of the 19th century, mothers, because of time spent in the home, were considered to be most closely bonded with their children and thus more capable of caring for them.

Such thinking was probably supported in no small part by Freud's theories and those of his followers; accordingly, a mother would have to be proven "unfit" before custody was given to a father. With the advent of the women's movement in the 1960s and its response among men, along with economic conditions that made it necessary for households to have two incomes, women have been working outside the home in increasing numbers, and as a result parents have shared child-rearing responsibilities a bit more evenly. No longer could the courts rely on the fact that a father was less available to the children than a mother. During this same period, "permission" was given to men to be more emotionally involved with their families and to women to have interests beyond the children, home, and hearth.

These economic and social changes impacted many areas of late 20th century culture. In addition to the increase in the divorce rate and its subsequent effect on court caseloads, the old framework on which courts had based child custody decisions could no longer be relied on. The courts were increasingly being put in a position of deciding for families what would be in the best interests of their children. Courts had more factors to weigh in this equation than they had in the past. With this circumstance came an awareness that evidence that had been traditionally relied on was insufficient to help the courts resolve individual custody disputes.

The courts began to increase their dependence on mental health practitioners to assess families and assist in the decision. On the face of it, this shift made sense because it was these practitioners who had education and training in many relevant areas (e.g., child development, family dynamics, psychopathology, diagnosis). However, the mental health community was a bit unprepared for these events.

It had been traditional for courts to rely on psychiatrists to provide evidence in a range of matters. This reliance was naturally extended to the area of child custody. There were, however, no procedures or guidelines for the kind of assessment required. Further, psychiatrists were under attack for their reliance on clinical inference and for the lack of the particular objective evidence the legal system prefers. Individual differences between professionals became a problem for the courts as the professionals themselves were so reliant on their own clinical expertise. At the same time, the legal system was becoming increasingly aware of the work of psychologists and, in particular, their use of testing, which provides more objectively ascertainable standards for the conclusions reached. The courts also began to rely on master's level professionals hired to serve in the conciliation courts, the predecessors of family court services.

In short, since the 1970s, two independent factors have come into play. First, child custody has been litigated at an increasing frequency. Second, the courts have become aware of the effectiveness of the assessment tools used by psychologists. Even so, psychology was no better prepared for this development than psychiatry had been. Both fields had to overcome the damage done by some colleagues who seemed to be for sale to the highest bidder, and both had to learn how to apply traditional procedures to a new area. Because the training of psychologists had not included the kind of broad assessment of family systems that would lead to decisions about how the custody of children would be apportioned to the parents, mental health professionals who came early to the field of child custody had to develop procedures that would best use the tools available to them and satisfy the basic need of the legal system for evenhandedness and objectivity.

Over time, such procedures have been developed. While areas of controversy regarding these procedures still exist, there has now been enough experience among a sufficient number of professionals to arrive at a consensus on a standard of care in regard to the methodology for child custody evaluations. This accomplishment is evinced in the books written in what is still a fledgling field, the journal articles appearing with increasing frequency, and the professional associations that have established guidelines for such work. Yet, these attempts to codify methodology have come after the fact. For a time, the ethics committees of relevant professional organizations were forced to address complaints in this field, about which few committee members had any experience. Indeed, these committees found themselves needing to seek consultation from practitioners who performed this work; ultimately, many have mandated that there be at least one member of the committee with such expertise. This need became evident as complaints mounted at a rate commensurate with the work being done.

This field has become one fraught with danger for the practitioner. Child custody-related complaints now outpace complaints from any other area of practice. Lawsuits and complaints to licensing boards as well as to ethics committees are frequent. The noted child psychiatrist Richard Gardner (1989) made the point that in no area of his practice other than child custody had he been subjected to complaint; yet, because of the pain resulting from dealing with such complaints, he wrote that he would no longer perform child custody evaluations. The nature of the population with whom one works in performing child custody evaluations contributes to a greater risk for complaints and suits than in other areas of practice. The lack of previous codification of procedures within the profession may have abetted this circumstance.

It is important, however, to understand that not only child custody evaluators are at risk. Therapists may, in the course of their work with patients, children and adults, find that they are also being asked to address custody issues. Subsequently, they have found themselves at risk of suit and formal complaint. This chapter is written as much for the therapist as for the custody evaluator. It is not meant to instruct how to perform a child custody evaluation. The areas it takes up are those to which more attention needs to be devoted to guide ethical practice and to limit questioning practitioners' work.

Critical Areas

The guidelines adopted by some state associations (New Jersey Board of Psychological Examiners, 1993; North Carolina, 1994, rescinded in 2004; Pennsylvania, a draft only, never adopted) and by the American Psychological Association (APA) (1994) and the Association of Family and Conciliation

Courts (AFCC) (2006) have great commonality among areas identified as having received the most complaints, although some guidelines provide more detail than do others in how to conduct a custody evaluation.

Because of the nature of child custody work, mental health professionals must be educated and experienced in a variety of areas. Certainly and obviously, mental health professionals conducting child custody evaluations must be knowledgeable in the areas of child development, psychological diagnosis, and family dynamics. Absent such knowledge, it will not be possible to perform a valid evaluation because mental health professionals have to know how each of these areas is relevant in the specific cases assessed to make custody determinations. Until fairly recently, there was little formal education or training available on the integration of these knowledge bases relevant to child custody evaluations.

While it was once necessary for those practicing in this area to fend for themselves and to develop the procedures and attitudes necessary to assist the court in a child custody case, that is no longer the circumstance. Child custody work has now been done for a sufficient length of time that, as noted, a number of experts are available to provide supervision and more formalized training. It is incumbent on the professional new to this work to seek adequate supervision and, when needed, formal training before attempting to perform custody evaluations. Furthermore, because special issues may be raised in the course of an evaluation, it is incumbent on the evaluator to seek consultation in any area that resides outside his or her expertise.

It is important to remember for whose benefit the evaluation is being performed. In all jurisdictions of which I am aware, the evaluation is identified as being performed to serve the best interests of the child; accordingly, neither parent is the client, even though one or both parents may be paying for the evaluation. To emphasize, the evaluation is to serve the *child* of the family and to provide the basis for recommendations to the court regarding what is in the child's best interests.

Perhaps the court can be considered a second client since it will be the recipient of the evaluator's data and conclusions. It is the responsibility of the evaluator to provide the court with sufficient data to evaluate the conclusions drawn by the mental health professional. It may also fall on the mental health professional (e.g., through court testimony) to explain the reported conclusions to the court. It is not in the service of the court for the mental health professional simply to defend the conclusions reached or the methodology used; rather, the mental health professional must explain the conclusions to the court for its own scrutiny of the work done and inferences made so that the court may ultimately reach its own ruling based on the evaluator's data, along with any other evidence presented.

Most prominent in all of the guidelines is the importance of objectivity. The mental health professional, as evaluator or therapist, must show objectivity. Procedures must be established by each practitioner to ensure this objectivity from the very first contact. So important is it for the evaluator to be in an objective position from the very beginning of the evaluation that the first contact is most significant in this regard.[1] As an example, when a colleague asks to be trained or supervised on a custody case that may have been referred, I first establish the nature of whatever contact has already been made before agreeing to act as a supervisor.

The first contact is usually made by one of the representing attorneys, although in some cases attorneys for the parents arrange a conference call so that one is not speaking with the evaluator ex parte. If the attorney for one party calls, the attorney for the other party should be contacted immediately, thereby establishing that both attorneys share the same understanding of the request being made of the evaluator. Similarly, when an attorney has been assigned to the child or children in a case, that attorney must be contacted also for the same purpose. When a parent makes the first contact, it is advisable to get the name of the parent's attorney and ask that you be allowed to coordinate through the attorneys. It is important that, in conversation with a single attorney or parent, no substantive issues be addressed; in practice, only the logistical issues pertinent to the beginning of the evaluation should be discussed. Such issues might include how you will go about scheduling the first appointment for the parents, how the attorneys will get documents to you, fee arrangements, and other matters of that kind.

It might not be comfortable to cut off an attorney who wants to explain his or her client's position in the matter or to cut off a parent who is feeling pressed to inform you of his or her particular needs and view of the situation; however, it is essential to do so all the same and to explain that permitting an attorney or a parent to continue could be interpreted as a breach of your objectivity. In practice, attorneys generally appreciate this intent to protect the objective position, and parents often feel comforted that the other parent also will not be permitted to impress the evaluator prior to the beginning of the process.

This objective stance must be maintained throughout the evaluation. Procedures administered to one parent will almost always be administered to the other as well. This practice is necessary to ensure that objective and equivalent data, on which the ultimate conclusions will be based, be obtained from each parent. In addition to helping parents and their attorneys understand that the evaluator has maintained an objective position throughout, the court's interests are served by being presented equivalent data on both parents by the evaluator through the submitted report or court testimony. To repeat, it is important to administer the same tests to both parents and, throughout the evaluation, not to permit discussion of substantive material with only one attorney. Inevitably, though, once the evaluation is begun, time will be spent alone with each parent.

It is not possible to ensure that both parents will continue to perceive the evaluator as objective once the recommendations are released since by that time the evaluator has taken a position. That position may be disliked by one parent or by both, and thus they may become angry with the evaluator. Rather, what is important is that the evaluator does whatever can be done to avoid any perception that he or she has not been objective in arriving at a final recommendation.

Another matter that is related to the objectivity reflected in the evaluator's procedures is his or her position before the first contact is made. For example, if the evaluator has had previous contact with the family or any of its members, the issue of multiple relationships (APA, 1994, 2002) may arise. If a mental health professional has seen a member of a family in therapy, it may be presumed that some bias will exist. Arguably, the presence of bias is less clear when the child was the therapist's patient since it is the child whose interests are to be served by the evaluation, just as in therapy. Even so, many potential conflicts can still present themselves. For example, did the evaluator have significantly greater contact with one parent during the child's therapy, such that views could have been formed about this parent relative to the less-frequently contacted parent? While these notions may prove, in the end, to have been accurate, it is also possible that they will be false or misleading. In either case, should a professional enter the evaluation with a set of ideas about a particular family, bias may ultimately create difficulties. It may be necessary, even in circumstances in which it can be argued that the child is still the one being served, to excuse oneself from the evaluation.

Arguably, when one has seen a couple for mediation of custody issues, there may not be a problem of one's having developed a relationship with the evaluator to the exclusion of the other; thus, it may be possible for the parents to feel that they can begin the evaluation on an equal footing. Further, the parents may share a trust in this professional with whom they have both worked, may feel that this professional will already have a grounding in the dynamics of their family, and prefer that this professional perform the evaluation rather than give decision making regarding their family over to a stranger. Finally, although mediation might have failed to bring the parents to agreement, it remained the responsibility of the mediator to make recommendations; this is also the ultimate responsibility of the evaluator.

This scenario presents one of the many gray areas that are endemic to custody work. It can be argued that the position that would most protect the professional (i.e., to refuse the evaluation) would not best serve the family. If one were to consider performing an evaluation in this unusual circumstance, it would at least be necessary to establish that the parents were coming to you of their complete free will, and that one has not been pressured into it by the other parent or by his or her own attorney.

In rural areas where there may be only one mental health professional to serve the community, residents may be more used to contacting a mental health professional for any and all of their mental health needs. The unique position of the rural mental health professional has been recognized by the APA (2002) in its most recent ethics code; even so, great care should be taken.

Such an issue also affects the therapists who are asked to advocate for their patient, either through a letter, which will be turned into a formal declaration filed with the court, or by providing actual court testimony. The Nebraska guidelines (1986) gently suggest that the position of a therapist may be presumed to be biased, and that the therapist and the court should both be aware of this fact. The mental health professional should address this issue forthrightly in any communication about the custody issue.

Most important, the therapist must remember that while he or she may be free, assuming an appropriate release has been signed by the patient, to comment about the patient, this does not hold true for any comments the therapist might be tempted to make about the other parent or about the needs of the particular child in question. It violates ethical principles (APA, 2002) to make statements about persons who have not been clinically evaluated. Further, child custody requires that a comparative choice be made. Without equivalent information that permits such comparison, no comment can be made regarding custody. A therapist may say that the patient has the ability to be an appropriate custodial parent but may not recommend that the patient have custody. The latter remark is a comparative one about an individual with whom the therapist has not had the same level of contact. Such statements constitute the most common way in which therapists find themselves subject to suit or formal complaint over custody issues.

Therapists and patients together must also determine whether it is in the best interest of the patient for the therapist to have any input into the custody proceedings. It is likely that patients may be opening all of their records to scrutiny were they to ask the therapist to become involved. As a result, issues and events that might be interpreted negatively in the custody case might ultimately be revealed. Further, the therapist may not feel able to portray the patient as positively as the patient desires, which could threaten the patient's treatment. It is incumbent on therapists to attempt to discuss these issues with patients before blindly responding to a request that they release information in order to affect the custody dispute.

Another kind of bias for which warning is in order has to do with the political or societal bias that may automatically accrue to the benefit of one parent. Professionals involved with custody cases have learned that no rule applies across the board. By the time a pending divorce has moved beyond the parents' own discussions, beyond the attorneys' efforts to assist the couple in resolving areas of dispute, and beyond the efforts of the court mediator and is then referred to a mental health professional for evaluation, it can be assumed that there are unique circumstances operating in the family that must be considered. Indeed, it is necessary to assess each family and its specific circumstances undeterred by assumptions. Those who disregard these peculiarities and subtleties are not likely to practice for long in the child custody arena.

Psychological testing as used in child custody cases has become something of a controversy. There are those (Brodzinsky, 1993; Weisman, 1991) who point out that the usual personality measures have not been standardized for child custody populations and thereby argue to limit the applicability of these tests to this special population. In spite of this argument, these tests are used commonly by custody evaluators. Accordingly, it is necessary to be aware that the tests on which mental health professionals have relied do have some limitations when applied to a special population; indeed, such limitations are regularly discussed. Certainly, no student has taken a course in psychodiagnostic testing without being so informed. It has always been the responsibility of the mental health professional to determine how applicable a test score is to the individual being tested, and this responsibility is emphasized when test data are being used in making child custody decisions.

There are those who are working to develop tests specific to custody evaluations (see Bricklin, 1992). Even though these tests have not undergone the

usual standardization procedures, to date they may serve as useful structured interview formats. Until such tests have undergone rigorous standardization procedures to determine the confidence level of their usefulness,
however, they must be relied on only with great care by the evaluator.

All published guidelines emphasize the importance of having a variety of data sources in conducting child custody evaluations. Interviews,
observation, and testing should be utilized as often as possible. The 1994
APA guidelines suggest that the evaluator should document issues from
at least two sources. Although such documentation is not always possible, attempts should be made to seek it. Certainly, information should be
sought from professionals who have worked with members of the family
on custody-related issues. Other professionals—for example, a pediatri-
cian—may really have nothing to offer the custody evaluator; however,
in some cases, the medical condition or the care a child receives from his
parents is a significant issue, one involving matters that are important for
an evaluator to assess. As indicated, it may be that a therapist or a parent
will not wish to release information. In the usual child custody case, the
judge may not be in a position to order that the privilege be relinquished.
Even so, the therapist, after determining the possible usefulness of a data
source, should attempt to gain that information.

Still another possible data source involves people who have been close
to the family being evaluated, including members of the extended family, neighbors, family friends, and others. Some mental health professionals object to such sources, viewing such information as of limited
worth (Ackerman, 1995; Gardner, 1982; Stahl, 1994), or as going beyond
the bounds of psychological practice and turning evaluators into private
investigators. Others find this type of collateral information most useful.
It is likely that there will be cases in which information of this kind is useful, whereas in other cases it will not be. The evaluator will have to decide
whether to proceed with collateral information in each evaluation.

Stepparents or significant others living in the household in which a parent resides should also be interviewed. Some practitioners routinely test
such individuals, just as they do the parents. The extent to which these
individuals are evaluated depends largely on the circumstances of the
case—whether any objection has been raised by one of the parents about
such individuals and to what extent the custody decision should turn on
this figure as opposed to the parents themselves.

Allegations of alcohol and drug abuse are not uncommon in custody
cases. While it may not be possible for a mental health professional to
order drug testing as a medical procedure, it is still possible to request that

this be done voluntarily by the parents. In other cases, it is possible for the court to order that they submit to testing. Information from the results of such testing is a most useful data source.

Finally, although it may sound too obvious to be included in this chapter, interviews and observation of the children with each of the parents are basic requirements. Although there may be an occasional case in which the court orders that such contact not take place—usually in extreme situations of alleged abuse—the evaluator should otherwise make certain that these data are acquired during the assessment. It is mentioned here only because often when evaluators have not done so, they have suffered repercussions for the omission.

The product of the evaluator's work is usually a written report. Many mental health professionals also communicate directly with the attorneys, and others communicate results directly to the parents. Whatever manner is chosen, it is necessary, as is commonly true in other areas of practice, to be mindful of who will receive the information and how it will be used. Some jurisdictions seek to limit the availability of the report, although court files are usually a matter of public record. In San Diego, measures are taken to ensure that parents do not see the full report, which will include a description of their former spouse in psychological terms. (Such information seems to get broadcast when parents do have the report available to them.) Even so, the court cannot always ensure that a parent not receive a copy of the report; certainly, this is the case when one of the parents is representing himself in the action. In that instance, the parent/attorney has a right to all the evidence that might be addressed in the legal proceeding. In other instances, certain attorneys feel that it is their responsibility not to keep from their clients something in their own case files.

Mental health professionals should determine usual practices in the local jurisdiction and plan accordingly. Even though steps can be taken to protect families from themselves, ultimately, once the report is directed to the attorneys and to the court, it is not possible for mental health professionals to control further.

It is also incumbent on mental health professionals to protect the integrity of the tests used and to attempt to release data only to those trained to interpret such data; however, this is not always possible. When performing a forensic evaluation, ultimately, the attorneys have a right to examine all evidence. It is common practice to ask attorneys seeking the evaluation data for permission to send the data to an expert of their choosing to review the data and assist them in preparations for trial rather than to the attorneys themselves. Occasionally, attorneys seek consultation to determine the advisability of going to trial; however, the attorney is not obliged to seek consultation or to acquiesce to the request that data be sent to another mental health professional. Rather, the attorney may legitimately require the evaluator to forward the data directly or through a copy service. Again, mental health professionals can take steps to follow professional guidelines, but the legal system might require that those guidelines be breached. The most recent APA ethics code (2002) finally recognizes that such a circumstance no longer places psychologists in jeopardy of an ethics violation.[2]

Another controversy within psychology is the nature of recommendations made following a custody evaluation. Some mental health professionals feel that a schedule of contact between children and each parent should be designed and offered to the court. Others feel that this is outside the scope of psychology, and that it is sufficient to offer the court a description of the family members and the dynamics within the family. It is likely that the nature of any recommendations will depend on the desires of the jurisdiction in which a mental health professional is working.

Conclusion

The focus of this chapter is to address issues commonly at the center of lawsuits and formal complaints arising out of child custody work. Evaluators should make full use of available guidelines and standards: the "Ethical Principles of Psychologists and Code of Conduct" (APA, 2002); the *Specialty Guidelines for Forensic Psychologists* (Committee on Professional Practice and Standards, 1991); the *Guidelines for Child Custody Evaluations in Divorce Proceedings* (APA, 1994); and the *Model Standards of Practice for Child Custody Evaluation* (AFCC, 2006). All of these, and others from state associations listed among the references, are relevant to work connected with child custody.

It is also important to emphasize the need for practitioners to be clear on their own position and boundaries in each case. Attorneys who are doing their jobs in representing their clients and who are not mindful of the professional responsibilities and constraints pertaining to the mental health professional will jeopardize the position and boundaries of a professional who is not willing or able to be very clear on these professional boundaries. In addition, the circumstances of different cases may serve to further shade those boundaries.

The complexity of this work is such that an ethical code regarding child custody work probably will not be possible to develop. Shadings required by many cases make hard-and-fast rules impossible to apply. The common grievance of those who do this work is that anything can go awry in a custody battle and often does. Even those with years of experience in the field will usually seek to consult with colleagues when difficult situations arise that are not readily codified. Consultation remains the best course of action because the actual circumstances of the custody case at hand are not likely to fit neatly into the limited guidelines offered by the APA, the AFCC, and the individual state associations brave enough to make the attempt. Also, occasionally circumstances may arise that suggest the prudence of seeking consultation with an attorney regarding points of law or procedure.

Notes

1. In the forensic psychology course I teach to doctoral students, 2 hours are focused on the manner of the first contact alone.
2. I take one extra step to control at least parts of the report since they could be sought directly. While the parents routinely sign releases of information so that the report will go to the attorneys and to the court counselor, they do not sign releases to each other. As a result, no parent can get, from me, a copy of those parts of the report that discuss the other parent.

References

Ackerman, M. J. (1995). *Clinician's guide to child custody evaluations*. New York: Wiley.

American Psychological Association. (1994). *Guidelines for child custody evaluations in divorce proceedings*. Washington, DC: Author.

American Psychological Association. (2002). Ethical principles of psychologists and code of conduct. *American Psychologist, 57*, 1060–1073.

Association of Family and Conciliation Courts. (2006). *Model standards of practice for child custody evaluation*. Retrieved from http://www.afccnet.org/resources/standards_practice.asp

Bricklin, B. (1992). Data-based tests in custody evaluations. *American Journal of Family Therapy, 20*, 254–265.

Brodzinsky, D. M. (1993). On the use and misuse of psychological testing in child custody evaluations. *Professional Psychology: Research and Practice, 24*(2), 213–219.

Committee on Professional Practice and Standards. (1991). Specialty guidelines for forensic psychologists. *Law and Human Behavior, 6*, 655–665.

Gardner, R. A. (1982). *Family evaluation in child custody litigation.* Cresskill, NJ: Creative Therapeutics.

Gardner, R. A. (1989). *Family evaluation in child custody mediation, arbitration, and litigation.* Cresskill, NJ: Creative Therapeutics.

Nebraska Psychological Association. (1986). *Guidelines for child custody evaluations.* Lincoln, NE. Retrieved from http://www.nebpsych.org/resources/childcust. htm.

New Jersey State Board of Psychological Examiners. (1993). *Specialty guidelines for psychologists in custody/visitation evaluations.* Available from New Jersey State Board of Psychological Examiners, 124 Halsey Street, Newark, NJ 07102.

North Carolina Psychological Association. (1994). *Child custody guidelines.* Raleigh, NC: Author. (Rescinded in 2004 and no longer available)

Pennsylvania Psychological Association. (n.d.). *Roles for psychologists in child custody disputes.* Unpublished draft. (No longer available and not adopted by the association)

Stahl, P. M. (1994). *Conducting child custody evaluations.* Thousand Oaks, CA: Sage.

Weisman, H. N. (1991). Child custody evaluations: Fair and unfair professional practices. *Behavioral Sciences and the Law, 9*, 469–476.

7

Acting as a Special Master in High-Conflict Postdivorce Child Custody Cases

S. Margaret Lee

Introduction

The use of special masters (also called custody commissioners in Hawaii, "wise persons" in New Mexico, and "med-arbs" in Colorado) in the context of child custody cases is quite recent and raises questions regarding the appropriate relationship between the special master and the court; the appropriate qualifications a professional should have to function as a special master; and myriad ethical considerations in such diverse areas as informed consent, dual-role relationships, and general standards of care. Given the power invested in the special master and the highly conflictual nature of the clientele, the increase in ethics complaints filed regarding child custody evaluations is not unexpected. The challenge of functioning as a special master is heightened by the very limited literature focusing on it (Lee, 1995; Stahl, 1995) that is available and by limited formal training opportunities as well. Some guidance can be obtained through the superior court jurisdictions that have developed standardized orders (e.g., Santa Clara and Marin County Superior Courts in California).

Special mastering is a legal concept originating in the federal court system, in which judges transferred their decision-making powers to an expert in cases requiring a high level of specific, technical expertise. The concept of utilizing an expert to determine the "best interests of the child" in child custody cases expands this original concept to include both an ongoing relationship between the special master and the litigants (in these cases, the two parents) and adding mediative, educational, and therapeutic elements to the process. Thus, although a special master is most often a psychologist, he or she can be another mental health professional, mediator, or family law attorney who specializes in helping high-conflict post-divorce families resolve disputes through such processes as mediation, developmental education, untangling intercouple communication, and quasi-therapeutic intervention. When such efforts fail, the special master, as a judicial officer, can make decisions in the manner a judge would, subject to an appeals process that is similar to review available following a court decision.

Use of a special master might be considered when (a) other avenues of conflict resolution have not resulted in parents' being able to make decisions about their children; (b) disagreements persist about such issues as schedules, overnight visitation, choice of schools, extracurricular activities, troubles at the point of transferring the child, holiday scheduling, and the handling of the child's or children's behavior, religious training, and health issues; and (c) problematic behaviors on the part of one or both parents continue. Most often, the family has already participated in a child custody/access evaluation, has been in front of the judge numerous times, and is likely to be seen as a high-conflict family. *High-conflict* families, as defined by Johnston (1994), who represent a small percentage of the divorcing population, are those in which the potential for extremely negative impact on children's adjustment to divorce is great.

A second group of families appropriate for the service are those in which serious concerns regarding child abuse, parental fitness, or major impairment of one or both parents that require ongoing monitoring exist. A third type of families appropriate for the appointment of a special master are those in which there is a young infant or toddler whose rapid changes in developmental needs will require frequent adjustment to visitation schedules along with significant communication between parents to coordinate such parental tasks as weaning, toilet training, and forms of discipline. In such instances, the parents would never or not yet have had the opportunity to develop effective problem-solving mechanisms between themselves.

The work of a special master includes meeting with parents, sometimes meeting the children, and reviewing evaluations and other documents to orient themselves to the family and the types of problems that have occurred. When disputes occur, the special master will initially attempt to help the parents mediate the conflict. The special master must have access to information such as the child's opinion as well as information from doctors, therapists, schools, or other caretakers. If the parents are unable to reach agreement through a mediation process or utilizing information obtained during the mediation process, the special master then makes a decision. Decisions that do not result in substantial changes in time sharing or do not have a significant impact on either parent's relationship with their children are immediately implemented and are considered equivalent to a court order. For major decisions, such as a change in basic custody, a decision about one parent's relocating, or a significant change in the visitation schedule, the special master will submit a recommendation (not a decision) to the court. The judge will review the opinion and make a decision. The use of special masters has been increasing over the past decade and is currently being accepted as an appropriate alternative method for conflict resolution in several states.

In most jurisdictions, there is no code that accurately describes the functioning of a special master and that addresses issues such as more flexible gathering of evidence, the informality of the hearing process, and the mixed functional role encompassed within this work. As viewed within the family court system, the special master concept is a hybrid, having some similarity to those roles defined in state codes pertaining to arbitrators, referees, mediators, expert witnesses, and guardians *ad litem*. For example, each of the relevant sections in the California code accurately describes some aspects of the process, but either fails to provide the decision-making capacity or imposes unrealistic requirements on the special master. These unrealistic requirements include publicly posting notice utilizing a court reporter and prohibiting the special master from testifying in court. The solution to this absence of an appropriate code has been for court or attorneys either to create their own orders, mostly by stipulation, describing the process, power, and requirements of the special master, or to utilize existing codes with multiple modifications stipulated by the parents.

Appointment of a special master, whether it is based on codes for expert witness, referee, arbitrator, mediator, or guardian *ad litem*, provides the special master with *quasi-judicial immunity*. The concept of quasi-judicial immunity "bars civil action against judges for acts performed in the exercise of their judicial functions, and it applies to all judicial determinations" (Lurvey, 1990, p. 11). The courts can extend absolute immunity to persons other than judges if those persons act in a judicial or quasi-judicial capacity. The court's delegation of its decision-making function, accompanied by protection against civil suit, are the factors that make the special master role a powerful one. Because the special master has great influence, he or she has potential to benefit families when performing wisely. At the same time, the special master can do great harm to families while protected from having to take responsibility for their actions. In this role, psychologists are understandably vulnerable to having their work closely inspected and monitored for ethical practices.

Once a special master has been appointed, he or she can only be removed on the agreement of both parents, by the expiration of their term, by their own resignation, or by order of the court. When one parent has concerns about the professional standards of the special master or the quality of work performed, some courts have established local court rules for an appeals process within the court of jurisdiction. At this time, a dissatisfied parent may also lodge a complaint with the state licensing board governing the special master or file an ethics complaint with their professional association.

A special master should be a professional who is a recognized expert in the areas of family systems, child development, and psychology of divorce and custody and who also has familiarity with the legal concepts used in his or her state and local family courts. Mediation training is helpful, as is membership in state or national professional organizations that ensure commitment to their discipline's ethical principles and allow an avenue for consumer complaints. The current lack of any adopted guidelines defining appropriate qualifications is concerning as it allows anyone accepted by the court to act as a special master.

Ethical concerns to consider when working as a special master include the avoidance of potentially damaging dual roles, informed consent, ex parte communication with attorneys and judges, community standards of care, avoiding harm, confidentiality, and record keeping.

Dual Roles

Given the nature of the special master role, which encompasses such varying functions as mediator, developmental consultant, evaluator, and decision maker, the potential for engaging in unethical dual relationships is great. The pressure to be all things to all members of the family can be strong. The special master is in the position of assessing and understanding the needs of the children, the dynamics of the parents, and mechanisms by which conflicts arise. In addition, the special master may have had a previous relationship with the family. While prior relationships are ethically justifiable, they are somewhat debatable. Although one might be conservative, taking the position that a psychologist should only become a special master for a family if there is no prior relationship, this position would preclude a change in function that many special masters have found exceedingly useful—the change from court-ordered custody evaluator to special master. The American Psychological Association's (APA's) ethics code (2002) requires that we avoid engaging in multiple roles that will either "impair the psychologist's objectivity ... or otherwise [risk] exploitation or harm to the other person" (p. 1065). A distinction should be drawn between a sequential change in role from child custody evaluator to special master as opposed to a concurrent appointment. When a concurrent appointment has been made, the professional is in the potential position of gathering data, making recommendations, and then deciding on those recommendations. This concurrent appointment would appear to be an inappropriate transfer of the court's mandate to guard the children's interests.

Clearly, any prior relationship with family members that would raise the issue of bias or appearance of bias would be contraindicated. Accordingly, if a mental health professional had been the therapist for either parent or had been in a consulting role to either parent or their attorneys, or if the special master had a social relationship with either parent, to accept the family as a special master case would be unethical. Although one might argue that having been a child's therapist could provide a mental health professional with valuable insight into a family's dynamics and might facilitate making determinations regarding the best interests of a particular child, there are two reasons why such a role shift would be unwise. The first is that once a mental health professional becomes a special master, that mental health professional is no longer available to the child as a therapist. Children in high-conflict families frequently require intermittent treatment as they work through family issues at subsequent stages of development. Thus, children who were caught between warring parents at age 6 and struggled with issues of balancing their alliances between divergent parental expectations will likely need to revisit these issues as they enter preadolescence. The second reason for not mixing the role of child therapist with special master involves issues of the child's retrospective view of the therapist. Thus, a child may have developed a trusting therapeutic relationship with a mental health professional and experienced treatment as a haven to sort through the many conflicting feelings and issues associated with that child's family situation. If that same therapist later is placed in the middle of the family and legal maelstrom and is making decisions, the child might come to view some of the decisions as wrong; might come to see the mental health professional as siding with one parent; or might feel that material from the treatment influenced the decision making, which could result in feelings of guilt or concerns about having too much power within the family. Further, the child may experience betrayal if any private material from the treatment process is seen as having been incorporated into the decision reached or the justification for the decision.

Prior roles that appear justifiable include that of having been the custody evaluator, a developmental consultant to both parents, or a coparenting counselor. The advantage to a role shift from one of these services is that the prior role has been neutral and nontherapeutic yet has allowed the parents access to the mental health professional's manner of thinking, personality style, and fund of knowledge. Since appointment as a special master is most frequently determined through stipulation by both parents, prior knowledge of the mental health professional can allow for truly "informed consent." Thus, the parents know to whom they are giving decision-making power and know that this is a person with whom they can work effectively. The mental health professional who has worked in a prior role with a family must ascertain that neither parent is agreeing to the assignment out of a sense that he or she must do so to appear cooperative and must make the implications of changing roles clear.

After one's role of special master has been accepted, the potential for falling into unethical dual relationships does not abate; in fact, it is during one's tenure of actual service as a master that one must be most vigilant. The following example provides a common scenario:

Example 1

Dr. Smith had worked as a special master with the Jones family for several years. The work had progressed very successfully, resulting in the family's ability to make many routine decisions on their own. The parents had developed improved avenues for communication with each other and felt grateful to Dr. Smith for their harmonious interchanges and the wise decisions that Dr. Smith had made. During her work with the family, Dr. Smith had maintained contact with their 14-year-old son, Adam, to obtain his feelings about various issues that had arisen over the years. Adam was also very appreciative, crediting Dr. Smith with bringing some calm to his previously contentious family life. During one session with the parents, they requested that Dr. Smith meet with Adam and his father to sort through some issues involving limit setting and, more important, help Adam express his thoughts more openly to his quite powerful father. Dr. Smith agreed. The conjoint session was a poignant and meaningful experience for both father and son. Adam was able to express himself quite fully, and this somewhat constricted, diplomatic youngster was able to be angry with his father and then to cry out his feelings of not having a way to explore his own identity due to feeling overpowered by Dad. Following such a dramatic session, which was seen by all family members as extremely useful, the parents asked that Dr. Smith continue conjoint work for several additional sessions.

Dr. Smith wisely refused to continue the work with the father and son, correctly understanding the unethical dual relationship that would arise from providing such a service. Had Dr. Smith established a therapeutic relationship in addition to the special master relationship, a number of potentially harmful events could have occurred. As mentioned, later decisions could result in a feeling of betrayal on the part of Adam, who might feel that information from therapy was used to make such a decision. The special master process could deteriorate in such a manner that one parent remained so angry or distrustful of the mental health professional that the latter's resignation would be indicated but would then also require the cessation of any therapeutic involvement; the mother could feel that a bias toward the father had developed, arising out of an alliance with the father and resulting in undue emphasis on the father-son relationship when making decisions; or the mother could feel suspicious merely because there might be an "appearance of bias" due to the special master's greater involvement with the father, even when none existed.

Not all dual relationships arise out of multiple roles with the family. They can also arise out of the relationships the mental health professional has with the participating attorneys. When working in family court, the professional community tends to be closely knit. Except in big cities, the number of evaluators, family law attorneys, and judges is limited. The tendency for mental health professionals to get referrals repeatedly from specific attorneys or judges is common and makes sense; thus, an attorney who has experienced a mental health professional as competent is likely to refer to that same professional in the future. In such communities, social relationships may develop out of business lunches, working together on cases, and long hours waiting in court corridors.

During the special master process, the special master may have significant contact with attorneys. The most successful cases are those that involve the attorneys working in concert with the special master to facilitate the clients' acceptance of decisions, to provide the special master with information, and to assist the special master in obtaining the compliance of the parents. For this work to be most effective, there are often times when the special master will speak privately with only one attorney about an issue. A strong possibility for a bias to emerge exists in working with a family when the special master has a closer relationship to one attorney than to the other attorney, thereby creating a potential influence on how decisions are made. Even when there is no actual bias, the appearance of bias can affect the nature of the relationship with the parents. When only one parent has legal representation, it is wisest to maintain minimal communication with the other parent's attorney in order to maintain the trust and sense of fairness for the parent who does not have legal representation.

Indeed, when a special master has a closer, more familiar relationship with one parent's attorney, the potential impact on decision making is unpredictable. The special master may be inclined to rule "against" the parent, knowing that the attorney will be helpful in gaining the parent's cooperation. Conversely, the special master may rule "for" the parent in order to maintain the good relationship with the attorney. Particularly when decisions are arbitrary and do not involve the children's interests directly, potential influence from the relationships with attorneys must be safeguarded against.

Informed Consent

When individuals enter therapy, they most often come with a set of understandings of how that process will work and the parameters of the work. Thus, they expect the therapeutic work to be private, to be driven by the goal of helping them with their conflicts, and to follow certain agreed-on scheduling and fee structures. Likewise, when clients enter a courtroom, they hold a set of understandings about the legal process: It is an adversarial situation; the judge is neutral; evidence must be produced in a particular way; and communication is defined by a set of rules. When people enter into a relationship with a special master, they are usually rather desperate, have been in a prolonged state of crisis and conflict, and accept the process because their attorneys or the judge has convinced them that this is their only alternative. Depending on their own personal experiences, they may view the special master in widely divergent ways. Often, these people have already been in psychotherapy, have been with mediators, have undergone evaluation, and have been in the courtroom many times. Within these arenas, the issues of real-world power, psychological power, confidentiality, and lack of cooperation in decision making arise but are differentially treated depending on which process is occurring. Frequently, the attorneys have spent their efforts on convincing the client to accept a special master rather than educating the client about the special master process. Such clients will often enter the relationship with the special master with many misconceptions. Given the newness of this work, many special masters themselves will have misconceptions about their role, scope of power, and responsibilities. It is the special master's duty to carefully review with the clients the scope of power being given to him or her, the lack of confidentiality, the process for review of decisions, and the relationships that will exist among the special master and the client, children, attorneys, and the court. The court order, if well constructed, provides a framework defining the special master's function. Sample orders being used in the Marin and Santa Clara Superior Courts in California have been thoughtfully developed. Failure to provide such informed consent would constitute a violation of section 3.10 of the APA ethical principles and code of conduct (APA, 2002). An example demonstrating the assurance of informed consent follows.

Example 2

Dr. Jones accepted the referral of the Winter family. The Winters, who had been divorced for many years, were the parents of two daughters, ages 10 and 12. Both parents had remarried, and there were several half- and step-siblings in the two homes. These parents hated each other, had nothing positive to say about the other parent, blamed the other parent for all the difficulties with the children, and when placed in a room together their anger tended to escalate quickly. The special master was engaged following an incident in which the older daughter ran away from the mother's home following an argument. She ran to her father's home and complained that her mother had been abusive toward her and never listened to her, and that she wanted to live with Dad. Her father had no trouble accepting his daughter's view of her mother as abusive and insensitive and allowed the child to stay with him. The mother, on the other hand, stated that her daughter was in need of therapy, and that the daughter was creating false allegations of abuse to avoid the consequences in Mom's house for the misbehavior that had caused the fight between them. The family was referred in a crisis requiring immediate action regarding whether the daughter should be returned to her mother's home.

Dr. Jones offered an appointment to meet with the parents to explain the special master process and to begin to unravel the current crisis. There was a court order in place that clearly set forth the powers of the special master, the limits to confidentiality, the term of appointment, and the relationship of the special master to the court. In that initial meeting, despite parental pressure to engage immediately in the crisis, Dr. Jones first reviewed the order with the parents and then proceeded to address the crisis. After Dr. Jones collected some information about the history and the current situation and obtained an evaluation of the child, he ordered that the child enter treatment, and that the child be made to spend time in her mother's home despite her wish to remain solely with her father. On receiving the decision, the father immediately filed an ex parte motion to block the decision and levied allegations that Dr. Jones had acted unethically as he had not shared all of the information obtained with both parents. Because Dr. Jones had reviewed with the parents the appropriate appeals process and had discussed the manner in which he would meet individually and not necessarily share all of that information, he could be confident that there had been no ethical violation, and he urged the court to support his authority to make such decisions. The court refused to hear the matter brought by the father and supported the special master process.

In the initial stages of the special master process, there are often immediate crises that must be attended to and actions required to restabilize the family. Within this context, it is often difficult to ensure that the parents really understand the nature of the work and the scope of the special master's power and rules for functioning. Particularly for less-experienced special masters or special masters in jurisdictions that lack court definition of the special master process, there is a chance that the special master will not have a clear understanding of these issues, which may have an impact on the informed consent process. The special master's lack of clarity, by definition, implies an inability to obtain informed consent.

When the concept of using a special master in postdivorce families originally arose, special masters often rolled up their sleeves and just dealt with whatever problems emerged, defining the process as the work progressed. This approach led to situations in which parents were forced to accept decisions with no idea that the special master had the authority or power to make such decisions; thus, understandably, they felt angered by the power the special master wielded, leading to situations in which special masters were vulnerable to complaints. Further, given pressure from the court and attorneys to resolve crises immediately, some special masters have made decisions prior to receiving a filed order. To act in this way makes the special master vulnerable to a malpractice action. The following example is one demonstrating the failure to obtain informed consent and failure to clarify the scope of decision making:

Example 3

Dr. Doe, an experienced clinician, had just begun to work as a special master. In one of his initial cases, he was given a referral for a family with a very young child and an accompanying court order that basically stated that he had been appointed as a special master to make child custody decisions for an undefined amount of time. Dr. Doe worked quite successfully with this family for over a year, facilitating communication and increasing the father's time with his child in a developmentally appropriate manner. However, there then arose an incident involving a serious allegation of sexual abuse made by the child against the father. Dr. Doe issued an order requiring supervised visitation and curtailing the father's visitation. The father disputed the order, believing Dr. Doe to have acted outside of the scope of his power, and the special master's relationship completely unraveled. Given the lack of definition of the special master role, it was unclear whether Dr. Doe was making decisions outside of the scope of his power; as a result, there was a failure to obtain informed consent regarding the types of decisions to which the parents were agreeing to abide. Failure to define the master's scope of work resulted in lengthy court hearings, which further escalated the toxic conflict between the parents.

Lack of Community Standards of Care

The example from the preceding section not only highlights a concern about informed consent but also raises the question of standard of care. The use of special masters in postdivorce custody disputes, as a concept, has been established without uniformity in different jurisdictions; there is a lack of established guidelines and standards. Further, this work entails the use of mental health professionals who must become familiar with legal concepts and attorneys who must become familiar with clinical issues. Section 2.01 of the APA (2002) ethics code requires the following:

> In those emerging areas in which generally recognized standards for preparatory training do not yet exist, psychologists nevertheless take reasonable steps to ensure the competence of their work and to protect clients/patients, students, supervisees, research participants, organizational clients, and others from harm. (p. 1064)

Various jurisdictions have attempted to develop a recommended set of credentials and qualifications for psychologists seeking appointments as special masters, but as of this writing, no known guidelines have been adopted. Suggested qualifications considered by the California Superior Court in Marin County include 3 years' postlicense experience in child and family therapy and 3 years' experience in diagnostic evaluations for family court, juvenile court, or family mediation services, with a minimum of 10 evaluations or 3 years' experience in court-based family mediation. Further, psychologists are recommended to be expert in family systems, child development, psychology of divorce, and custody and to have a working knowledge of custody laws and local court rules, with a minimum of six cases working with attorneys or court appointments. Recommendations further include familiarity with ethical issues of custody disputes and membership in the relevant national or state professional association to ensure a commitment to such ethical principles. Last, training on mediation is thought to be helpful.

As evident in such recommended standards, the work of a special master is highly complex and draws on expertise from many clinical areas in addition to requiring that the clinician become an expert in forensic concepts and practices. Given the relative novelty of this work, the dearth of formal, comprehensive training available, and the scarcity of available experts with whom one can consult, it becomes the ethical responsibility of the individual psychologist to obtain the knowledge and training, even if this must be acquired in a piecemeal fashion. Failure to develop such comprehensive expertise, especially given the decision-making power inherent in the work, creates significant risk of doing harm.

Example 4

Faced with the crisis in mental health practice stemming from the advent of preferred provider organizations (PPOs) and a dwindling general clinical practice, Dr. Harpo decided to expand her work to include the provision of services for the family court. Dr. Harpo had some experience working with children, and as is true for many clinicians, she had dealt with families in which divorce was an issue. She started setting up luncheon engagements with local family law attorneys and, after one such lunch, received a call from an attorney with a request that she act as a special master for a family. Dr. Harpo accepted the referral and blindly accepted the court order drawn up by the attorneys. Although Dr. Harpo was an experienced clinician and managed to avoid getting drawn into the fray or pulled into one-sided alliances, she soon found that she did not really understand what legal concepts should be the basis of her opinions and had no idea how to think through the child's developmental needs as they related to custody and visitation arrangements. The case fell apart when she ordered the 3-year-old child to go back and forth between the parents' homes on an every-other-day basis, which met some developmental needs but failed to account for the difficult transitions, the escalation of conflict caused by such a schedule, and the parents' inability to have the needed minimum contact with each other. Dr. Harpo was deluged by phone calls from both parents and their attorneys, demanding that she make decisions about the daily crises that were occurring. Dr. Harpo's failure to have adequately prepared herself for this work resulted in damage to the child and left the parents with a more acrimonious relationship than had existed prior to her work. Further, the family, having become very disillusioned with that avenue of conflict resolution, was unwilling to agree to another special master. These consequences indicate an ethical violation of Section 3.04 (APA, 2002), related to avoiding harm.

Ex Parte Communications With Attorneys and Judges

In standard legal practice, a trier of fact does not engage in separate communications with attorneys or parties. Communications either involve direct, conjoint communication or are presented in written form, copied to the other party. During a child custody evaluation, attorneys in many jurisdictions are prohibited from initiating contact with the evaluator on any substantive matters without prior agreement by the other side. The evaluator, however—and specifically the special master assigned to a case—is allowed to initiate such contact while being aware of the potential for allegations of bias or appearance of bias. Special masters, as they conduct their evaluative practice in some jurisdictions, see their functioning as involving direct and separate work with the individual attorneys. As has been mentioned in this chapter, special masters may wish to discuss their thinking on a particular issue and may wish to enlist the attorneys' help in gaining client compliance or in the parent's acceptance of an upcoming decision or discussion. These discussions with attorneys occur separately for justifiable reasons. They can serve to maintain equilibrium in a family system, and they can facilitate compliance that promotes a successful process. If all communications involve both attorneys, attorneys can be placed in an ethical dilemma with their clients by withholding information at times or failing to be the client's advocate. For example, if information is brought forth in a conjoint session, it is the attorney's responsibility to inform his or her client of that information, whether or not that information will be well used by the client. The concept of such separate discussions is highly at odds with the thinking of many attorneys and also with many parents who have already been involved in numerous court hearings. It is important that all interested parties understand such deviation from standard practice, and that the special master be impeccable in maintaining a neutral stance and avoiding any bias that could arise from these relatively protected conversations. Despite that protection, all parties must be informed regarding the lack of confidentiality in the special master process. The special master should also maintain written records of these separate discussions in the event that there is an appeal or court review of the special master's work. The advantage of ex parte communication is noted next.

Example 5

Dr. Post had worked with the Smiths for several years, helping the parents develop a way to exchange information about their 2-year-old child and working to adjust the visitation schedule as the child aged. The Smiths were a very angry couple who had only been together for a short time prior to the pregnancy and were legally separated prior to the birth. Mr. Smith was an intensely narcissistic man prone to outbursts of rage, and Mrs. Smith was suspicious and tended to overreact to the "normal" upsets in her child, finding fault in the father's actions. Following statements made by the child about her father touching her "butt," Mrs. Smith contacted Dr. Post with allegations of sexual abuse against the father. Dr. Post did see the child and, supported by his additional information about the family, was of the opinion that there was no cause for concern regarding child abuse. Dr. Post explained to the mother his reasoning and some other possible explanations for the child's statements. Dr. Post also contacted and discussed the issues with Mrs. Smith's attorney. It was agreed by all that they should pay close attention to any future statements made by the child, but that there was no requirement to make a report to child protective services or take any further action. The Smith family continued to work with Dr. Post for several years. Had Dr. Post included Mr. Smith and his attorney, rather than confining himself to ex parte discussions with Mrs. Smith, there would have been a significant risk of a breach in the avenues of communication and the tenuous coparenting relationship that had been developed. Further, there would have been a significant risk that one or the other parent would make unforgivable statements and that what little trust existed would have been eroded, ultimately leading to potential harm for the child.

Confidentiality

Generally, the special master process does not include the premise of communications being confidential. In certain jurisdictions, the special master can be compelled to testify in court, either during an appeals process of a particular decision or if divorce disputes that interface with the special master's realm of decision making are brought to court. There are, as well, times when the court must decide financial issues, such as payment for day care, and thus requires information regarding the children's needs, such as the need for a certain amount of day care or a certain type of day care. Further, in the routine work of the special master, any information that is obtained in separate interviews with parents, obtained from collateral parties, or learned from attorneys may be disclosed in mediation efforts or disclosed as part of the justification for a particular decision. Typically, special masters do not routinely testify in court; however, in incidents when the special master process unravels and the family reenters the court process, it is often useful to inform and update the court on the family's progress, issues that have been dealt with during the special master's tenure, and the causes of the breakdown in the special master process.

A potentially important function of a special master is to provide a buffer for a child's therapy. Child therapists who work with children of divorce often find themselves pulled into the arena of custody decisions and are called on to make recommendations regarding what is in the best interests of the child. With the appointment of a special master, a protection of that relationship can occur, allowing the therapists to provide the special master with their understanding of the child but clearly delineating the functions of helping a child as against making recommendations that bear on decisions about that child. Many special masters require, as part of their work, an agreement from the parents that the communication between the special master and the child's therapist remain confidential. This condition is not unlike the condition required by many child therapists that the parents must relinquish their right to know what the child says in treatment, thereby allowing the child to have a confidential relationship with the therapist. Some orders for special masters define the master as the holder of the child's therapeutic privilege, which further protects the therapy but significantly increases the power accorded to the special master.

Example 6

Dr. Mack became a special master for the Jordan family. The Jordans shared custody of their 8-year-old son, who had been in treatment with Dr. Tool for several years. They had agreed to a special master on the recommendation of Dr. Tool, who had found herself barraged with questions regarding changing the child's visitation schedule because of difficult transitioning between parents and who had been asked to render recommendations about extracurricular activities, telephone access between the households, and vacation planning. Dr. Tool found herself focusing on addressing these concerns rather than focusing on the issues the child brought to treatment, the original referral involving significant alienation from his mother. Following Dr. Mack's involvement, he became the magnet for the barrages, which allowed Dr. Tool to perform her work with the child. After several months, based on communication between Dr. Mack and Dr. Tool, Dr. Mack ordered that the child spend more time with the mother as part of the effort to decrease this child's alienation. The child had begun talking with his therapist about the father's "brainwashing" and about secret yearnings to reconnect with his mother. Mr. Jordan was quite upset by this decision, stating that the child hated his mother and never wanted to see her, and that spending time with her would be damaging. Dr. Mack refused to discuss the information obtained through discussions with the therapist, citing the confidential nature of that information. It was Dr. Mack's opinion that if the father were to know of his son's fragile wishes to reconnect with his mother, the father would increase the pressure on his son. Fortunately, Dr. Mack had established at the beginning of his work with this family the understanding that information regarding the child's treatment would remain confidential.

That the special masters may hold some information confidential and utilize that information as a basis for decision making puts them in a position of power that is frightening if misused. Further, given the special masters' quasi-judicial immunity, they enjoy qualified protection from civil litigation.

The other side of the confidentiality issue involves the manner in which clients will assume confidentiality or privacy within the context of a sense of trust and alliance with a mental health professional; thus, in an individual meeting with a trusted special master, either parent may let down his or her guard and provide information about himself or herself that either has no intention of providing to the other parent. If this information is later divulged to the other parent, the informing parent may feel that the special master has been unethical, even though the latter has not in fact operated in an unethical fashion. As long as the lack of confidentiality has been made clear, there is justification for the release of the information; thus, there has been an attempt on the special master's part to avoid doing harm (APA, 2002, Sections 3.04 and Principle A).

Bias, Its Sources, and the Special Master's Responsibility to Manage It

There are several major factors that can contribute to bias in the special master process. These include the flexibility of the standard for the best interests of the child, the lack of guidelines for the special master process, and countertransference on the part of the special master.

The legal principle that underlies all decisions regarding child custody is the best interests of the child. This legal standard is encoded in a quite flexible manner and allows judges broad judicial discretion. Although defined differently in different states, in California the court's determination of the best interests of the child is defined as follows:

> In making a determination of the best interest of the child in any proceeding under this title, the court shall, among any other factors it finds relevant, consider all of the following: (a) The health, safety, and welfare of the child. (b) Any history of abuse by one parent against the child or against the other parent. ... The nature and amount of contact with both parents. (California Civil Code, 2005, §3011)

The standard allows judges to prioritize and emphasize different factors in any particular family or circumstance. The flexibility in the law allows recognition of the many issues that may be involved in what is "best" for a particular child, in a particular family, given a particular situation. However, this same flexibility allows judges to be driven by their own beliefs, biases, and values. As is true for the judiciary, child custody evaluators and special masters can likewise be driven by their biases in making recommendations and decisions. Thus, biases such as a preference for sole rather than joint custody, a belief that infants can or cannot handle overnight visits with the nonprimary parent, or a belief that avoiding nasty transitions outweighs a child's experience of more frequent contact with both parents can determine what decisions are made. With the lack of well-constructed research in this arena, experts must rely on theory, clinical experience, and their own beliefs about what is best for children.

Example 7

Dr. Maple had a strong belief that joint custody with shared parenting was in the best interests of all children. As a divorced father who was deeply committed to involvement with his children, Dr. Maple had successfully worked with his ex-wife to establish a 50/50 visitation arrangement by which they regularly communicated about the children and made decisions about day care, activities, and education. In his work as a special master, Dr. Maple routinely made orders requiring joint custodial arrangements (e.g., varying the type of schedule, the blocking of time, the manner of transitioning the child, and modes of interparental communication) based on the individual family. Dr. Maple worked diligently with these families in helping them accept his orders and in building the tools needed to allow for more successful coparenting. Dr. Maple accepted the assignment of the Smith family. The Smiths had been engaged in an extremely protracted and hostile custody battle. They had little respect for each other, their relationship had been marked by violence, and they had no way to communicate about their daughter, Stephanie. Stephanie, a temperamental child, was slow to adapt to new situations, had difficulties with transitions, and tended toward a more anxious, pessimistic stance in life. She had witnessed many frightening exchanges between her parents and experienced a pervasive sense of instability and uncertainty in her postdivorce life. Both Mr. and Mrs. Smith, however, were devoted to their daughter. Dr. Maple made decisions for this family that supported the involvement of both parents. Although he improved the situation by making all transitions occur through the school, by establishing strict rules about telephone access for Stephanie, and by blocking her time with parents in a manner that involved fewer transitions and longer periods for adjustment to each household, Stephanie remained highly anxious and the parents continued their war. Dr. Maple's insistence on maintaining a coparenting arrangement, because of his own beliefs, resulted in placing Stephanie in a continuously traumatizing situation. Her temperament, her parents' history, and their lack of tools to manage such an arrangement should have been determinative rather than the belief that shared parenting is best for all children. This would be a violation of Section 2.04 of the ethics code (APA, 2002), which states that "Psychologists' work is based upon established scientific and professional knowledge of the discipline" (p. 5).

Another source of bias arises out of the potential countertransference reactions of the special master. This type of work involves the development of intense relationships with families within a context of significant power over their lives. Parents work hard to make the special master their ally, to pull the special master onto "their side" of disputes. The parents are dependent on the special master to manage their lives vis-à-vis the children. These families are often in crisis, and at times the amount of emergency phone calls and demands for actions are overwhelming. Given the rich context in which issues of power, dependency, demandingness, and anger are the daily fodder of the work, it is extremely difficult for special masters to maintain a neutral, objective stance at all times. It is for this reason that it is recommended that only those psychologists who are well seasoned and have extensive experience working in the area of divorce engage in such a role. The potential for losing one's objectivity is great, as is the potential to make decisions based on one's own psychology rather than the actual situation. To do so puts the well-being of the clients at risk and is unethical, as defined by Section 2.04 of the ethics code (APA, 2002). The following example is a case in which the special master's own feelings prompted unprofessional conduct that resulted in damage to the involved families.

Example 8

Dr. Johnson had worked as a special master for the Green family for several months. Mrs. Green was a somewhat immature, demanding woman who constantly contacted Dr. Johnson with weekly complaints and concerns. As soon as one issue was resolved, another emerged. Mr. Green, although a somewhat self-centered man, was much less demanding, accepted the decisions of the special master and could wait until scheduled meetings to address conflicts. Dr. Johnson had grown up in a family with a somewhat overbearing mother who constantly intruded in his life. Dr. Johnson had learned to cope with his mother by placating her while developing a stronger attachment to his father. Despite years of therapy as part of his training to become a psychologist, remnants of the anger felt toward his mother remained. In his work with the Green family, Dr. Johnson worked hard to listen and respond to Mrs. Green's concerns and never attempted to set limits with her regarding the phone calls. On Monday mornings, he would cringe as he checked his answering machine, steeling himself against the expected crisis or complaint. A dispute arose regarding whether the children should go to one or another school. Without fully investigating the issue—Dr. Johnson was very busy writing up a custody report, so he paid less attention to the issue that he normally might—he rendered a decision "against" the mother and allowed himself a small glimmer of pleasure in being able to get back at her in this manner. It turned out that the school decision resulted in implications Dr. Johnson had not anticipated, and a period of chaos resulted for the children.

Record Keeping

It is the obligation of forensic psychologists to maintain records that can be made appropriately available should there be a need to review the basis of their thinking and decision making. "The standard to be applied to such documentation or recording anticipates that the detail and quality of such documentation will be subject to reasonable Judicial scrutiny; this standard is higher than the normative for general clinical practice" (APA, Division 41, 1991, p. 3). Given the manner in which a special master is empowered to make decisions about children, it is particularly important that data relied on to make those decisions be well documented. Frequently, the articulation of the basis underlying a particular decision is included in the special master's order. When a special master is required to make major decisions or recommendations to the court, such as school placement, changes in the regular visitation schedule, or the requirement of a family member to obtain psychological intervention, it is wise for the special master to delineate the sources of data and the justification for the decision made. This practice ensures greater likelihood of compliance in addition to providing an accessible file should the court be asked to review a decision in the event of an appeal on the part of one parent.

In some jurisdictions, it is routine for orders to be filed with the court, becoming a permanent part of the family's court file. In other jurisdictions, orders are provided to the county's family court services or merely provided to the parents or their attorneys. Regardless of the dissemination of the orders, the special master should inform the parents, during the initial setup of the case, about the manner in which orders will be handled. In the instances when the special master is making immediate and often minor decisions, such as whether the pickup will be at 10:00 a.m. or 11:00 a.m. on Thanksgiving Day, no formal order will ordinarily be produced.

A special master's file should include detailed notes from meetings with the parents, notes about contacts with collateral parties, and orders made. A useful mechanism is to write a summary memorandum following each meeting that documents the topics of discussion, items agreed on by the parents, and orders made.

If called on to testify in court, a special master should take steps to protect sensitive material, such as notes on contacts with therapists and raw test data. Protections can include ensuring that the courtroom is closed to the public and that testimony regarding sensitive material occurs in chambers with the judge and attorneys, excluding the parents. This situation becomes problematic when either or both parents are unrepresented by attorneys. Failure to provide these parents with the data on which a decision is made limits their right to due process and disclosure; however, providing such data could permanently damage existing therapeutic relationships. Discussion with and guidance from the court of jurisdiction is helpful in such situations.

Summary

The use of psychologists as special masters within the family courts provides an alternative conflict-resolution mechanism for those high-conflict families that engage in ongoing and entrenched hostilities. Growing literature on the impact of conflict on children (Cummings & Davies, 1994) and on the predictive negative impact of interparental conflict on children's adjustment to divorce (Brotsky, Steinman, & Zemmelman, 1988; Johnston, 1994; Johnston, Kline, & Tschann, 1989) has resulted in professionals seeking alternatives to the standard court process. While mediation is a process that many families can use to resolve disputes in a more cooperative, less-adversarial manner, the lack of decision-making power on the part of the mediator often results in stalemates with parents who are intent on disagreement. The multifaceted nature of the special master process, which includes mediative efforts, education regarding children's needs, addressing the parents' dynamics, and decision making, has proven effective with many of these families. Other sorts of families, such as those in which there is a need to monitor a parent's behavior or the safety of a child or if families need to make frequent decisions due to the child or children's age or special needs, can also benefit from this process.

Potential positive outcomes of psychologists functioning as special masters are dependent on psychologists using their roles in an ethical and responsible manner. Training focusing on objectivity, data collection, neutrality, and analyses of multiple sources of data can prepare psychologists to perform effectively as special masters. However, holding the power to effect real changes in peoples' lives and determine the structure of children's lives must be accompanied by a recognition of the need to work at the highest professional standard and to be vigilant about limits of expertise and ethical pitfalls that may arise. In the exercise of such work, ethical issues most commonly stem from its nature and from the novelty of using psychologists as officers of the court. Among the potential ethical dilemmas arising from the nature of this work are those relating to multiple, untenable roles, informed consent, and issues involving privacy, confidentiality, and record keeping. The relative novelty of this work for psychologists, which has developed since the 1990s, raises questions about guidelines for training and needed expertise, the lack of community standards, and the paucity of readily available supervision and consultation. The potential power inherent in the role of a special master requires psychologists to maintain the highest ethical standards, both to protect courts and clients and to protect themselves. Their work in the family courts has led to increasing complaints to ethics committees and licensing boards; some of these complaints are justified, while others have been vengeful or frivolous. Complaints filed against special masters are surely likely to increase as the courts more frequently adopt this alternative process to conflict resolution.

References

American Psychological Association. (2002). Ethical principles of psychologists and code of conduct. *American Psychologist, 57*, 1060–1073.

American Psychological Association, Division 41. (1991). Specialty guidelines for forensic psychologists. *Law and Human Behavior, 15*, 655–665.

Brotsky, M., Steinman, S., & Zemmelman, S. (1988). Joint custody through mediation: A longitudinal assessment of children. *Conciliation Courts Review, 26*, 53–58.

California Civil Code, §4608 (1994).

California Civil Code, §3011(2005).

Cummings, E. M., & Davies, P. (1994). *Children and marital conflict*. New York: Guilford Press.

Johnston, J. R. (1994). High-conflict divorce. *The Future of Children, 4*, 165–182.

Johnston, J. R., Kline, M., & Tschann, J. (1989). Ongoing postdivorce conflict in families contesting custody: Effects on children of joint custody and frequent access. *American Journal of Orthopsychiatry, 59*, 576–592.

Lee, S. M. (1995). The emergence of special masters in child custody cases. *Association of Family and Conciliation Courts Newsletter, 14*, 5.

Lurvey, I. (1990). Case of the issue. *Family Law News, 13*, 1, 11.

Stahl, P. (1995, April). The use of special masters in high conflict divorce. *California Psychologist*, pp. 29–30.

8

Ethics in Performing Criminal Forensic Evaluations

Richard Romanoff

Introduction

The "Ethical Principles of Psychologists and Code of Conduct" (herein-after referred to as the ethics code or the code) as most recently revised by the American Psychological Association (APA) (2002), in combination with the "Specialty Guidelines for Forensic Psychologists" (Committee on Ethical Guidelines, 1991; hereinafter referred to as specialty guidelines), provides invaluable guides for the work of criminal forensic psychologists. While no code of ethics or set of guidelines can, by itself, answer all questions or address all potential difficulties, the ethics code and specialty guidelines provide psychologists who work in the forensic area with a thoughtful set of principles that can guide work often affecting people's most basic rights and freedoms. This chapter is written in an effort to apply the ethics code and specialty guidelines to issues that arise in criminal forensic assessments. It is not, and cannot be, a complete resource that covers all situations that might arise; rather, it is intended to serve as a starting point for further deliberation on ethical conduct in forensic psychology, an important and growing specialty.

Psychologists have had a code of ethics to guide their day-to-day work since 1953. That first code was developed, and has continued to evolve, in an effort to meet the needs of academicians, researchers, and clinicians. The 1992 APA ethics code revision was the first to have a specific section devoted to ethical issues in forensic work, and that ethics section has been expanded in the 2002 revision (APA, 2002). Added attention to forensic issues within the ethics code responds to the rapid growth in this psychological specialty and to the realization of the impact that such work can have on people's lives. The criminal courts are an increasingly common setting in which psychologists function. Federal and state statutes and judges determine what roles psychologists can have as well as which credentials are necessary for a psychologist to be deemed an "expert."

Forensic psychologists perform a wide range of assessment and treatment tasks. This chapter focuses mainly on ethical issues related to psychologists' roles in assessment. In this role, psychologists may be called on to help determine whether a defendant is competent to stand trial (or competent to waive a specific right, execute a specific legal document, or make a specific legal decision); legally insane; capable of forming the specific intent on a particular crime at the time the crime was committed; or dangerous to others. They could also be asked to respond to a variety of other questions that emerge in the course of criminal proceedings in which psychological expertise is deemed relevant to the trier of fact.

Psychologists who perform such work can be in private practice, employed by academic or government institutions, or employed by some private agency. In general, the ethical responsibilities of psychologists, regardless of their work settings, are similar, if not identical. Psychologists working in settings where policies are developed by nonpsychologists must strive to ensure that their work conforms to ethical practice. It is important to develop policies that do not conflict with the current ethics code and to work toward modifying existing policies that might lead to conflicts with the ethics code. In particular, special attention must be given to issues of confidentiality, and careful consideration must be given to explicating who the "client" is in any given situation (see Melton, Petrila, Poythress, & Slobogin, 1997; Monahan, 1980) and to making this clear to all parties concerned.

Expertise

In general, a judge is left to decide whether a particular psychologist meets the criteria to be deemed expert. The central issue rests on the ability of the expert to aid the trier of fact via the use of specialized knowledge, experience, and training (see Caudill & Pope, 1995, pp. 399–406; Lilly, 1987, pp. 483–485; Stromberg et al., 1988, pp. 647–650). Psychologists are now routinely recognized by the courts as possessing such specialized skills. The importance of specialized training and the provision of ongoing supervision and consultation for psychologists who operate in this arena are discussed in greater detail in this chapter.

For each case on which a psychologist works, he or she must decide if he or she possesses an appropriate level of scientific knowledge and competency to become involved in that case. While the court will have the final say regarding this decision, it is important to recognize the ethical responsibility psychologists have in evaluating, for themselves, whether they have such expertise. In particular, Section 2 of the 2002 ethics code (APA, 2002) and Section III of the specialty guidelines (Committee, 1991) speak to the importance of pursuing work only when competence is deemed to be present.

The formal ethical responsibilities for a particular case begin at the moment when someone involved in the case contacts the mental health professional. Most often, this contact will come from an attorney who is already involved in the case. In the event that the contact is made by the defendant, by a family member of the defendant, or by some other interested party, it is ethically appropriate to ask whether an attorney is involved and to request that the attorney contact the mental health professional if his or her services are desired. It is important to understand that the criminal arena is best understood by appropriately trained attorneys, and that the general rules followed by mental health professionals in other areas of practice may lead to unintended and even harmful consequences for the defendant. For example, when a client comes for treatment, it is reasonable for the mental health professional to inquire about any relevant topic; however, in a forensic setting, there are carefully developed rules of evidence that must be followed to avoid unanticipated harm to your client. Thus, any forensic work planned by a mental health professional should under almost all circumstances be reviewed by the appropriate attorney before it is undertaken.

If no attorney has been retained or assigned, then the mental health professional should advise the contacting person to begin with this step before proceeding further. If a particular problem has developed in finding an attorney, then referral should be made to a local bar or other attorney association to help the defendant proceed. One important exception to this procedure would develop when information about imminent danger to self or others has come to the attention of the mental health professional and some immediate response is indicated. Such involvement may preclude that mental health professional's later involvement in that case.

Once an attorney has been retained or assigned and contact made, the attorney and psychologist should first review the basic facts of the case together, and then the psychologist must decide whether to accept the case. The ethics code (APA, 2002) is quite clear in its guidelines in this regard. First, the specific issues involved must fall within the scope of expertise of the psychologist. Relevant past training and supervised experience are necessary since it is ethically unacceptable to be learning at the expense of the client. An increasing number of formal forensic training programs have emerged. The American Board of Forensic Psychology requires 1,500 hours of relevant training, and for example, California courts require 5 years of experience in the area of claimed expertise. While these requirements do not serve as hard-and-fast rules, they can serve as guides to psychologists, helping them decide whether they have the necessary background to accept a particular case. Most centrally, psychologists must honestly ask themselves whether they believe they can address the issues raised in a particular case at a standard of service deemed to be "genuinely competent."

Dual Relationships

Other important issues to consider before accepting a case include making certain that there is no dual relationship with the retaining attorney, the court, or the opposing attorney, as well as with the defendant or victim, that might ultimately prove to undermine the psychologist's objectivity or the appearance of objectivity in that case. Every effort should be made by the mental health professional to avoid accepting cases that might lead to future entanglements that might compromise the ability to operate in an objective fashion.

It is particularly important to point out the inadvisability of serving as both evaluator and therapist. These roles are in frequent conflict, so it is almost impossible to maintain both roles in an uncompromised fashion. While it is not an automatic ethical violation to accept both roles, the likelihood that this dual role will ultimately lead to an ethical violation is extremely high. The difficulties of avoiding certain dual roles in more rural areas have consistently been used to argue against an outright ban on such practices. The arguments against this ban are less relevant in the criminal arena, in which the relatively short duration of work on a particular case can almost always allow for someone to be brought in who does not have some actual or perceived conflict of interest. It is also important to note that mental health professionals serving a therapeutic function should be wary of involvement in court as an expert witness on behalf of their clients because they often lack access to the broader evidence needed to form more objective opinions. In addition, such mental health professionals often have a greater interest in the well-being of their clients that can conflict with the need to provide potentially negative input to the trier of fact.

When beginning work with an attorney, one should clarify the objective nature of psychological assessment and one's own neutrality of the mental health professional. The attorney should be told explicitly that no advance guarantees can be provided regarding the outcome of the assessment. It is also useful to advise the retaining attorney in advance on the nature and extent of one's background and training in the area. Any limitations or concerns that can be anticipated as a result of one's introduction into the case should be reviewed. For example, if the issue of intoxication has been raised and a relevant question centers on how this may interact with a particular medical condition, then it is important to suggest, early on, that a specialist in this area of focus is needed. It may also be important to notify the attorney that some outside life event, such as a recent conviction of the mental health professional for driving under the influence, has bearing.

Fee Arrangement

It is incumbent on the psychologist to work out a clear fee arrangement at the initial contact. Often, a third party is involved; thus, issues of who will have access to the results of the assessment must be clarified for all parties concerned. Often, a retainer system is employed in the legal arena, and there is nothing unethical about this type of fee arrangement. In general, accepting cases on a contingency basis (the mental health professional is only paid if the retaining attorney prevails) has been viewed as unethical. In essence, the actual or perceived pressure that such a fee arrangement, as noted, might have in coloring the mental health professional's findings has been seen as unethical.

The ethics code (APA, 2002) urges that psychologists provide some work on a low-fee or no-fee basis to enable indigent clients to benefit from psychological expertise. Issues of time frame, availability, and anticipated vacations should also be reviewed. Once these issues are clarified, and if one is retained, a letter should be sent to the attorney that spells out the nature of the case, the services one has agreed to provide, the confirmed fee arrangements, and any additional details relevant to the case.

Case Materials

Either in the initial contact with the attorney or at the earliest convenient time, a discussion should be held to determine what materials are needed to enable a competent assessment in a case. The forensic guidelines highlight the need for objective, thorough, and comprehensive opinions; thus, a full range of materials should be reviewed. Typically, the arrest report, prior arrest reports, if available, and probation reports, transcripts from preliminary hearings, statements made by interviewed witnesses or by the defendant, interviews with important collateral contacts, past medical records, past school records, and other information specific to a case can all be relevant. What is most important in this decision process is that the mental health professional pursue review of any materials deemed relevant for a comprehensive and objective assessment. It is vital actively to pursue both the good news and the bad news and not to omit consideration of the full range of information in forming conclusions. It is also important for the mental health professional and attorney to agree on the nature of access that the mental health professional will have to information deemed relevant by the mental health professional. For example, if the defendant informs the mental health professional that there is a taped confession that the mental health professional did not know existed, it would be important to have clarified with the attorney in advance the importance of free access to relevant information. If such an agreement has not been reached with the attorney, and if the mental health professional feels that an objective and comprehensive review is impossible without a particular piece of evidence, then it is likely unethical to continue with the case.

While psychologists are not attorneys and cannot hope to master the intricacies of the law, it is vital for forensic criminal psychologists to have a thorough working knowledge of the laws and rules that govern confidentiality and privilege in the jurisdictions in which they work. When not sure, they should ask. Sometimes, the retaining attorney will be equally unclear, and it is important for a forensic psychologist to maintain contacts with other psychologists and with other attorneys whose expertise may be called on in the course of ongoing work. When this is done, it is vital to adequately document with whom you have consulted and what was concluded. It is also important, before the psychologist proceeds with any work, to understand the guidelines related to discovery by expert witnesses from the relevant evidence codes and from past case law. Thus, interviews with other relevant witnesses should always be cleared with the attorney who has retained you before you pursue the interview. There are times when an ethically acceptable role might lead to decisions that would at least temporarily preclude the psychologist from proceeding with interviews deemed to be essential. For example, if retained to work on the penalty phase of a capital case before the guilt phase of that case has concluded, it may be ethically and professionally necessary to refrain from interviewing certain key witnesses in an effort to avoid contaminating their testimony in the guilt phase.

Assessments with child victims and child witnesses are now considered a distinct area of specialization by forensic psychologists, and a wide range of ethical issues must be carefully considered before pursuing work in this area. Review of these issues is beyond the scope of the present chapter; however, views of what is or is not appropriate are changing with such speed that it is important to proceed carefully in this area (see Fisher, 1995; Koocher et al., 1995; Melton et al., 1995; Saywitz & Goodman, 1996; Saywitz, Goodman, & Lyon, 2002).

There are also times when the pursuit of a psychologist's work can lead to unforeseen consequences that must be communicated to the attorney (and, within legal and ethical demands, to other parties). For example, an accused child molester who had initially disclaimed involvement in the molestation might, on interview, acknowledge his involvement in the molestation, indicating that he wants to change his plea from innocent to guilty. Such a change must be communicated to the attorney as soon as possible (namely, that day).

The first meeting with the defendant must begin with certain steps. As with any client, the work must begin with a verbal or written informed consent. In this introduction, the mental health professional must spell out the nature and purpose of the assessment or interview. The defendant should be told who retained the mental health professional and what limitations to confidentiality are present. The defendant should be informed of his or her right to refuse to participate in the interview and what implications might follow from such refusal. For example, refusal to participate in an assessment of competence to stand trial might result in involuntary hospitalization or the continuation of court proceedings even when the defendant is incompetent.

A cautionary note emerges from this last consideration. At times, despite the best efforts of the mental health professional, a defendant will be unable to think meaningfully or intelligently about the issues at hand. When this happens, the mental health professional has a special responsibility to communicate with the attorney and to obtain the attorney's consent before proceeding. The issues involved in this type of situation are in many ways similar to the issues that develop in work with young children. In essence, mental health professionals must ask themselves what *they* believe to be in the best interests of the defendant. When there is a disagreement between the mental health professional and attorney about how best to proceed, consultation with other attorneys and mental health professional colleagues is indicated.

Record Keeping

Issues of record keeping are important in forensic work. In general, the guidelines are evolving toward higher expectations for maintaining written records. In forensic work, maintaining comprehensive records is all the more important, at times conflicting with what attorneys want. Often, in an attempt to minimize discovery by opposing counsel, they may want minimal or no records kept. However, the ability to recall material over months and sometimes years, where details will be requested, requires the taking of thorough notes. In certain key interviews, there is increasing use of audio- and even videotaping, a practice that is fully consistent with ethical guidelines.

Psychological Testing

Often, mental health professionals will make use of psychological testing when conducting assessments. They should only use tests with which they are familiar. Tests must be appropriate for the setting, and the norms must be generalizable to the population at hand. Mental health professionals should be familiar with reliability and validity issues for the tests chosen, and they should keep current on new developments with the tests they use (e.g., new editions and standardization samples). In general, it is wise to choose tests that have either been specifically developed and normed in forensic settings or to choose tests that have often been used in forensic settings (see Gacono & Meloy, 1994; Melton et al., 1997; Pope, Butcher, & Seelen, 2006). At such times, it is important to be aware of the scientific literature on how test interpretation can be affected when a specific test is used in a forensic setting. It is also important to have a solid understanding of test development theory and general issues of reliability and validity that pertain to all psychological tests.

The issue of computer scoring also warrants some discussion. Forensic settings elicit somewhat different performances on some standardized tests; however, hypotheses generated by most computer scoring programs assume that the client is being seen in a clinical rather than a forensic setting. It would be important to communicate with any scoring service or program developer to get the official policy on the use of their specific program with a forensic population. If no policy exists, then a mental health professional needs to exercise great care before proceeding.

Another important issue in any forensic assessment follows from the need to understand the rules of evidence and relevant case law for particular issues and in particular jurisdictions. For example, if retained to determine a defendant's competency to stand trial, it is vital for a mental health professional to understand the importance of *not* asking questions about that person's mental state at the time of the alleged offense. In effect, pursuing discovery of issues not germane to the request at hand can lead to serious difficulties for the client. At times, attorneys will request information about both competency to stand trial and mental state at the time of the alleged offense. At such times, the mental health professional should clarify the difficulties with this approach to the attorney before proceeding. In general, a good rule of thumb is to have the attorney produce a specific set of questions that the attorney wants to have answered. This request should lead to some interaction between the mental health professional and the attorney to find a set of questions that are both of concern to the attorney and possible for the mental health professional to answer effectively.

Records that are obtained must be secured in a safe and confidential manner (i.e., locked in a protected venue). Any employee or other professional with whom the mental health professional interacts about such materials must understand the confidential nature of the materials reviewed. Agreements with all employees, psychological assistants, or independent contractors must be developed to ensure that they understand that the need for them to maintain confidentiality is identical to that of the mental health professional conducting the assessment.

When an assessment has been completed and feedback to the attorney is indicated, both the ethics code (APA, 2002) and the specialty guidelines (Committee, 1991) urge psychologists to provide maximally unbiased opinions and conclusions. Questions must be answered in a comprehensive and honest manner. The code is quite clear that, to the extent psychologists fall short of this goal, they are falling short of optimal ethical behavior. Limitations to any conclusions must be provided as part of the general feedback given. For example, an argument can be made that, in any particular forensic evaluation, the results may be invalid owing to possible malingering or misrepresentation by a defendant, who might be trying to reduce his or her criminal responsibility. The typically limited duration of the assessment and the high motivation of the defendant (consciously or unconsciously) to provide a distorted account of events remain constant possibilities; thus, ethical practice requires great awareness and sensitivity to this possibility. Similarly, it is important to keep in mind that psychology remains far from an exact science, and that much remains to be learned, especially as relates to forensic practice.

Malingering

It is important to address the issue of malingering, including the necessity to carefully consider it as a possibility in each and every case. To do so, one may use normed tests designed to detect malingering (see Rogers, 1990, 1997), interviews with collateral contacts to confirm statements made by the defendant, review of records to see if they support statements made by the defendant, and other indicators. However, it is vital in each assessment to outline the specific steps taken to detect malingering and the findings and conclusions drawn by the mental health professional as a result of that review. If an interview with a victim is pursued in an effort to comprehensively assess a defendant, the victim should be informed that information obtained might be used to reduce the criminal responsibility of the defendant.

Appropriate Feedback

Mental health professionals must also strive to explain their views to all parties in a fashion that facilitates understanding. Thus, the avoidance of jargon and terms that might be misunderstood by the attorney or the trier of fact is important. A particular difficulty may arise in criminal forensic work in the process of providing feedback to the defendant. The ethics code (APA, 2002) calls on psychologists to provide feedback to clients after an assessment in terms that the client can understand. In most criminal cases, the defendant is not actually the client (see Monahan, 1980) and, in this sense, has no direct right to such feedback. Even so, to the extent possible, and after discussion with the defendant's attorney, appropriate feedback may not interfere with any legal issue and may help to serve the clinical needs of the defendant.

In some situations, important information discovered by the mental health professional will be suppressed by the attorney. For example, a defense attorney may choose not to make use of a confidential assessment that the attorney feels would harm the best interest of his or her client. Mental health professionals, in the course of their evaluations, can uncover evidence of guilt or dangerousness that they believe should be released. In general, the ethical guidelines in this area are similar to those in other areas. Specifically, in the absence of some legally mandated obligation or authorization, mental health professionals must maintain the confidentiality of the information gathered. Issues of attorney-client privilege must be clearly understood and respected by mental health professionals who work in this area. Mental health professionals have, at times, been retained by opposing counsel after discovery has been made by that attorney that the mental health professional was retained and then not used by the other side. Accepting this role is likely an ethical violation and may also be a violation of attorney-client privilege. For example, a defendant who was initially interviewed by a mental health professional on behalf of a defense attorney might speak more openly to that mental health professional. If the mental health professional had not reviewed the possibility that he or she might serve as a witness for the opposing counsel, the defendant could justifiably feel that he or she had been manipulated and treated unethically.

It is also important to communicate clearly to the attorney (a) any additional information that one feels is needed to complete the assessment and (b) how failure to pursue that lead might limit the conclusions that can be drawn. In general, all information that should be pursued to answer the original referral question, or to respond to any clinically important issue (e.g., the danger of clients to themselves or others), should be identified to the attorney. Providing detailed verbal feedback to the attorney prior to producing a written report is ethically appropriate.

In general, most cases will require the writing of a report to summarize the opinions and conclusions that have been made. As with the noted verbal feedback, these written reports must strive for maximally objective and comprehensive information to respond to the referral questions. Reports should contain a clear presentation of the findings used to arrive at any conclusions or opinions. Any limitations to these conclusions must also be entered into the written record. It is important to recognize that courts are far more interested in the thinking that contributes to a conclusion than in the conclusion. In effect, the goal is to allow the triers of fact to form their own conclusions, armed with specialized knowledge provided by the psychologist to aid them in their task. Providing draft copies of written reports to the attorney is an ethically appropriate action that can give the defendant and the attorney an opportunity to raise any issues or concerns that may necessitate further consideration before a final report is produced. This practice is akin to responding to concerns raised by any client regarding the accuracy or validity of any assessment report. All earlier draft copies of reports should be maintained as part of the permanent record.

One must focus on which findings and content belong in the report and which do not belong. In general, any information needed to answer the original referral questions should be included, and information that does not speak to one or more questions should be left out. If unsure about the relevance of a particular finding, it may be useful to consult with a colleague and to document this consultation. However, mental health professionals must maintain complete records of their work products, including material not included in the final report, as part of the permanent record maintained for that case.

Reports should also strive for clarity and avoidance of jargon. Essentially, reports should be written so that the readers can clearly understand the conclusions as well as the rationales that contributed to those conclusions. It is ethically problematic to provide conclusions and opinions that are not anchored in some reportable set of observations (behavioral, historical, test data, etc.). For example, it is inappropriate to conclude that a client is dangerous without spelling out the specific factors relied on by the psychologist that led to that conclusion. The written report must include any limitations that are considered appropriate and that reflect the scientific literature related to the issues at hand.

Some discussion is warranted on the issue of providing conclusions to ultimate issue questions (i.e., sanity, capacity to premeditate or harbor malice, and the like). Many courts have held that providing ultimate issue conclusions usurps the role of the trier of fact. In general, courts are more interested in providing judges and juries with more and better information to enable them to arrive at *their* conclusions to the ultimate issues. At least some jurisdictions no longer allow mental health experts to testify to certain conclusions before the trier of fact (e.g., California Evidence Code, §720 et seq.). Thus, if the report is going to the trier of fact directly, then the evaluator must know whether such conclusions should be omitted. Even so, a strong case has been made for omitting such opinions as a general rule of thumb (Melton et al., 1997). In effect, difficulties emerge when translating legal concepts into psychological concepts (and vice versa), stemming from differences between the more probabilistic science of psychology and the more black-and-white nature of legal decision making. In general, if clear reviews of the findings that led to conclusions are provided and all relevant limitations to the conclusions are given, and if it is legally allowed to provide those findings in a particular jurisdiction, then the reason not to give ultimate issue conclusions is essentially not an ethical one, although not precluding a given psychologist from choosing to avoid providing such conclusions on bases other than ethical ones.

On the Stand

If the attorney comes to believe that, based on the results received via verbal and written feedback, expert testimony is desired, the next, and in some ways most difficult, phase of the work will begin. For most mental health professionals, it is this phase that is most stressful and aversive. It is vital to have a clear understanding of ethical guidelines as they pertain to professional involvement in this phase. It is here that the mental health professional has the least control over how the proceedings will unfold. Essentially, it is here as well that mental health professionals are confronted with the reality that they are visitors in someone else's house. As such, they must abide by the rules and customs of that house. The impetus behind the development of the rules of the criminal justice system are quite different from the impetus behind the development of the ethical code for psychologists. Conflict is inevitable.

On the stand, mental health professionals can only answer questions that have been put to them. Thus, to a large extent, attorneys have effective control over the specific information that emerges. In addition, rules of evidence and case law also affect what can or cannot be asked (e.g., ultimate issue questions in some jurisdictions). Accordingly, psychologists may have a desire to provide more comprehensive recitals than will ever take place. Doing so, however, can result in testimony that leads to misunderstandings for judges and juries. Nevertheless, the 2002 APA ethics code encourages psychologists to avoid making misleading statements. Mental health professionals can minimize this problem by apprising attorneys before testimony begins of the nature of the testimony that will be provided. Efforts can be made to obtain agreement on the full extent of the testimony that will be offered. Efforts to anticipate cross-examination questions and to have these questions asked by the attorney on direct examination is desirable. It is reasonable to explain to the attorney, if need be, that one's credibility is enhanced when potentially damaging information is brought out on direct examination. There are also other advantages to having the information emerge on direct examination rather than risk its emergence during the later cross-examination. This strategy would be viewed as maximally consistent with the standards set by the ethics code. In this regard, it is important to note that review of anticipated direct examination, cross-examination, redirect, and recross with the retaining attorney is both ethical and advisable.

The pressures created during the direct examination and cross-examination process are likely to be the most intense relative to any other phase of the criminal forensic assessment. In essence, from the defendant's and attorney's perspectives, this is the phase that is of ultimate importance; thus, at this point there is the greatest potential for violations of the ethics code (APA, 2002). The exaggeration, overgeneralization, or misrepresentation of results in court testimony are unfortunately all too common. A perception has developed on the part of the public that experts can be influenced by the side that hired them, and further, that the subjective nature of the work may make it difficult for judges and juries in their decision making.

At such times, careful study and consideration of the ethics code (APA, 2002) and the specialty guidelines (Committee, 1991) become critical. It may be helpful to review these documents periodically (and, in particular, to do so before offering testimony) and think through how particular segments of the specific testimony about to be offered might need to be reconsidered in the context of the code. It is at this point that consultation with well-regarded colleagues can be invaluable. When doubts arise, it is important to work toward clarifying the issues involved with all relevant parties before any testimony begins.

The demeanor of the mental health professional while testifying is also important. The science of psychology is not precise, and it is crucial that a presentation not overstate the basic limitations of current knowledge. Courts often reward individuals who have an ability to project an air of self-confidence and certainty. There is a powerful pull to present findings in the strongest possible terms, based both on pressures from the involved attorneys and personal needs to be perceived as competent and important. While it is ethically responsible to state findings with both clarity and reasonable confidence, certain caveats should always serve to bolster one's statements. For example, it was common practice several decades ago to state with "reasonable professional certainty" that a given individual is or is not dangerous. Now, given the work of many researchers (e.g., Monahan,

1981; Monahan & Steadman, 1983), it is probably clear to everyone that such statements are scientifically unsupportable and constitute a violation of ethical principles. This example is raised to highlight the pull to exaggerate the state of knowledge and to caution against making similar errors with more current issues. For example, there is likely to be much less controversy over a well-researched issue, such as whether a particular person suffers from schizophrenia—and even this can be argued by well-trained and competent professionals—relative to whether a particular memory reported by a defendant or victim is accurate. In such matters, it is critical to maintain up-to-date knowledge of relevant scientific literature so that findings can be presented accurately for a particular case.

Follow-Up

Less frequently discussed, in relation to criminal forensic assessment, is the difficulty that arises because of the absence of follow-up with most cases. In effect, mental health professionals are forced to develop a set of hypotheses about defendants who are in the middle of a legal process that exerts unusual pressures on them that can lead to important misunderstandings of the "true" clinical situation. Rarely has this individual been known by the evaluator before the assessment begins and rarely will the assessor remain in contact with the same individual after criminal proceedings have ended. While no clear resolution can be found to this particular dilemma, one important strategy to minimize this problem centers on the criminal forensic expert's maintaining a nonforensic practice in which such feedback is more readily available. While such private practice does not eliminate the problem, it can serve to inoculate the mental health professional against forgetting how much can happen that was neither expected nor predictable.

Finally, as in other areas of practice (psychotherapy, academics, and the like), participation in active peer review with other colleagues on a regular basis and use of consultation when needed are essential for continued ethical practice. The potential for being blinded by the issues that can develop in a particular forensic case is as great as the potential for developing harmful countertransference reactions in psychotherapy. Ongoing training and discussion with peers in long and difficult cases become critical for maintaining a more objective and a clearer view on issues involved in such cases and how best to handle them.

Ethical practice by mental health professionals in forensic criminal assessment is a challenge that can be most successfully met when a strong commitment to integrity and competence is maintained. The substantial impact that this work can have on the life of an individual and the degree to which it brings close scrutiny to the individual clinician and the profession of psychology highlight the importance of regular review of the complex ethical issues raised by this type of work. This chapter has sought to identify some of the important issues in the ethical conduct of this work. Other issues that could not have been anticipated will come up on a case-by-case basis. When such issues arise, the immediate availability of a competent and trusted support system becomes critical since decisions may need to be made in a very short period of time that could have reverberations well into the future. Maintaining ethical practice in the area of forensic criminal evaluations calls for active and sustained vigilance.

Appendix

Vignette 1

Mr. Smith, a local attorney, needed a psychological assessment for one of his clients and was referred to Dr. Jones, a recently licensed psychologist. Smith called Jones and asked if he were available to perform a confidential comprehensive psychological assessment of his client. Smith noted that the assessment needed to be performed in a hurry, as there was a court date set for 3 days from that date. Smith noted that the judge had refused any further continuances in this matter. Smith went on to say that his client, Mr. A, had been charged with first-degree murder after allegedly stabbing his girlfriend 17 times. Smith noted that A was currently at the local jail and said, "I think they're giving him some medication." Smith went on to say that he wanted to know whether A was sane at the time of the crime and whether he was able to form the necessary criminal intent to be found guilty of first-degree murder. He noted that he wanted the information to help him decide how best to defend his client. Without further discussion, after agreeing that he would receive his full fee, Jones accepted the case. He requested copies of all relevant records from Smith, who said he would have them delivered by messenger the next morning.

When Dr. Jones arrived at his office the next morning, the package was waiting. To his surprise he found that the records consisted only of a brief arrest report, with no information regarding A's state of mind at the time of the offense, and of a transcript of the preliminary hearing. Jones gathered his materials and left for the jail. Following only minimal introductions, he began to administer the Minnesota Multiphasic Personality Inventory-2 (MMPI-2). After about 14 minutes, A stood up and began screaming. He stated that he knew that Dr. Jones was a "soldier of Satan" who would never succeed in his plan to destroy the world, and that he, A, would prevail at any cost in this battle, "even if I have to kill every one of you."

After a brief silence, A stormed out of the interview room and disappeared down the hall. On his return to the office, Dr. Jones contacted Smith, and informed him that he had completed his assessment and was prepared to testify that Mr. A was a paranoid schizophrenic who was delusional and likely insane at the time of the offense. Smith was delighted, and arrangements were made for Jones to testify the next day. Dr. Jones arrived and took the stand. On direct examination, he stated that he had examined Mr. A at the jail and had determined that he was currently psychotic and probably a paranoid schizophrenic. He stated that the defendant, A, suffered from delusions of persecution and delusions of grandeur. He stated that it was his opinion that A had stabbed his girlfriend as a result of these delusions and perhaps in response to command auditory hallucinations. He opined that Mr. A was insane at the time of the offense. Direct examination took about 1 hour and seemed to go fine.

Cross-examination took the rest of the day, and by the time it was over Dr. Jones swore he would never do another forensic assessment as long as he lived.

Vignette 2

Dr. Smith is a well-known forensic psychologist in his city. He was reading the newspaper one day and noticed a story about a man who had apparently stalked and killed a high-level city official. Later that day, he received a phone call from a defense attorney he had known from prior cases. The attorney asked him if he would be interested in evaluating the alleged perpetrator in this matter, who appeared to be mentally unstable. Smith accepted the case.

Dr. Smith reviewed the voluminous material accumulated by the police. He conducted a comprehensive assessment. During the interview, the defendant told him that he had killed the city official because that official had singled him out for psychological torture by placing listening devices in the walls of his home and by transmitting humiliating messages about him over the radio and television sets of everyone in the city. He also said that, for the past 2 months, he had noticed that people were laughing at him wherever he went. The defendant said that he was out of touch with his family and had no friends. He said that he had not been working and was receiving disability benefits for "mental illness." He denied any past history of alcohol or drug use.

A review of past records documented a history of multiple prior arrests with some prior violent felony arrests. There was no history of prior psychiatric hospitalizations. The psychologist noted that, at the time of the offense, the defendant had not exhibited any bizarre behavior and had told police that he would not answer any questions without his lawyer present. Smith also noted that the defendant had sustained several prior drug-related arrests. He discovered that a prior arrest had led the defendant to be diverted to a drug rehabilitation program; he requested that the attorney send for these records, which he then reviewed. He discovered that this individual had been seen as manipulative and insincere in the drug treatment program. These findings led him to become more suspicious of the defendant's account. He checked with the local Social Security Administration office and found that the defendant had applied for but been denied benefits.

Smith then administered a battery of psychological tests. He found that the validity scales of the MMPI-2 suggested a strong tendency to exaggerate illness. Other tests were administered to assess the possibility of malingering and to probe more thoroughly for the presence of psychopathy. Results yielded evidence of both.

Smith asked the defense attorney if any interviews had been conducted with other people who knew the defendant around the time of the offense. The attorney reported that several people who lived in apartments adjacent to the defendant's had been interviewed, and Smith reviewed these interviews. They suggested that the defendant had not exhibited any evidence of bizarre behavior prior to the arrest, and that many people often came to his apartment at all times of the day and night. One witness recognized a picture of the victim, who had come to the apartment on several occasions.

Smith decided to have another meeting with the defendant. In this meeting, he confronted the defendant with the evidence of past substance abuse. He wondered whether the defendant had known the victim prior to the killing. He wondered whether they had been involved in some type of ongoing relationship. He noted the results of psychological testing that suggested exaggeration of illness and possible malingering. The defendant became increasingly quiet and angry. He then stormed out of the room and informed his attorney that he would not meet with the psychologist again and that he did not want this psychologist to have any further involvement in his case.

Smith provided a feedback session to the attorney. He said that he had strong concerns about the authenticity of the defendant's current account and believed that there was likely some exaggeration of illness in an attempt to avoid criminal responsibility. He outlined the reasons for his concerns. The attorney thanked him for his work and requested that he not speak about his findings with anyone. The attorney told him that he looked forward to working with him in future cases. Dr. Smith did *not* testify in this case and quickly moved on to other work.

References

American Psychological Association. (1992). Ethical principles of psychologists and code of conduct. *American Psychologist, 47,* 1597–1611.

American Psychological Association. (2002). Ethical principles of psychologists and code of conduct. *American Psychologist, 57,* 1060–1073.

Caudill, O. B., & Pope, K. S. (1995). *Law and mental health professionals: California.* Washington, DC: American Psychological Association.

Committee on Ethical Guidelines for Forensic Psychologists. (1991). Specialty guidelines for forensic psychologists. *Law and Human Behavior, 15,* 655–665.

Fisher, C. B. (1995). American psychological association's (1992) ethics code and the validation of sexual abuse in day-care settings. *Psychology, Public Policy, and Law, 1*(2), 461–478.

Gacono, C. B., & Meloy, J. R. (1994). *The Rorschach assessment of aggressive and psychopathic personalities.* Hillsdale, NJ: Erlbaum.

Koocher, G. P., Goodman, G. S., White, C. S., Friedrich, W. N., Sivan, A. B., & Reynolds, C. R. (1995). Psychological science and the use of anatomically detailed dolls in child-sexual abuse assessments. *Psychological Bulletin, 118*(2), 199–222.

Lilly, G. C. (1987). *An introduction to the law of evidence* (2nd ed.). St. Paul, MN: West.

Melton, G. B., Goodman, G. S., Kalichman, S. C., Levine, M., Saywitz, K. J., & Koocher, G. P. (1995). Empirical research on child maltreatment and the law. *Journal of Clinical Child Psychology, 24,* 47–77.

Melton, G. B., Petrila, J., Poythress, N. G., & Slobogin, C. (1997). *Psychological evaluations for the courts: A handbook for mental health professionals and lawyers* (2nd ed.). New York: Guilford Press.

Monahan, J. (Ed.). (1980). *Who is the client? The ethics of psychological intervention in the criminal justice system.* Washington, DC: American Psychological Association.

Monahan, J. (1981). *Predicting violent behavior: An assessment of clinical technique.* Beverly Hills, CA: Sage.

Monahan, J., & Steadman, H. J. (Eds.). (1983). *Mentally disordered offenders: Perspectives from law and social science.* New York: Plenum.

Parker's California Evidence Code, §720 (1997).

Pope, K. S., Butcher, J. N., & Seelen, J. (2006). *The MMPI, MMPI-2 and MMPI-A in court: A practical guide for expert witnesses and attorneys* (3rd ed.). Washington, DC: American Psychological Association.

Rogers, R. (1990). The SIRS as a measure of malingering: A validation study with a correctional sample. *Behavioral Sciences and the Law, 8,* 85–92.

Rogers, R. (Ed.). (1997). *Clinical assessment of malingering and deception* (2nd ed.). New York: Guilford Press.

Saywitz, K. J., & Goodman, G. S. (1996). Interviewing children in and out of court: Current research and practice implications. In J. Briere, L. Berliner, J. Bulkley, C. Jennry, & T. Reid (Eds.), *APSAC handbook on child maltreatment* (pp. 297–318). Newberry Park, CA: Sage.

Saywitz, K. J., Goodman, G., & Lyon, T. D. (2002). Interviewing children in and out of court: Current research and practice implications. In J. Briere, L. Berliner, J. Bulkley, C. Jenny & T. Reid (Eds.), *APSAC handbook on child maltreatment* (pp. 379–402). Newberry Park, CA: Sage.

Stromberg, C. D., Haggarty, D. J., Leibenluft, R. F., McMillian, M. H., Mishkin, B., Rubin, B. L., et al. (1988). *The psychologist's legal handbook.* Washington, DC: Council for the National Register of Health Service Providers in Psychology.

Section III

Mental Health Professionals and Litigation

The third and final section of this book turns toward claims that practitioners must face as a result of working in a forensic setting. It begins by taking up the involvement of mental health professionals in litigation, including civil lawsuits and malpractice claims, plaintiffs with "false memories" of trauma, and ethics committees. The various forms of litigation that a mental health professional may face and how these different types of litigation can be quantified are discussed. The major types of sexual misconduct litigation are addressed, followed by a focus on such topics as dual relationships, failure to warn of a patient's danger, patient suicide, and unusual treatment techniques. The life cycle of a professional liability claim and historical claims data are described. Legal issues relevant to the therapist's treating "recovered memory" or "false memory" survivors are described in the context of testifying for the recanter or reporter of trauma, third-party duty cases with adult patients, child patients, and retractor cases. The ethics complaint procedure within the American Psychological Association and the structure and functioning of a state ethics committee are described, specifically noting background information and due process for the American Psychological Association and cooperating with state ethics committees.

9

When a Mental Health Professional Is in Litigation

O. Brandt Caudill Jr.

Introduction

Litigation against psychologists for alleged malpractice was a relatively infrequent occurrence before the *Tarasoff v. Regents of the University of California* decision in 1976. Following the *Tarasoff* decision, the nature and number of lawsuits against psychologists has proliferated geometrically. The types of lawsuits can be categorized as follows: (a) alleged sexual misconduct; (b) dual relationships; (c) failure to warn of a patient's violent behavior or threats; (d) patient suicide; and (e) use of bizarre or unconventional treatment techniques. Issues related to opinions expressed in custody proceedings are addressed in Chapters 6 and 7; implantation of false memories is addressed in Chapter 11.

Sexual Misconduct Claims

Given the prevalence of sexual misconduct litigation, it is somewhat surprising to realize that, as late as the mid-1960s, there were therapists who were openly advocating sexual relationships with patients.[1] The first case finding such sexual relationships to be unethical in California was not decided until 1975.[2] That civil statute was not limited to psychotherapists but also applied to a number of other professionals, including attorneys and real estate brokers. The most significant part of the statute is that it would appear to take causes of action for sexual harassment by a therapist outside the protection of California's Medical Injury Compensation Reform Act of 1975 (MICRA),[3] which imposed limitations on damages and various other protective provisions—limitations that are extremely significant in defending these cases.

In 1979, the first statute was enacted making sexual misconduct grounds for discipline. Since then, a progression of statutes has enacted stringent penalties for sexual relationships with present and former patients. Despite the fact that the statute of limitations would clearly seem to bar such claims, it is not uncommon to have sexual misconduct claims filed concerning acts that took place in the 1970s or early 1980s when standards were unclear or different. The major types of sexual misconduct litigation are (a) the therapist has been having sex with the patient while the therapeutic relationship is going on (and sometimes having sex in the office); (b) the therapist has been having a sexual relationship with a former patient; (c) the patient's spouse is suing but the patient is not; and (d) the therapist is being sued vicariously for the acts of an assistant or intern who is accused of sexual misconduct. In addition, in 1995 California enacted a statute (California Civil Code 51.9) that created a special cause of action for sexual harassment against a variety of professionals, including psychotherapists. Because this statute allows a plaintiff to recover attorney's fees, which cannot be recovered on a malpractice action, it has been extensively used since its passage, both in cases with true allegations and in cases with false allegations. Because sexual harassment claims are excluded from most malpractice policies, this statute is a powerful weapon for plaintiffs. One concern with the statute is that it applies to patient-therapist relationships or any relationship that is substantially similar. This vague language could extend the application of the statute to relationships such as coaching. This statute should be of concern to psychotherapists outside California because a number of California statutes have been the models for similar legislation in other states (e.g., the MICRA damage cap provisions).

Sex With Existing Patients

The first case to impose liability for sex with an existing patient in California was *Walker v. Parzan* in San Diego.[4] In that case, a psychiatrist had a lengthy sexual relationship with a patient and was allegedly using prescription medications to make her more susceptible to his advances. The defense argued that this was essentially a consensual relationship that was equivalent to "a roll in the hay." The jury awarded over $4.6 million, and the case was settled on appeal for a substantial amount. Ms. Walker then wrote a book called *A Killing Cure*[5] (Walker & Young, 1986) and established an organization called Victims Against Psychic Abuse. Seminars were put on regarding sexual misconduct claims, at which patients or prospective litigants were able to meet attorneys who wanted to handle their cases. The Walker case and the book were among the first books published with direct patient accounts of sexual relationships with therapists. One of the first professional books in this area is *Sexual Intimacy Between Therapists and Patients* (Pope & Bouhoutsos, 1989). This book is often referenced in depositions of therapists accused of sexual misconduct. Another helpful text is *Sexual Feelings in Psychotherapy* (Pope, Sonne, & Holroyd, 1993).

Typically, the factors that exacerbate the damages are the following: (a) the patient has a preexisting history of sexual abuse, including child molestation; (b) the therapist has previously or subsequently engaged in sexual relationships with other patients; (c) the patient has an eating disorder, and the sexual relationship exacerbates the eating disorder; (d) the patient is depressed, and the sexual relationship leads to suicidal attempts or gestures; or (e) the therapist involves the patient in bizarre or offensive sexual conduct, including sadomasochistic sex, urinating on the patient, anal sex, group sex, encouraging the patient to have extramarital affairs, and so forth.

The California Supreme Court has taken the position that a sexual relationship with a patient may involve some legal theories that are covered by MICRA and others that are not.[6] However, the special MICRA provisions on assertion of punitive damages contained in California Code of Civil Procedure §425.13 do apply to alleged sexual misconduct.[7] This section requires that before punitive damages can be asserted in a malpractice case, a noticed motion must be brought, supported by affidavits establishing that there is a reasonable probability that the plaintiff will be able to prevail on the punitive damage claim. The reason for the special statutory section is that so many frivolous punitive damage claims were filed in malpractice actions that the legislature was required to act.

If the therapist's sexual misconduct involves a minor, it is subject to criminal prosecution[8] and can give rise to claims on the part of the patient's parents because of their role in obtaining the therapy for the patient.[9] Where the sexual relationship did not occur, the major way of disproving it is by focusing on minutiae to establish that the relationship could not occur within the time period or in the manner specified. In this regard, the prior sexual misconduct claims by a patient or tendency to sexualize nonsexual contacts are particularly critical. In my experience, although there are no meaningful statistics, the vast majority of false sexual misconduct claims are brought by patients who have a borderline personality disorder.

Frequently, when allegations of sexual misconduct are supported by evidence, the relationship is one in which the judgment of a generally ethical therapist may be corrupted by the patient's adoration, to the point at which a sexual relationship occurred. The popular myth is that therapists who engage in sexual relationships with patients generally do so with more than one patient. The American Professional Agency, the broker for insurance for a variety of mental health professionals, has compiled statistics indicating that 85% of the true sexual misconduct claims involve one therapist and one patient, with no repetition (E. Marine, vice president of claims for the American Professional Agency, personal communication). There are numerous appellate cases from several states' misconduct claims.[10]

Sex With Ex-Patients

Until 1988, sexual relationships with ex-patients in California were not illegal or even unethical. In 1988, a statute was passed (California Civil Code 0§43.93) that expressly provided that, for a sexual relationship with a former patient to be legal, a period of 2 years must have elapsed between the termination of therapy and the beginning of the relationship. This statute included a specific section providing that no patient who had married a former therapist could maintain an action because of the fact that many patients had married former therapists. The old standard before this law was that if a therapist wanted to date a patient, that therapist needed to terminate the counseling and refer the patient to another therapist before dating could begin. In February 1987, the American Psychiatric Association published a survey indicating that almost 30% of responding psychiatrists believed that they could terminate therapy and start dating a patient immediately.[11] In my experience, such an attitude still holds for a small percentage of psychotherapists, along with the mistaken belief that the prohibitions against sexual relationships do not apply if theirs is "true love." Unfortunately, some therapists attempting to be ethical about posttermination sexual relationships have contacted their colleagues for advice in these situations and have been misinformed about the amount of time that has to occur between the end of the professional relationship and the beginning of a sexual one. The good faith of the therapist in relying on misinformation or ignorance of the law is not a defense to a suit of this type, although it would certainly be relative in consideration of punitive damages. This is one of the more common issues in sexual misconduct litigation and generally involves therapists who are attempting to comply with the law and act in good faith. Obviously, the length of time between the termination of therapy and the beginning of a subsequent relationship is critical. The shorter the period of time, the less likely it is to be seen as reasonable. The 2-year time period is an arbitrary one and may be subject to constitutional attack. At least one court outside California has held that if the therapy relationship is so brief that a trusting relationship did not arise, no sexual misconduct claim can be asserted by an ex-patient.[12]

Claims by the Patient's Spouse

There is a subset of cases in which the claim regarding the sexual misconduct is brought by the spouse of the patient, not the patient. An example is *Smith v. Pust*, where a husband and daughter sued over a sexual relationship the wife had with her therapist, but the wife herself did not sue.[13] The two key defenses to a claim by a spouse are that the action is barred by California Civil Code §43.5 and lack of obligation to the nonpatient spouse. This is the section that abolishes actions for alienation of affection, seduction, and breach of promise to marry. This code section has been construed specifically to hold that claims by the spouse are barred if the spouse was never a patient. Similarly, the courts have looked with favor on an argument that no duty for liability was owed to the nonpatient spouse. On the other hand, if the spouse is a patient, frequently the spouse involved in the sexual activity with the therapist often has a less-valuable claim than the innocent spouse because juries and judges tend to ascribe a certain percentage of fault to the participating spouse, particularly if there was a course of conduct to deceive the innocent spouse. One of the largest monetary verdicts in this area was *Ertel v. Kersenbrock* (1989). In that case, the then-president of the California Association of Marriage Family Therapists (CAMFT) was engaged in a sexual relationship with a patient. The patient and her spouse ultimately filed suit, and Mr. Kersenbrock denied everything. The wife's claim was settled for around $375,000. The husband's claim was taken to trial, and a jury awarded him more than $3 million dollars. Cases both in and out of California have held that a nonpatient spouse cannot maintain a civil action against a psychotherapist for a sexual relationship with a patient-spouse.[14]

Vicarious Liability

As the wave of sexual misconduct litigation grew, insurance companies began writing exclusions for sexual acts in the policies. This action led the plaintiff's bar to engage in a deliberate shift of tactics, from focusing litigation on the person who engaged in the sexual contact to focusing on those people vicariously liable for supervising or training the therapist who engaged in the misconduct.[15]

Because of the intentional nature of sexual misconduct, it would seem that such conduct could not be the basis for vicarious liability; however, a number of court decisions outside California have held that the risk of a sexual relationship between a subordinate employee and a patient is one that employers are required to assume.[16] The focus then shifted to the nature of the employer's investigation of the employee prior to hiring and the steps taken to train the employee to refrain from becoming involved in such relationships. This focus is at the core of sexual misconduct lawsuits that have been currently filed.

Dual Relationships

The concept of dual relationships was first invoked by the American Psychological Association in its 1981 ethical principles in prohibiting sexual relationships with patients. The concept was extended to nonsexual relationships in the 1992 ethical principles. The premise is that whenever a therapist engages in a secondary relationship with a patient there is potential for confusion and exploitation of the patient and for impairment of the therapist's judgment. The CAMFT has a specific ethical prohibition against dual relationships that are exploitative or impair the therapist's judgment.[17]

The most typical dual relationship is a sexual one, as mentioned. The second most frequent type of dual relationship involves business dealings with patients. Typically, these would consist of commercial transactions that have a profit motivation or employment of a patient either for pay or barter where the goal of the relationship is to fund therapy. Some licensing boards, such as two in California, frown on business relationships with patients and employment of a patient for any purpose. Since the two

California boards get a combined 1,500–2,000 complaints per year, they address the issue more frequently than do many other licensing boards.[18] Generally, however, bartering of products for psychotherapy is less problematic because the potential for exploitation is weaker owing to the readily ascertainable market value of the goods. The potential for exploitation is substantially greater in a service relationship. In various cases, experts have testified that the key factor in bartering is the purpose for the relationship and the ratio of exchange. In some cases, the ratio of exchange of patient services for therapy hours has been as high as 100 to 1. Further, the assumption is that the more menial the services by the patient, the more likely the possible exploitation. Among the services that have been the subject of lawsuits are patients cleaning houses, mowing lawns, painting houses, taking care of dogs, cutting hair, and running errands.

In terms of business relationships, my colleagues and I have seen cases in which therapists became involved in real estate transactions, Amway dealerships, securities transactions, soft drink delivery routes, psychological testing services, marketing software, and entertainment businesses. In one of the cases that we handled, a therapist not only had provided psychotherapy but also had acted as a travel companion, "gofer," travel agent, and art tutor to a millionaire who was seriously disturbed. Over the course of 10 years of therapy, the therapist was paid over a million dollars in fees and had no notes whatsoever to document the therapy.

Although not technically instances of a dual relationship, many cases involve issues of role reversal, wherein the therapist begins sharing his problems with the patient. Some articles have suggested that when a patient is in counseling with a Christian therapist, there is a potential dual relationship if the therapist begins taking on the role of religious or pastoral counselor as well as psychotherapist (Younggren, 1983). Other commentators, however, contend that since all therapy is influenced by the values of the therapist, whether admitted to or not, counseling within a Christian framework does not pose an ethical dilemma (Bergin, 1980). When litigation involves a Christian counselor or therapist, it is not uncommon to have an allegation that the patient's spiritual beliefs were damaged by the relationship.

Failure to Notify of a Patient's Danger

California was the first state to make a case for the standing of third parties to sue over a therapist's failure to warn them of a patient's violent threats.[19] This kind of failure was the primary issue in *Tarasoff v. Regents of the University of California* (1976), a case widely followed in other jurisdictions in the United States. Initially, the *Tarasoff* case posed the situation of an expressed threat by a patient to kill a specified individual, Tatiana Tarasoff. Importantly, subsequent cases somewhat expanded the theory, from duty to *protect*, to apply to a duty to *warn* anyone who is in a reasonable zone of danger derived from the patient's threats. This expansion reached its height in *Hedlund v. Superior Court* (1983), in which the court concluded that the duty to warn extended to a 5-year-old whose mother was the target of threats by a patient. The author handled that case after it came down from the California Supreme Court, and there was a hotly contested issue about whether a threat had been made. There was also strong evidence to suggest the plaintiff actually knew that the patient was a danger.

A third case of importance in dealing with these issues is *Jablonski by Pahls v. United States* (1983), in which a patient murdered his girlfriend. In that case, the Ninth Circuit Court of Appeals held that the therapists at a Veterans Administration Hospital were potentially liable for failing to obtain the prior medical records of the patient, which would have disclosed a lengthy history of violence toward women. It appeared, however, that Ms. Pahls was well aware of the defendant's violent tendencies, and that a warning would probably have been of limited effect. Ultimately, the California legislature limited the duty to warn by passage of a statute, Civil Code §43.92, which provides that if a patient makes a threat, the therapist must take steps to protect those individuals who are in the zone of danger along with the local police. If such notification has been provided, the therapist is then immune from suit for exposing the patient to danger. Finally, in *Ewing v. Goldstein* (2004) a California appellate court held that the duty to notify can be triggered by a threat communicated to the therapist by a member of the patient's family, even when the patient never directly communicates a threat to the therapist.

Those states that have adopted a duty to notify based on the *Tarasoff* rationale can use California appellate court cases in interpreting that duty. Some states have rejected the idea of a duty to warn, generally because of the impact on confidentiality. Failure-to-notify cases are somewhat infrequent but usually arise out of fairly dire circumstances and can therefore have significant potential damage exposure. Typically, the highest exposure is incurred when the patient kills a parent who has several small children dependent on him or her for support; however, attempts to expand the duty to notify to areas other than violence have so far failed. Among the issues to consider in these cases are how frequently threats were made, to what extent they were serious or clearly just expressions of frustration, the patient's access to weapons, the patient's access to the victim, and the time lag between when the threat was made and when the attack is carried out. In a somewhat bizarre twist, the California Supreme Court invoked the duty to protect to find that there was no psychotherapist-patient privilege governing communications between Dr. Jerome Oziel and the Menendez brothers when they threatened to kill him if he disclosed their confession of murdering their parents.[20] It should also be noted that there is little dispute in the psychological community that violence cannot be predicted.

Patient Suicide

As with failure-to-notify cases, patient suicide cases are somewhat infrequent but do pose a fairly high exposure when the decedent leaves minor heirs. There have also been cases in which patients who had unsuccessfully attempted suicide filed suit subsequently over the injuries that they had inflicted on themselves.[21] The California Supreme Court has recognized the distinction between potential liability of therapists who treat a patient in an inpatient setting, and thereby have control over the patient's environment,[22] and those who treat patients in an outpatient setting.

Generally, the potential liability of an outpatient therapist is somewhat limited due to the lack of control over the patient's environment. However, there are often warning flags, indicating that a patient is suicidal, that have been missed by the therapist. California law does not allow the therapist to disclose the patient's suicidal thoughts to other family members unless the manner of committing suicide, as described by the patient, would put the other family members at risk.[23]

Patients who are expressing suicidal thoughts and might be a danger to themselves or others can be involuntarily hospitalized under various state statutes. In California, that law is Welfare and Institutions Code §5150. The decision to involuntarily hospitalize or release a patient from involuntary hospitalization is subject to immunity.[24]

It is also not uncommon to have cases in which it appears that patients did not intend to kill themselves but simply miscalculated the dosage of medication that they were taking, resulting in an overdose. Through my experience, it is often in these cases that the people who are bringing the lawsuit are the people who were tormenting the patient in life,

and a secondary function of the litigation is to expiate their own sense
of guilt.

Unusual Treatment Techniques

A number of nonmainstream therapies have sprung up over the years; some
of these have become progressively more accepted, and some are still considered fringe therapy. Among the more popular current therapies are those
that involve New Age concepts such as energy balancing, past life regression therapy, entity releasement, use of spirit guides, primal scream therapy,
and naked mothering. For a period of time, a group in Orange County was
featuring therapy that involved, among other things, beating patients. This
practice led to extended litigation in which the California Appellate Court
said that no matter how clearly a consent form was drawn, it was against
public policy to let patients agree to be beaten.[25] A surprising number of
cases have dealt with psychotherapists' beating of patients.[26] It is always
a problem when a therapist is using a fringe therapy technique because of
the progressively more conservative attitude of experts on the standard of
care. Generally, there is always a contention that the patient should have
been advised in writing and given an informed consent that the therapy
was experimental or controversial, although such actions are almost never
taken. California law does require that all patients, both medical and mental health, receive an informed consent to treatment procedures.[27]

Past life regression therapy, which involves accessing the patient's prior
lives to determine how those prior lives influence the current life, is particularly controversial. Despite that fact, there is an association of such therapists that is based in Riverside, California, and the therapy is still used
around the United States. Spirit guides are also a particularly controversial technique. Depending on the particular therapist, this technique may
be described as only using the image of a spirit guide to assist a patient in
visualizing certain images as part of guided imagery. This approach represents the more mundane and acceptable explanation. Other therapists
actually believe that the spirit guides are disembodied spirits who return
to this life to lead or assist other people to obtain some higher stage of
enlightenment. Therapy of this latter kind is, of course, substantially more
controversial and difficult to defend.

Litigation Self-Defense

Against this backdrop, the question becomes, What can mental health professionals do to protect themselves from suit and to maximize their chances of prevailing if they do get sued or face a board complaint? Perhaps the most important protection is to maintain a good clinical record, which includes a written informed consent (and Health Insurance Portability and Accountability Act of 1996 [HIPAA] forms, where applicable), a written patient history form, and session notes. A history form in the patient's writing is particularly valuable because it shows what the presenting issues were, and what was not disclosed to the therapist can impeach the patient's credibility. The classic example is patients who omit to mention that they are involved in ongoing litigation, in which the therapist may end up being a witness and secondary gain may be an issue. In maintaining a good clinical record, all documents written by the patient, including diaries, letters, greeting cards, and phone message slips, should be preserved. If the therapist maintains computer notes, they should be printed off periodically, dated, and placed in the file to guard against a computer crash and to avoid later claims that they were prepared after a dispute arose. In a malpractice suit or a board action, the issue of whether the therapist met or fell below the standard of care is the subject of expert testimony. A good clinical file makes it easy for an expert to track the therapist's process and conclude that the standard of care was met. In some civil cases, motions can be brought to dismiss the case before trial based on such expert testimony. When no notes exist, there is little chance of having an action dismissed before trial, and the absence of notes becomes a standard-of-care issue in and of itself.

The next protection is consultation. Consultation is seen by reviewing experts as indicating a desire to comply with the standard of care because a consultant can sometimes see things the therapist is too close to see. Such consultations should be documented in the file. Obviously, any action that contradicts the advice of the consultant should be carefully explained.

Finally, unless it is unavoidable, there should be no relationship with the patient other than the therapeutic one, no matter how desirable, lucrative, or rewarding it may seem at the time. If a dispute arises, the existence of a secondary relationship will be problematic at best and could be catastrophic at worst.

Conclusion

This overview of the types of litigation mental health professionals may face suggests that a cautious approach to practice is necessary. The safest approach in these dangerous times is to maintain good clinical records, avoid dual relationships (no matter how innocuous they seem at the time), and engage in frequent peer consultation. While there is no way to insulate mental health professionals from all forms of litigation, these steps will help in any administrative or civil litigation.

Notes

1. See McCartney, J. L. (1966). Overt transference. *Journal of Sex Research, 2*, 227–237.
2. Cooper v. Board of Medical Examiners, 49 Cal. App.3d 931 (1975).
3. California Civil Code, § 51.9.
4. Case No. 437-631, which was decided in 1981.
5. See Walker and Young (1986). For other first-person accounts of sexual relationships between therapists and patients, see the following works: Bates and Brodsky (1989), Noël and Watterson (1992), and Freeman and Roy (1976).
6. Waters v. Bourhis, 40 Cal.3d 424 (1985).
7. College Hospital v. Superior Court, 8 Cal.3d 704 (1994).
8. People v. Bernstein, 340 P.2d 299, 171 Cal. App.2d 279 (1959).
9. Marlene F. v. Affiliated Psychiatric Clinics, Inc., 48 Cal.3d 583 (1989).
10. Cases outside California dealing with sexual relationships between therapists and patients include Simmons v. United States, 805 F.2d 1363 (9th Cir. 1986); Horak v. Biris, 130 Ill. App.3d 140, 474 N.E.2d 13 (1985); Rowe v. Bennett, 514 A.2d 802 (Me. 1986); and Mazza v. Huffaker, 61 N.C. App.170 300 S.E.2d 833, review denied 309 N.C. 192, 305 S.E.2d 734 (1983).
11. See Herman, Gartrell, Olarte, Feldstein, and Localio (1987).
12. Sisson v. Seneca Mental Health/Mental Retardation Council, Inc., 185 W.VA.33, 404 S.E.2d 425 (1991).
13. A similar case, Underwood v. Croy, was recently decertified by the California Supreme Court, meaning that it cannot be cited as a precedent, although the appellate court there reached the same result as in Smith v. Pust, 19 Cal. App.4th 263 (1993).
14. Smith v. Pust (1993); Weaver v. Union Carbide Corp., 378 S.E.2d 105 (W. VA 1989). Also see Mazza v. Huffaker, 61 N.C. App.70, 300 S.E.2d 833 (1983), in which a patient successfully sued a psychiatrist who had sex with the patient's wife; Kousoulas v. Axel, a New York trial-level decision with similar facts.

Cases outside California dealing with claims by a patient's spouse include Weaver v. Union Carbide Corp (1989) and Horak v. Biris, 85 Ill. Dec.599, 130 Ill. App.3d 140, 474 N.E.2d 13 (1985).

15. See Jorgensen, Bisbing, and Sutherland (1992). Cases outside California dealing with vicarious liability for sexual misconduct claims include Simmons v. United States (1986); Marsten v. Minneapolis Clinic of Psychiatry and Neurology, Ltd., 329 N.W.2d 306 (Minn. 1983); Noto v. St. Vincent's Hospital; Roy v. Hartogs, 81 Misc.2d 350, 366 NYS2d 297 (Civ.Ct. 1975), Aff'd 85 Misc.2d 891, 381 NYS2d 587 (App. term. 1976); and Zipkin v. Freeman, 436 S.W.2d 753 (Mo. 1968).

16. Marsten v. Minneapolis Clinic of Psychology (1982); Simmons v. United States (1986).

17. See Younggren and Skorka (1992).

18. See enforcement statistics provided by California Board of Behavioral Sciences, 2006, and California Board of Psychology, 2006.

19. See Simone and Fulero (2005) for an in-depth discussion of ethical and legal issues related to a therapist's duty to warn.

20. Menendez v. Superior Court, 3 Cal.4th 435 (1992).

21. Gross v. Allen, 22 Cal.App.4th 354 (1994).

22. Meier v. Ross General Hospital, 69 Cal.2d 420 (1968); Nally v. Grace Community Church, 47 Cal.3d 278 (1988).

23. Bellah v. Greenson, 81 Cal.App.3d 614 (1987).

24. Michael E. L. v. County of San Diego, 183 Cal.App.3d 515 (1986).

25. Rains v. Superior Court, 150 Cal.App.3d 933 (1984).

26. Dennis v. Allison, 698 S.W.2d 94 (Tex. 1985); Hammer v. Rosen, 7 N.Y.2d 376, 165 N.E.2d 756 (1960).

27. Cobbs v. Grant, 8 Cal.3d 229 (1972).

References

American Psychological Association. (1981). Ethical principles of psychologists. *American Psychologist*, 36, 633–638.

American Psychological Association. (1992). Ethical principles of psychologists and code of conduct. *American Psychologist*, 47, 1597–1611.

Bates, C., & Brodsky, A. (1989). *Sex in the therapy hour.* New York: Guilford Press.

Bergin, A. E. (1980). Psychotherapy and religious values. *Journal of Counseling and Clinical Psychology, 48,* 75–105.

California Board of Behavioral Sciences. (2006, July 3). Enforcement activity/statistics. Retrieved August 22, 2006, from http://www.bbs.ca.gov/enfstats.htm

California Board of Psychology. (2006). Overview of enforcement activity, 2001–2006. Retrieved August 22, 2006, from http://www.psychboard.ca.gov/enforce/stats.pdf

California Civil Code, §43.92.

California Welfare and Institutions Code, §5150.

Ertel v. Kersenbrock, San Diego Superior Court Cases 595257 & 588117 (1989, October 31).

Ewing v. Goldstein, 120 Cal.App.4th 807 (2004).

Freeman, L., & Roy, J. (1976). *Betrayal.* New York: Stein and Day.

Hedlund v. Superior Court, 34 Cal.3d 695 (1983).

Herman, J.L., Gartrell, N., Olarte, S., Feldstein, M., & Localio, R. (1987). Psychiatrist-patient sexual contact: Results of a national survey II: Psychiatrist's attitudes. *American Journal of Psychiatry, 144,* 164–169.

Jablonski by Pahls v. United States, 712 F.2d 391 (9th Cir. 1983).

McCartney, J. L. (1996). Overt transferance. *Journal of Sex Research, 2,* 227–237.

Noël, B., & Watterson, K. (1992). *You must be dreaming.* New York: Poseidon Press.

Jorgensen, L., Bisbing, S. B., and Sutherland, P. K. (1992). Therapist-patient sexual exploitation and insurance liability. *Tort and Insurance Law Journal, 27,* 595.

Pope, K. S., & Bouhoutsos, J. (1989). *Sexual intimacy between therapists and patients.* New York: Praeger.

Pope, K. S., Sonne, J. L., & Holroyd, J. (1993). *Sexual feelings in psychotherapy: Explorations for therapists in training.* Washington, DC: American Psychological Association.

Simone, S., & Fulero, S. (2005). Tarasoff and the duty to warn. In S. Bucky, J. Callan, & G. Stricker (Eds.), *Ethical and legal issues for mental health professionals: A comprehensive handbook of principles and standards* (pp. 145–168). New York: Haworth.

Tarasoff v. Regents of the University of California, 17 Cal.3d 432 (1976).

Walker, E., & Young, P. D. (1986). *A killing cure.* New York: Holt.

Younggren, J. N. (1983). Ethical issues in religious psychotherapy. *Register Report, 18*(4), 1–8.

Younggren, J., & Skorka, D. (1992). The non-therapeutic psychotherapy relationship. *Law and Psychology Review, 27*(3), 13–28.

10

Civil Lawsuits
Malpractice Professional Liability Claims Process and Claims History

Margaret A. Bogie and Eric C. Marine

Introduction

Mental health professionals, like all professionals, are subject to the law of negligence when rendering their professional services. Such professional negligence is more commonly called *malpractice*. The term *malpractice* specifically refers to negligent or unintentional acts by medical professionals. *Professional liability* refers to the negligent acts or unintentional acts of nonmedical professionals. For purposes of this chapter, malpractice and professional liability are used interchangeably when discussing claims and insurance coverage.

Like most professionals, mental health professionals carry professional liability insurance to pay the defense costs and to fund the financial liability associated with a finding of professional negligence by a court of law. Most mental health professionals will never be sued for malpractice and will never use their insurance coverage. Therefore, few mental health professionals know what to expect if they are sued. One purpose in writing this chapter is to reduce the mystery associated with professional liability claims against mental health professionals. Being sued for malpractice is unpleasant. Having some insights into the process and outcomes can reduce some of the anxiety associated with malpractice litigation.

This chapter addresses two aspects of professional liability claims against mental health professionals. First, it describes the life cycle of a professional liability claim. How long will it take? What can be expected to occur and when? Who is responsible for what actions? What can go wrong? How could mental health professionals prepare themselves to face a professional liability claim? Second, it discusses the historical claims data regarding professional liability claims for mental health profession-als' professional liability claims from the oldest continuing, and largest, program for mental health professionals' insurance coverage. For what do mental health professionals get sued? Which claims are the most expen-sive? How have claims against mental health professionals changed since 1976? What can practicing mental health professionals do to limit their exposure to future malpractice litigation?

The Professional Liability Claims Process

The claims process is best understood by first describing a "perfect" law-suit moving through the claims and legal systems. In reality, few lawsuits are this straightforward, but it is helpful to have an overview of the process before discussing the problems, exceptions, and intricacies at each stage of the claims life cycle.

The claim process starts when the mental health professional is served a complaint alleging malpractice. The complaint may be preceded by notices required by statute in many states. The complaint is a document filed with a court of law that identifies the plaintiffs and the defendants and other factual information, contains allegations of wrong-doing, and requests compensation in the form of monetary damages. The complaint does not have to be factually true; it contains allegations that are presented as the belief of the person bringing the suit. Its validity will be determined by the trier of fact, either a judge or a jury. The act of service begins the malpractice insurance claim because all professional liability insurance contracts stipulate that they provide a legal defense and payment of dam-ages in the event the insured is a defendant in a lawsuit alleging profes-sional misconduct.

The first step to take is to note the date and time the complaint is received and how it is delivered. Whether the mental health professional received proper service will be an initial consideration when the defense attorney receives the complaint. The next step to take, after being served with a complaint, is to read it. The mental health professional should note (a) the identity of the plaintiffs; (b) the identity of the defendants; (c) the exact time period of professional services rendered; and (d) the alleged wrongful acts. Armed with this information, mental health professionals should contact their insurance company immediately to start the reporting procedure. All professional liability insurance contracts require that an insured provide notice of a claim as soon as possible. The complaint itself requires that the mental health professional (defendant) respond to the allegations within a prescribed period of time. Therefore, time is of the essence when notifying an insurance company of a lawsuit.

Most professional liability insurance contracts with mental health professionals are administered by a third party, a program administrator, rather than directly by the insurance company underwriting the policy. In a few instances, the insurance company does administer the policy, and for purposes of this section, the terms *program administrator* and *insurance company* are interchangeable. Although most professional liability insurance contracts specify that written notice is required, it is highly advisable to telephone in advance of filing written notice of a claim.

Program administrators will vary somewhat on the content of the written notice. Usually, notice should be given on letterhead and contain the insurance policy number, the names of plaintiffs, the first and last dates of professional service, a summary of the circumstances that gave rise to the claim, and the date the lawsuit was served on the defendant. The summary should be succinct, should describe the circumstances factually, and might also contain the mental health professional's opinions regarding the cause of the lawsuit. It need not be a clinical analysis or contain a copy of the patient's records; those come later. This letter, along with a copy of the complaint, is forwarded to the program administrator for handling. Although not required by the insurance contract, sending notice by overnight mail is recommended as an important safeguard. Not only does it arrive faster, but also the insured has a receipt that his or her notice has been received.

The program administrators are responsible for completing the notice of claim. They will verify coverage and attach any insurance contracts in force during the period of services. They also record the notice of claim within their own claims tracking system. The completed notice of claim is then forwarded to the insurance company's claims department for handling.

The time required for completing a notice of claim varies by program administrator. Due to the external and internal mail-handling process, it may take up to 10 business days before the insurance company will contact the mental health professional. A few jurisdictions require an answer to a complaint in a relatively short time period. In those circumstances, the program administrator will try to expedite the process. Once the mental health professional reports a claim to the program administrator, it becomes the program administrator's responsibility to process the claims notice and avoid default by not missing deadlines. An insurance company that defaults by missing deadlines on a claim is likely to be the target of a successful breach of contract suit from the insured, so deadlines are critically important in claims administration. Keep in mind that the responsibility for meeting deadlines is contingent on reporting the claim soon enough to provide adequate time for the insurance company to respond.

The insurance company's claims department is responsible for determining coverage under the terms and conditions of the insurance contracts in force for the time of service. If a claim is not covered, the insurance company will contact the mental health professional immediately with a denial of coverage. The insurance company is required by law to provide the contractual reasons for denial and advise the insured of the available appeals process. It is important to understand that less than 5% of all professional liability claims are denied by insurance companies. The most common reason for denial is that the policy or policies were not in force during any part of the period of service. Coverage also is denied when the alleged acts are specifically excluded under the contact. For example, criminal charges cannot be covered by any liability insurance policy.

After the insurance company determines the coverage that is in effect, it confirms claims coverage by letter and assigns a defense attorney to the claim. This letter, sometimes called the "reservation-of-rights" letter, is an important but frequently misunderstood document.

Insurance law requires that the insurance company advise the insured (i.e., the mental health professional) of any potential liability exposures that, if proven, would not be covered by the insurance contract at the outset of the claim. If the initial complaint requests a multimillion dollar damage award and the policy limits are $1 million, the insurance company will inform the insured of its ability to pay only up to policy limits. Since an insurance company cannot alter or deny coverage midway through the litigation on known allegations, it is not unusual to see boilerplate language reserving a list of contractual rights as part of the insurance company's initial response. Although it may seem foreign to the insured, a reservation-of-rights letter is standard operating procedure for most claims departments. The reservation-of-rights letter should not be construed as an attempt by the insurance company to avoid paying the claim. In most instances, the rights reserved by the insurance company do not have any impact on the claim.

The insurance company also provides the name and contact information for the local defense attorney it has assigned to the claim. Typically, the insurance company maintains a national panel of attorneys who specialize in professional liability defense litigation. In the case of mental health professionals, this panel has expertise in mental health care law. "Local" is a somewhat liberal term. If the insured lives in an urban or suburban area, the attorney is likely to be in the same city or in a nearby location. If the insured lives in a rural or remote area, the attorney will probably be located in the nearest large town or city. Proximity to the assigned attorney is a key consideration for the insurance company since the insured will be working directly with the attorney on the claim.

At this point, the assigned defense attorney becomes involved in the claim. One of the first acts the attorney probably will perform on the mental health professional's behalf is to request more time to answer the complaint. This is a routine request, and an extension of time to respond usually is granted automatically by the opposing counsel. The extension of time allows the attorney to review the complaint, meet with the defendant, research any issues, and craft an answer to the complaint.

Before meeting with the attorney, the mental health professional should make copies of all written records that the mental health professional has pertaining to the plaintiffs. Telephone logs, clinical records, correspondence, billing records, and appointment calendars should be copied for the attorney's use. The mental health professional should review all these materials and become familiar with them. If more records or materials are found after meeting with the attorney, the defendant should forward copies to the attorney immediately. Complete disclosure of records is critical to defending the claim.

Personal expertise is crucial in helping the attorney defend the claim. The insurance company has little or no interaction with the mental health professional after attorney assignment. The insurance company's claims department is paying the defense attorney, assisting him or her as needed, and monitoring the progress of the claim. The mental health professional's concern from this point is focused on working with the attorney.

The lawsuit moves into the discovery phase after the answer has been filed with the court. Discovery allows each side in the lawsuit to have access to appropriate records, documents, and witnesses. Disagreements regarding what is or is not discoverable in the course of a lawsuit are resolved by the court. Attorneys will obtain information primarily through interrogatories (i.e., written sets of questions that require responses and supporting documents) and depositions (i.e., sworn statements taken in interview form). During the discovery period, both sides may commission reports from experts on the standard of care. The reports of these expert witnesses will become discoverable if the experts testify in a trial.

Typically, a professional liability lawsuit is dropped, dismissed, or settled at some point during the discovery period (Danzon, 1985, 1991; Danzon & Lillard, 1982). Discovery allows the relative merits of the claim to be scrutinized by both parties and by the court. It is unusual for any professional liability suit to go to trial; if, however, the lawsuit does go to trial, the judge's or the jury's verdict will determine the final outcome. If there is a settlement or a compensatory damage award, the insurance company pays the amount due subject to the liability limits of the insurance policy. The insurance company also pays the defense attorney's final fees and expenses, such as expert witness fees. From the insurance company's perspective, the life cycle of the claim is complete. A resolution to the allegations contained in the initial complaint has occurred. The insurance company is not obliged to pay for any appeals should the mental health professional receive an unfavorable verdict at trial.

The claims life cycle described is "perfect." In reality, a malpractice claim does not proceed quite as smoothly. The process is fraught with potential problems, exceptions, and important intricacies that complicate the claim's life cycle. Moreover, these complications add time to the claims process. It is reasonable to expect that the simplest claim will take at least 1 year to resolve. More complicated claims may take far longer, sometimes 4 or 5 years to resolve (Calfee, 1992; Helliczer, Lorenzen, & Lambert, 1993). This long life cycle is particularly frustrating for many mental health professionals, but it is virtually unavoidable because the process is controlled by other people (namely, the plaintiff and his or her attorney), contracts (one or more insurance policies), and the volume of litigation on the court docket.

The controlling element in any malpractice litigation is the complaint filed by the plaintiff. The allegations in the complaint constitute one of the criteria by which the insurance company determines coverage. A poorly drafted complaint can cause great difficulty for a mental health professional because it may allege acts specifically excluded by the professional liability policy. An example of this problem would be a complaint alleging "intentional acts" of malpractice. Most professional liability policies exclude coverage for acts committed with the knowledge that they are wrongful acts. In other words, there is no insurance coverage if a mental health professional deliberately decides to harm a patient. Unintentional or accidental wrongful acts are covered. Thus, if the complaint only alleges intentional acts of malpractice, the insurance company may deny the claim. The plaintiff's attorney can amend the complaint and refile it once he or she learns that no insurance coverage is available for the alleged misconduct. Since the allegations in the complaint, regardless of merit, must be answered, the insurance company will probably assign an attorney, but reserve its rights while it determines if the allegations are covered by the insurance policy. In very rare instances, mental health professionals may have to hire attorneys of their own to handle the complaint until such time as coverage can be established.

A second complication to the professional liability claims is the variation of insurance contracts that may cover a particular claim. Until October 1, 1991, most mental health professionals were insured through one source of insurance, an occurrence-based policy underwritten by the American Home Assurance Company, administered by the American Professional Agency, and endorsed by the American Psychological Association Insurance Trust. When this business relationship ended, both the American Professional Agency and the American Psychological Association Insurance Trust offered competing programs to mental health professionals for both occurrence-based and claims-made coverage. In addition, other insurance companies entered the marketplace at regional levels during the 1990s.

Most complaints allege professional misconduct over the entire course of therapy, so the beginning and ending dates of service determine the policies that provide coverage for the claim. If the policy form (occurrence based or claims made) or insurance company changed during dates of service in the complaint, the insured may be dealing with two or more different companies or insurance contracts. These companies will have to determine if the claim is covered under their respective insurance policies and, if so, will have to work together on their shared liability. Sometimes, insurance companies can handle a shared claim with little friction. Sometimes, there can be friction between insurance companies over attorney assignment and reimbursement as well as over shared liability arrangement. No insurance company is going to pay more than what it deems to be its fair share of a claim. Not only do different levels of coverage under existing contracts complicate claims administration among multiple companies, they may also involve multiple lawyers. While the insurance companies cannot leave an insured in limbo while they resolve issues related to a shared claim, the presence of multiple insurance companies is likely to slow the claims process.

Another key difference among the insurance companies has been the coverage clause for sexual impropriety allegations. Most professional liability policies are similar except for this clause. All insurance companies provide a full defense against such allegations; however, the amount of liability coverage for settlements or damages is generally limited to $50,000 or less, if the coverage even exists. The reduction or absence of liability coverage for sexual impropriety allegations is detailed in the reservation-of-rights letter sent to the mental health professional by the insurance company when the claim is filed.

A number of states have provisions in their laws for special counsel to be provided when there is limited or no liability coverage available for a claim. In these states, the insurance company has the right to assign an attorney to defend the claims, but the insurance company also must pay for a second attorney of the mental health professional's own choosing to protect that defendant's interests if the reservation of rights is based on "outcome determinative" issues. The logic behind this provision is related to an inherent conflict of interest if the insurance company controls the defense in which there may be covered or uncovered allegations. An insurance company could be motivated to try to push the defense so that only uncovered acts are found to be the cause of a damage award. While the insured always have the option of filing a lawsuit against their insurance company for a breach of contract if a vigorous defense is not provided, this is not an optimal way to resolve a conflict of interest. Some states try to remedy the conflict by allowing for special personal counsel.

Personal counsel is not automatically provided when any contractual rights are reserved by the insurance company. State laws on judicial precedent dictate when special counsel is provided. The addition of a second counsel to the claims process may not speed up the litigation. Some insureds elect not to have a personal counsel for this very reason. However, a second counsel can be helpful when dealing with multiple insurance companies and insurance contracts that may or may not cover settlements or damages for specific acts, such as sexual impropriety. Of course, a mental health professional can always associate a personal counsel with the litigation at the practitioner's own personal expense.

Attorney assignment, in and of itself, is a sensitive issue. Most mental health professionals' professional liability insurance companies retain the right to assign an attorney. The insurance company's position is that their money is at stake, whereas it is the mental health professional's reputation at stake in a malpractice claim. An infinitesimally small number of malpractice claims are settled or have damages awarded in excess of the insurance policy's liability limits. Thus, from the insurance company's perspective, it has significantly greater loss exposure than does the insured and consequently must take steps to retain quality legal counsel to defend its insured.

The attorney assigned to the mental health professional will be sensitive to any potential conflict of interest in representing both the mental health professionals and their insurance company. Insurance companies maintain national panels of experienced attorneys who specialize in the defense of the professionals being insured and are trained to be strong advocates for their clients. The defense attorney will be committed to providing a vigorous defense that preserves the mental health professional's reputation while limiting the insurance company's liability exposure.

The potential conflict of interest faced by assigned defense counsel is small because of policy language and state insurance laws that protect the insurance consumer. For example, most professional liability insurance policies for mental health professionals stipulate that the insured must consent to settlement except under specific circumstances. Insurance companies want those they insure to consent to settlements whenever possible. If the insurance company withdraws from a claim because an insured refuses to settle and the insured prevails at trial, the insurance company could face a breach-of-contract and bad faith suit from the insured. In most cases, insurance companies will not risk facing such a suit to achieve a forced settlement. In addition, nearly all state insurance laws protect the insured from unfair claims practices and take strong legal action against insurance companies that do not live up to their contractual obligations.

While there is no guarantee that the personalities of the attorney and the client will be a perfect fit, generally speaking the relationship between an insured and the assigned defense attorney is positive and professional. Most defense attorneys are vigorous advocates for their clients. If an insured is unhappy with assigned counsel, the insurance company will investigate and may assign new counsel. The insurance company does not want an adversarial relationship between the assigned defense attorney and the insured.

There are two common situations that do not initiate a malpractice claim but involve interaction with the mental health professional's insurance company on coverage issues. Some insurance companies have started offering limited legal fee reimbursement for licensing or administrative board actions filed against the mental health professional. Such complaints are not malpractice claims, even though the allegations contained in them are similar to those found in a lawsuit. The claim is triggered when the insured is notified by an administrative or licensing board that a formal complaint has been filed. The insured selects an attorney, and the insurance company reimburses this attorney up to the limit stipulated in the insurance policy. Licensing or administrative board actions do not provide monetary compensation for the complainant. This coverage feature is the exception, with coverage provided without a lawsuit being filed.

Threat of a lawsuit, or a situation in which a lawsuit seems likely to occur, does not initiate insurance coverage; however, all professional liability insurance policies require notice of an actual or a potential claim as soon as practicable. If mental health professionals have a reasonable belief that a lawsuit is imminent, they must report the particulars as a potential claim to the program administrator. Reporting a potential claim is not a blemish on the mental health professional's insurance record; the insurance company does not report potential claims to outside sources such as managed care organizations. In addition, the insurance renewal should not be prejudiced by reporting potential claims. Early reporting of potential claims is important because program administrators and insurance companies do evaluate potential claims when they are filed. Although the insurance company has no contractual obligation to do so, it might provide a defense attorney prior to filing of an actual claim. Obviously, the individual circumstances of the claim will predicate the insurance company's decision regarding assignment of counsel.

Perhaps the most frequent complaint about professional liability claims process from those mental health professionals who have been sued is that the process takes too long. Depending on the jurisdiction and the complexity of the claim, the claim life cycle can span from 1 to 5 years or even longer. In all likelihood, legal action on the claim will progress in fits and starts, with short periods of action followed by long periods of inaction. The situation is frustrating because the system is slow.

What can mental health professionals do to help themselves when malpractice litigation ensues?

1. They should resign themselves to the likelihood that the claim will take time and energy to defend and try to accept that it is not something that the mental health professionals can control.
2. They should not try to work things out with the plaintiff. Regardless of anger, indignation, or guilt, there is rarely any benefit in attempting informal resolution. Usually, contacting the plaintiff after a lawsuit is filed only complicates matters.
3. They should not contact or try to work things out with the plaintiff's attorney. Not only might the mental health professionals prejudice their position, they also might violate the conditions of the malpractice insurance policy. The insurance policy contains language in which the insured agrees to assist and cooperate with the insurance company. The insurance company will want the assigned defense attorney and only

the assigned defense attorney to talk to the plaintiff's attorney on its insured's behalf.

4. It is strongly recommended that the mental health professional follow the advice rendered by the defense attorney. The legal system is an alien forum for most mental health professionals. The defense attorney is an expert on the system and will try to manipulate it to the mental health professional's advantage.

5. The mental health professional should never alter files or records after a claim has been filed. The records may not be perfect, but alteration of records after the fact is unethical and illegal, apart from appearing self-serving and suspicious.

6. The mental health professional should not discuss the lawsuit with anyone other than the attorney or insurance company. This stricture is difficult because the temptation to talk about the lawsuit will be great.

7. Mental health professionals should make efforts to alleviate their stress. If a mental health professional wishes to enter psychotherapy with another mental health professional, the one being treated should be sure that relationship is privileged before the process is initiated. Mental health professionals should try to engage in activities or hobbies that take their minds off the malpractice suit. Since the lawsuit is not going to disappear quickly, the mental health professional should take steps to live through this experience in as positive a manner as possible.

Historical Loss Data

We turn next to the historical data on professional liability claims against mental health professionals, with the data drawn from the records of a major insurance program. The American Professional Agency has been the program administrator for the oldest continuing and the largest program for mental health professionals' insurance coverage in the United States.

Starting in February 1976 and continuing until the present time, the American Professional Agency has managed more than 30 years of psychologists' claims losses on a national basis. The program's size has varied over the years from a low of 10,000 insureds in 1976, to a high of nearly 45,000 in 1991, to a level of about 30,000 insureds in 2006. Until October 1, 1991, the American Professional Agency's program was offered on an occurrence basis only, making it the likely source of coverage for any malpractice claim against a mental health professional occurring on or before October 1, 1991. While American Professional Agency's aggregate of insureds has an inherent selection bias, if viewed as a sample of all mental health professionals, the sheer size and age of the program suggest that it is reasonably representative of mental health professionals buying insurance coverage over the past 30 years and more.

It is relevant to note that the data analyzed contain some notable idiosyncrasies. These data were collected by the program's managing general agent, Richard C. Imbert, certified insurance counselor, for insurance administration purposes, not scholarly research. Claims are categorized by the primary reason for a lawsuit. The category selection is a judgment call by the claims examiner reading the lawsuit. The complaint may allege two dozen wrongful acts; the claims examiner must select the primary, secondary, and tertiary reasons. Most complaints use "boilerplate" language when alleging wrongful acts, which can make their categorization difficult because the allegations may be vague as well as numerous. Sometimes a boilerplate claim would have its category reassigned when additional information became available; however, this action may not have been taken consistently since 1976.

Claims categorization may not be consistent among examiners over the past 30 years. Claims examiners will differ regarding the cause of a claim. Furthermore, the categories have increased over time as new causes for litigation have developed in significant numbers to justify a unique category. For example, child abuse reporting only became a unique category in the late 1980s. These data were not recoded to reflect changes in the coding system.

It is also important to understand that the claims are categorized by allegation only. These data do not provide any determination of the validity of the allegations; thus, they describe what mental health professionals are sued for, not what malpractice acts mental health professionals have actually committed. This distinction is a critical one since about one third of all claims involve defense fees only, and about half of all claims dollars paid under this program are for defense fees. One of the purposes of having professional liability insurance is to have a defense against any allegation of professional negligence, not just accurate allegations of professional negligence.

The data reported in this chapter focus on dollars expended for each type of claim. Unlike the figures discussing frequency, for which each claim reported counts as one, the actual dollars expended on legal fees, settlements, and damage awards for each claim are counted in the total. These figures include data on both open and closed claims. The open claims are still accruing expenses, and the cost distribution is more likely to be changed by a few large claims losses in any claims category. As noted, claims take time to reach resolution, so a 5-year life cycle is not unusual. The cost figures are volatile because of the length of the claim life cycle. Claims figures for the last 5 years must be treated with considerable care because recent claims are still in the immature phase in their development, particularly data regarding total cost.

The dollar figures reported are not adjusted for inflation. Obviously, a dollar paid in 1976 has a different value from a dollar paid in 2006. To compensate for the lack of constant dollars, the claims are analyzed in relationship to each other rather than noting average or median claims costs by claims category. Similarly, the method of settlement is not taken into consideration. Lump sum settlements have given way to structured settlements, wherein annuities may be used to fund payments to the plaintiff. Settlements have not been adjusted for present value in cases for which payments are actually being made over time.

Any review of these data should consider the impact of the change in policy forms that started on October 1, 1991. Prior to that date, the American Professional Agency's psychologist program was written on an occurrence basis. The transition from the occurrence to claims-made policy took 1 year, as the individual insurance policies renewed year round, on the first day of each month. The change in the policy form is an important distinction because claims are recorded separately under each program. Accordingly, it is important to understand that two separate data sets are being used: a mature data set for the occurrence program of approximately 30 program years and a less-mature data set for the claims-made program of approximately 15 program years.

The transition period poses problems in claims data analysis because there is no universal cutoff date between programs. In addition, some claims occurred over a time period that overlapped the two programs. As a general rule, claims are booked against the policy in effect at the earliest point of treatment. The data do not double count claims that can fall into either program and do not try to second guess the assignment to a particular data set.

Clearly, these data are imperfect from a scientific standpoint. Nonetheless, they are the largest and oldest data set available for psychologists' malpractice claims. It is our opinion that these data tell an interesting story about malpractice litigation against mental health professionals.

Figure 10.1 shows the frequency of the most common claims reported to the American Professional Agency between February 1, 1976, and January 1, 1991, in the occurrence program. They represent approximately 3,000

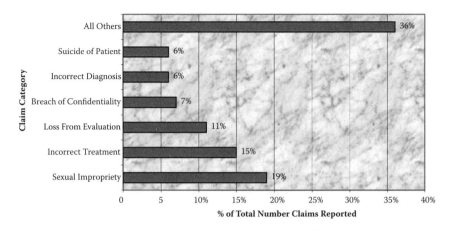

Figure 10.1 Most frequent claims losses by category, February 1, 1976, to January 1, 1991. Reported as of January 1, 1991. Source: American Professional Agency. Used with permission.

claims. The claims categories used are those available as of January 1, 1991, for the primary allegation in the initial complaint.

Sexual impropriety represents 19% of all claims filed. This claims category includes any actual or alleged erotic physical contact, attempt thereat, or proposal thereof between the therapist and the patient or member of the patient's immediate family. The misconduct alleged under this category ranges from verbal suggestion to hugging to intercourse. Incorrect treatment follows with 15% of total frequency. This claims category included allegations that therapy was ineffective or inappropriate. The allegations constituting incorrect treatment can be specific, but more often are general claims that therapy did not yield the expected results. Loss from evaluation represents 11% of claims frequency. Claims under this category involved testing and evaluation activities, particularly in the areas of job performance/promotion and security clearances. Breach of confidentiality follows with 7% of total frequency. The breach-of-confidentiality category covered a broad range of professional settings, including group therapy, employment evaluations/employee assistance plans, and treatment of children. Incorrect diagnosis and suicide of patient tie for the fifth most frequent type of claim at 6% of total frequency. Incorrect diagnosis is self-explanatory. Some claims allege that a physical problem (e.g., a brain tumor) went undiagnosed, while other claims allege that a diagnosis of a specific mental condition was inappropriate. Suicide of patient covered suicide attempts as well as actual suicides. The remaining 36% of total claim frequency falls into 30 other available categories, none of which have more than 4% of total frequency in any category.

For the purpose of analysis, Figure 10.1 serves as a baseline for comparison of how claims frequency has developed and changed by category. It reflects the losses for the occurrence program just as it was reaching the peak of its participation. However, because claims take many years from the date of the alleged malpractice to the date the claim is reported to the insurance company, these data have not fully matured.

Figure 10.2 shows the most costly claims reported between February 1, 1976, and January 1, 1991. The claims categories used are those available as of January 1, 1991, for the primary allegation in the initial complaint. These data include claims that were completed (i.e., closed claims) and claims that were in progress at the time (i.e., open claims). Given the lack of constant dollars and the potentially volatile impact of open claims on average dollar figures for the period, considering the categories as a ratio of the whole database seemed most appropriate. In our opinion, the actual dollars expended are less important than the proportionate cost of the claim type when compared with other claim types.

Sexual impropriety claims were far and away the most expensive claim to cover. At the time, almost 48% of all claims dollars paid were for this claim category. After sexual impropriety, there is a significant drop-off in

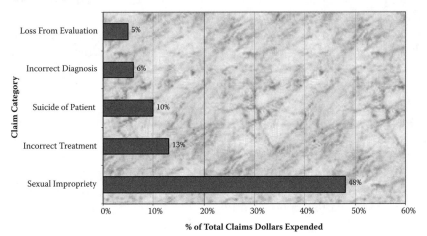

Figure 10.2 Most severe claims losses by category, February 1, 1976, to January 1, 1991. Reported as of January 1, 1991. Source: American Professional Agency. Used with permission.

the amount of money spent on any particular claim. Only two other categories reflected 10% or more of total claims dollars expended. Incorrect treatment followed with 13% of all claims dollars, and suicide of patient amounted to 10% of all claims dollars. Incorrect diagnosis and loss-from-evaluation claims comprised 6% and 5%, respectively, of total claims dollars expended as of January 1, 1991. The top five most expensive claims consumed 82% of all claims dollars at that time. All of the remaining categories amounted to 3% or less of total claims dollars.

Figure 10.2 serves as a baseline for comparison of how claims severity has developed and changed by category. This figure reflects the losses for the occurrence program while it was still dominated by sexual impropriety claims. Although policy sublimits that reduced settlements and damage awards for sexual impropriety claims to $25,000 had been introduced starting in 1985, it was too soon to judge the impact of the new sublimits on overall severity. In addition, sexual impropriety had incurred the greatest severity among high-dollar claims. At that time, the only $1 million claims paid in the mental health professionals' program concerned allegations of long-term sexual impropriety on the part of the therapist.

The difficulty in having such a large proportion of claims dollars paid out in one category is that all other categories are greatly diminished by comparison. The magnitude of sexual impropriety claims on severity suggests that controlling such losses should be the primary focus of mental health professionals and their insurance companies. The next two figures challenge this conventional wisdom.

Figure 10.3 shows claims for which treatment occurred between February 1, 1976, and January 1, 1996, and that were reported as of January 1, 2000, for either the occurrence or claims-made programs. The total number is approximately 8,000 claims reported for both programs. The claims categories used are those available as of January 1, 2000, for the primary allegation in the initial complaint. What a difference a few years have made on claims frequency distribution.

By 2000, sexual impropriety, with 19% of reported claims, had been surpassed by improper treatment, with 21% of reported claims, as the most commonly leveled allegation against psychologists (see Figure 10.3). Loss from evaluation amounts to 12% of total frequency. Suicide of patient and breach of confidentiality each represent 6% of the claims frequency. All remaining claims categories account for 36% of the claims frequency, with no category representing more than 3% of total claims.

It is not surprising to see sexual impropriety maintain its leadership position in claims frequency. Historically, sexual impropriety claims had

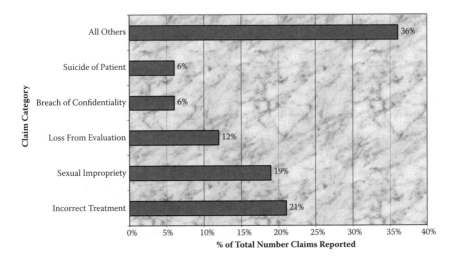

Figure 10.3 Most frequent claims losses by category, February 1, 1976, to January 1, 1996. Reported as of January 1, 2000. Source: American Professional Agency. Used with permission.

dominated claims frequency in the early years, but over time there has been a radical reduction in the number of allegations of sexual impropriety and therefore a small decrease in frequency in a database of this size or age. However, incorrect treatment allegations did increase by 5% of all claims frequency when compared with their share of claims shown in Figure 10.1. One impetus for this change might be the growth in the treatment of "recovered memory," which started in the late 1980s (see Dalenberg, Carlson, & Caudill, chapter 11, this volume). Since most recovered memory claims contain allegations of incorrect treatment in eliciting, treating, or implanting memories of prior abuse, such claims typically were assigned to the incorrect treatment category.

Another impetus for the change is the impact of the sexual misconduct limitation language in the policy. Savvy lawyers have started alleging improper treatment, which is subject to the full policy limits, rather than sexual misconduct, which is covered by a small sublimit or excluded completely from damage awards or settlements. Unfortunately, we cannot deduce which incorrect treatment claims include an element of sexual impropriety. The other categories of common claims remain virtually unchanged from the data shown in Figure 10.1.

Figure 10.4 shows severity of claim in proportion to total claims dollars for the entire occurrence program reported as of January 1, 2000. In the

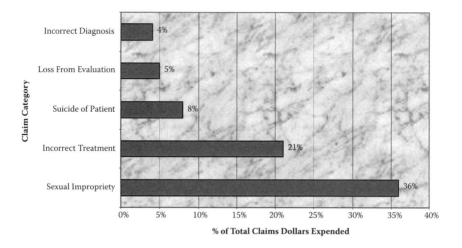

Figure 10.4   Most severe claims losses by category, February 1, 1976, to January 1, 1996. Reported as of January 1, 2000. Source: American Professional Agency. Used with permission.

9-year interval between the terminal dates for reports in Figure 10.2 and Figure 10.4, many of the open claims became closed claims, and more new claims were reported. Although the top categories have not changed, the proportionate cost of their claims has shifted. Sexual impropriety claims remain the most expensive type of claim in the program, but the category represents only 36% of the total claims dollars expended by 2000. The policy sublimit of $25,000 for settlements and damages was making an impact by 2000. Given that sexual impropriety claims consumed the majority of claims dollars in the 1970s and 1980s, it is not surprising that this claim category would dominate claims severity, even though its financial impact may be decreasing. The remaining top categories show some variation in the percentage of total dollars from 1991 but still comprise 38% of claims expenses by 2000. The proportion of total dollars expended on claims of incorrect treatment grew, which would be expected given the increased claim frequency. The decrease in suicide of patient claims since 1991 probably is immaterial. Suicide claims are, on average, the most expensive claim a mental health professional might face. They also tend to be volatile because the settlements or damages paid in suicide claims often are influenced by the surviving family rather than simply by the standard of care for the treatment rendered. Incorrect diagnosis and loss from evaluation have had only immaterial changes.

Changes in the type of claims being reported become clearer when focusing on recent data. Otherwise, the long history of the program may mask emerging trends. Figure 10.5 shows the most frequently reported claims involving treatment that commenced on or after January 1, 1992, and were reported as of January 1, 2006. The claims data are maturing and reveal some striking potential trends.

Incorrect treatment has become the most commonly alleged claim, at 29% of total frequency. As noted, these claims use boilerplate pleading language to create a question of fact to maintain the lawsuit in court. The lawsuit may be amended in the future with more specific allegations of negligence. Often, such pleading language is used to create a viable legal reason for bringing claims by nonpatients, such as relatives of patients with recovered memory claims. They allege improper treatment to the patient and resultant damage to another party. Such claims represent an attempt to set a professional duty on the part of the psychologist to a party who is not a patient. Another reason for this type of allegation is an attempt to plead around claims that are barred by governmental immunity, such as child abuse reporting. Again, it is important to keep in mind that Figure 10.5 describes what psychologists are being sued for, not the validity of the allegations.

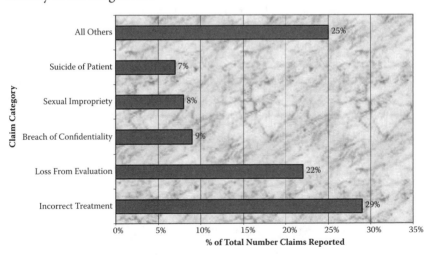

Figure 10.5 Most frequent claims losses by category, January 1, 1998, to January 1, 2006. Reported as of January 1, 2006. Source: American Professional Agency. Used with permission.

Loss-from-evaluation claims and breach-of-confidentiality claims have nearly doubled in frequency from the levels shown in Figure 10.3. The most significant contributor to these two categories is the treatment of children. The claims arise from the parents' conflict and the perceived alliance of the therapist to one party or the other. These claims also represent increased complaints about child abuse reporting and child custody evaluations. The use of these allegations of breached confidentiality or substandard testing allows these processes to be reviewed absent direct conflict with statutory protection.

Figure 10.5 shows claims for which treatment occurred between February 1, 1976, and January 1, 2006, that were reported as of January 1, 2006, for either the occurrence or claims-made programs. The total number of claims is approximately 11,000 reported for both programs. What is striking in Figure 10.5 is that sexual impropriety claims have dropped precipitously to 8% of the frequency of all reported claims for recent years. The decrease in the frequency of sexual impropriety claims may be attributed to the efforts by the profession to educate the public and professionals that sexual contact should never be part of therapy. It may also reflect the growth in the number of female therapists providing services. Female therapists are far less likely than male therapists to be sued for this type of claim. Suicide of patient accounts for 7% of the claims frequency in Figure 10.5. This category has ranged consistently between 6% and 8% of total claims frequency in all the figures describing claims frequency over time. Since suicide of patient involves allegations of negligence associated with a specific action taken by the patient rather than the more generalized allegations of negligence associated with incorrect treatment, it appears that claims frequency is remarkably stable over time.

Figure 10.6 is based on the most expensive claims resulting from treatment provided after January 1, 1992, and reported as of January 1, 2006; the categories used are those available as of the latter date. The frequency of claims is shown in Figure 10.5. The most expensive claim category for this time period is incorrect treatment, which accounts for 25% of all claims dollars paid on recent claims. Suicide of patient reflects 20% of the claims losses. As discussed, suicide or attempted suicide tends to be a definite act with a clearly definable loss. Many plaintiffs in suicide cases are highly sympathetic. Clearly, the decline of payments for sexual impropriety claims, a mere 12% of claims dollars expended or one quarter of the claims costs attributed to this category in Figure 10.1, has been reflected in the growing severity of loss in other claims categories. Reporting abuse to authorities, a category that does not even appear among the top five in claims frequency for

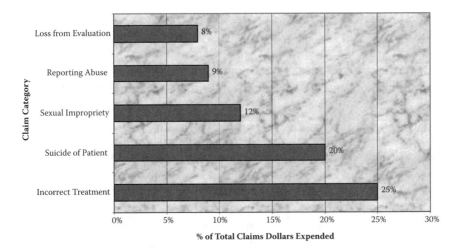

Figure 10.6 Most severe claims losses by category, February 1, 1976, to January 1, 2006. Reported as of January 1, 2006. Source: American Professional Agency. Used with permission.

the period, accounts for 9% of the total claims dollars expended. Similarly, loss-from-evaluation claims are consuming more of the total claims dollars, with 8% expended on this category of claims by 2006.

Incorrect treatment shows the influence of the recovered memory claims wending their way through the legal system. As noted in this chapter, many incorrect treatment claims are an attempt to create a professional duty to someone who is not a patient, such as an aggrieved family member. Therapists who treat patients with "repressed memories" of abuse increasingly are the targets of the alleged perpetrators. In addition, a number of patients have recanted their repressed memories and have accused their therapist of implanting "false memories." Although the frequency of recovered memory claims is on the rise, the length of the claims life cycle is such that their final impact on severity cannot be measured for many years.

Sexual impropriety claims have a less-significant role in claims severity by 2006. This reduction in cost suggests a greater awareness on the part of psychologists of the need to avoid sexual intimacy with their patients as well as significant changes in the insurance contract that limit the impact of settlements and damage awards, although sexual impropriety still retains a disproportionate ratio of payout to claims presented. This disparity is the recognition of the expense of the defense of these claims since settlements and damages have been limited to $25,000 per claim.

Claims in the reporting-abuse-to-authorities category reflect problems with the child abuse reporting system. The issue of abuse has received national attention. A variety of laws exists regarding child abuse reporting and may be in effect even though the alleged abuse occurred years ago. Allegations of child abuse tend to be highly inflammatory, often pitting family members against one another or against institutions in their community. It comes as no surprise that psychologists working in this professional area are becoming the targets of lawsuits brought by patients, their patients' parents or custodians, or other members of patients' families. While many child abuse reporting laws provide some immunity from litigation for reporting, no laws provide complete immunity, particularly if willful and wanton negligence can be proven. The tort system is the method our society uses to determine the validity of allegations and the level of compensation, if any, that may accrue to valid ones.

The loss-from-evaluation category also shows an increase in the severity of claims in 2006. However, while category frequency has doubled over time, as reflected in comparing Figure 10.3 and Figure 10.5, the claims dollars are not expanding at the same rate. Evaluations tend to produce finite results that can be linked directly to decisions. Evaluations performed as part of job fitness reviews or child custody disputes can result in malpractice litigation against psychologists. However, the typical settlement or damage award tends to be low in loss-for-evaluation claims because many of the claims in this category only incur legal fees when the psychologist prevails in the dispute.

Perhaps the most interesting point to consider in analyzing these data is that most of the dollars expended are for legal defense costs. While some damages and settlements are included in the total claims dollars expended, most of these claims have not completed the claims life cycle. As a rule, almost half of all dollars spent on malpractice claims are for defense costs. The data reported in Figure 10.6 represent approximately 70% defense costs as against 30% settlements or damages. Thus, the data shown in Figure 10.6 can be considered to be a maturing data set, not to be relied on as a strong indicator of the trends of damages and settlements for years to come.

Predicting future trends for mental health professionals' malpractice claims is similar to gazing into a murky crystal ball. Although more than 30 years of claims history is available, it would be naïve simply to expect a linear progression of current claims trends. Because malpractice claims are a reflection of their times, they involve certain sorts of disputes between people. The nature and the setting of these disputes evolve over time as the views of people and society change. Since malpractice occurs when there is a breach of the standard of care, as provided by the average practitioner under identical circumstances at the time, the historical context of malpractice claims is a critical consideration. Past claims provide us with some expectation of the future trends, but only to the degree of similarity obtaining between past and future professional practice.

What can mental health professionals do to limit their exposure to future malpractice litigation? Malpractice lawsuits are too random to predict on the basis of any particular personal or practice characteristic. Good practitioners operating within the standard of care do get sued. Should mental health professionals simply accept random distribution as their professional destiny? We do not agree with such a passive approach toward malpractice claims. In our opinion, mental health professionals can take proactive steps to help themselves and their profession on malpractice-related issues. Such steps include active participation in professional discourse through local, state, and national professional associations, keeping abreast of risk management topics, and focusing on ethical practices. The best defense to a malpractice claim is professional practices that hold to the standard of care for the profession. For the mental health professional, such practice involves a commitment to ongoing and unending professional development.

References

Calfee, B. (1992). *Law suit prevention techniques*. Cleveland, OH: ARC.

Danzon, P. M. (1985). *Medical malpractice: Theory, evidence and public policy*. Cambridge, MA: Harvard University Press.

Danzon, P. M. (1991). Liability for medical malpractice. *Journal of Economic Perspectives, 5*(3), 51–69.

Danzon, P. M., & Lillard, L. (1982). *The resolution of medical malpractice claims: Modeling and analysis*. Santa Monica, CA: The Rand Corporation.

Helliczer, J. R., Lorenzen, D., & Lambert, P. W. (1993). *Legal risk management for counseling and mental health professionals in Florida*. Eau Claire, WI: Professional Educational Systems.

11

Treatment of Patients With Recovered Memories of Trauma and With False Memories

Constance Dalenberg, Eve Carlson, and O. Brandt Caudill Jr.

Introduction

Available survey data suggest that large numbers of survivors who report a history of child abuse also report a period of amnesia or lack of awareness of that history. While the exact percentage of such individuals varies from study to study, over 50 surveys have established that the percentage is substantial, ranging from 20% to 60% of reported victims (cf. Brown, Scheflin, & Hammond, 1996). A reasonable consensus regarding the potential accuracy of such memories has emerged (cf. Knapp & VandeCreek, 1996), and early extremist statements that recovered memories of abuse are virtually always credible or virtually never so have all but disappeared in the professional literature. Less than 8% of experimental psychologists and less than 5% of clinical psychologists believe that accurate recovered memories of trauma are not possible (Dammeyer, Nightingale, & McCoy, 1997).

By the mid-1990s, virtually every relevant professional organization had accepted the potential accuracy of these "new" memories. The American Psychological Association (APA) Working Group on Investigation of Memories of Childhood Abuse (Alpert et al., 1996) concluded that it was "possible for memories of abuse that have been forgotten for a long time to be remembered" (p. 1), joining the American Psychiatric Association (1993) and many professional societies that focus on trauma. Those who reject the very concept of recovered memory (e.g., Ofshe & Watters, 1994,

1999) tend to be journalists and some academics outside psychology. Given the state of near-unanimous agreement among scholars, it is arguably now malpractice for a professional to state to a patient or to testify in a forensic case that a recovered memory is on its face (due to status as recovered) *necessarily* true or false. The ethical professional is thus confronted with several complex clinical situations that are explored here.

Setting aside for now the huge literature on the plausible mechanisms accounting for the recovered memory experience, the clinician specializing in trauma can expect (a) that some clients will have had a phenomenological experience of recovery of a memory of trauma prior to therapy and (b) that some clients will report such an experience within therapy.[1]

The extent of the problem of "false memory" of trauma is much more difficult to ascertain. There appear to be no well-conducted surveys on the phenomenological experience of false memory from trauma (cf. Pope, 1996), although it is described as an epidemic by some authors (e.g., Goldstein & Farmer, 1992). Nonetheless, the anecdotal literature on retractors, those who now believe their memories of childhood trauma to be false, again raises the possibility that therapists will confront such phenomena.[2]

The quotation marks in the headings of the "Recovered Memory" and "False Memory" sections are not meant to imply that either patient type is not exactly what he or she seems. Instead, they are meant to emphasize that we are attempting to address the ethics of treatment for patients who *report* a particular experience—either the experience of amnesia and return of traumatic memory or the experience of acceptance and then rejection of a memory. The former patient, according to varying theorists, could be lifting a repression (Dalenberg, 1994); recovering from dissociation (van der Kolk, van der Hart, & Marmar, 1996); experiencing state dependency of memory (Bower, 1981); reconstructing a true memory from poorly encoded fragments (Jacobs & Nadel, 1998); or constructing a false memory with or without external aid (Loftus & Ketcham, 1994). The retractor could be rejecting a painful truth for motivational reasons (Erdelyi, 1993), again with or without external aid; recovering from a noxious environment in which he or she was pressured to accept a false belief (Loftus & Ketcham, 1994); or simply coming to a different (correct or incorrect) point of view on history based on new evidence (cf. Spence, 1982). Often, the therapist will be in the position of not initially knowing the mechanism that created the patient's experience; in many instances, it will never be known.

The more vociferous battles among recovered memory experts have largely moved into the arena of specific mechanism, for example, critiquing experiments and case studies alleging support for repression and dissociation (Loftus, Joslyn, & Polage, 1998) or critiquing research alleging support for suggestion and false memory (Olio & Cornell, 1998). Pezdek and Banks (1996) compare the debates to "religious wars" (p. xii). Careful thinking that does not confer premature closure on confusing clinical phenomena is necessary for ethical practice.

Ethics and the Treatment of a "Recovered Memory" Patient

The Patient With Suspicion but No Memory of Abuse

We agree with Courtois (1999) that the clinician treating a patient who enters therapy to explore her believed, but unrecalled, history of abuse should first attempt an unbiased assessment of the source of the client's beliefs. At times, the patient who states, "I think I was abused, but I don't know for sure," will reluctantly report a variety of clear and continuous memories of events that are legally defined as abusive, but that the patient is most hesitant to label in this manner. Such initial disclosures may also be a way to "test the waters" with a new therapist—that is, to find out if the therapist will see parental behavior as justified. Since abuse experiences, particularly incest experiences, are frequently associated with shame (Courtois, 1996), such testing of the therapist is quite understandable. A therapist who responds that the existence of doubt or prolonged amnesia is a conclusive sign of the truth or falsity of the recovered memory is not only making an empirically indefensible statement, but also may be missing the point for this patient (cf. Dalenberg, 2000), as well as imposing his or her own version of reality. Such a stance does not show the respect for individual rights and dignity that is one of the foundational principles (Principle E) of the ethical code for psychologists (APA, 2002).

Other reported sources for client's believing in their own abuse (absent memory) are media, popular texts, or support groups who claim the ability to identify abuse victims from checklists of multidetermined symptoms (cf. Gardner, 1992, 1995). Again, passionate belief in the client or faith in unreliable and invalid instruments can push the therapist toward premature confirmation or disconfirmation. The question, "Was I abused?" should not be answered by the therapist for a patient without memories, despite pressure to do so from one in pain because of the disequilibrium such doubt may cause. Gardner's parental alienation syndrome, allegedly useful for identifying false allegations or memories generated by a malicious spouse, has been held by some courts to be not properly admissible.[3]

Another source for client belief without memory may be the wish to have a coherent narrative, a reason for persistent symptoms that both suggest the possibility of a cure and relieve some of the responsibility for psychological difficulties (cf. Spence, 1982). Some authors conceive therapy to be a rewriting of client narrative, and this may be accurate; if so, however, there should be no question regarding who is first author of this biography. The clinician must keep in mind that the client's disclosed reasons for suspicion that he or she was abused may be inadequate for a scholar to affirm the inference as necessary, but this does not mean that other, undisclosed reasons are not more adequate or that firm alternative inferences cannot be drawn that the client was not abused. A parallel may be found in the psychopathology literature, in which it has been shown both that depressives quickly and falsely fear that people have lost sympathy and patience for them (Beck, 1967) and that many people indeed do lose sympathy for such patients (Coyne, 1976; Joiner & Coyne, 1999). Given these reactions, therapists might inadvertently undermine the patient's reality testing by assuming that a conclusion seemingly arrived at through faulty reasoning is necessarily incorrect. Insufficient evidence for presence (insufficient evidence that abuse occurred) is not evidence for absence (evidence that abuse did not occur) and should not be presented as such to the patient. The therapist, on client request, can be a gentle source of alternative hypotheses for the patient without putting therapeutic weight behind only one of these hypotheses. The ethical principles expressing the clinician's duty to show respect for the patient (Principle E, APA, 2002) include the duty not to claim privileged knowledge of the patient's psyche that can be substituted for the patient's self-discovery.

McNally and colleagues conducted a series of studies on repressed memory patients who stated that they believe that they may have been abused as children but who do not recall the abuse (McNally, Ristuccia, & Perlman, 2005). This group epithet is problematic since there is no evidence that this patient group is repressing memories, will recover them, or even that its members have been abused. Even so, McNally's studies focused on a critically important group, one that may be vulnerable to a therapist's suggestion. In general, McNally's research concluded that the repressed memory group reports more depression, dissociative symptoms, and posttraumatic stress disorder (PTSD) symptoms than do those with continuous trauma memories and controls. Thus, patients entering therapy with suspicion of abuse may be highly symptomatic, creating pressure both from the patient and from the concerned therapist to find a coherent and treatable source for the distress.

The patient's decision to hunt explicitly for memories also deserves careful ethical evaluation by the individual clinician, specifically including informed consent obtained from the patient. Pope and Brown's (1996) text on treatment of such patients includes examples of informed consent documents as appendices. Caution is warranted in such a search because some of the techniques that might be used—for instance, hypnosis (Lynn & Nash, 1994) and repeated questioning (Ceci, Huffman, Smith, & Loftus, 1994)—have been empirically linked to increased false reports and increased confidence in the truth of the new material. Nonetheless, in some cases, the patient and therapist might come to a decision that the cost/benefit ratio is weighted in favor of struggling to recover some past information. For example, if an actively suicidal patient who has not responded to standard therapeutic strategies also shows a pattern of symptoms that fit posttraumatic profiles, strategies might be considered, despite their risk of increased false reports, in service of efforts to intervene before the patient seriously harms or kills himself or herself or another. In such cases, the therapist should clearly document the decision to use the technique and would be well advised to seek consultation. The APA (2002) ethics code does provide for the possibility that psychologists will be forced by circumstances to choose techniques and procedures that have not been scientifically established or strategies that do have risks (see Standard 10.01), but stricter requirements for disclosure of the developmental stage of the treatment are required when the treatment is untested (particularly if more well-established treatments are available).

The Patient Reporting a Previous Recovered Memory of Abuse

Given the incidence mentioned (in Brown et al., 1996), the odds are quite good that any therapist conducting therapy in areas related to recovery from trauma will be confronted with a patient reporting a recovered memory experience. Since patients may make life decisions on the basis of such memories, the issue also arises regarding whether the therapist owes a duty to a third party (e.g., the perpetrator accused within the recovered memory) to assess the veracity of this memory and to take a position regarding its likely truth. Although most attempts to assert such a duty through malpractice claims by parents of accusing children have not been successful, particularly when the therapist was not the source of the memory and when the parents had no prior contractual relationship with the clinician (Knapp & VandeCreek, 1996), this ethical question may be a difficult one. The therapist's role as champion of the patient's improved capacity to find personal truths may involve combating the biases of members of the patient's present or previous support system who have demanded disbelief in memories of a patient (perhaps to defend an alleged perpetrator) or demanded belief in memories from a patient struggling with indecision and skepticism. The therapist's advocacy role is not for an end point—namely, that the memory must be true or must be false— but instead for a process that includes reasonable reality-monitoring skills, openness to consideration of alternate explanations of one's own experience, and willingness to tolerate ambiguity in circumstances in which unknowns will continue to exist. The avoidance of declaring knowledge of the client's past, based on symptoms, is suggested by the ethical principle to base one's work on scientific and professional knowledge (Standard 2.04, APA, 2002).

We would argue that the decision to seek external validation also should be made by the patient, who may choose to live with uncertainties rather than force the issue with parents who are physically or mentally ill or who are perceived to be dangerous. It should be noted that in several of the cases in which retractors have successfully sued their therapists, the therapists had engaged in some direct parent contact (such as accepting payment, engaging in confrontation sessions, or mediating in family communication). In one California case, a court of appeal held that when a therapist goes beyond the role of providing therapy to assuming a quasi-prosecutorial or quasi-investigative role, that therapist may be vulnerable to litigation, which again suggests a legal risk in becoming a partner in the investigation to confirm or disconfirm memories.[4] Out-of-the-office field trips to investigate allegations of abuse are particularly likely to lead to liability. The APA (2002) standards on avoiding multiple and exploitative relationships are particularly relevant here (Standards 3.05 and 3.08).

While we join Herman (1992) in her statement that work with victimized people requires a committed moral stance, the therapist as witness, as companion in a difficult journey, need not dictate the nature of that journey. Empathy, which we suggest that therapists display in a clear and strong message, is directed toward the difficulty of the struggle itself and the limited success that is at times achieved.

As the client reexamines memories that emerged in previous therapeutic contexts, the comparison of the present therapy to the previous one is common and may provide the fuel for many ethical missteps. What therapist (what teacher, what poet, what author, what human being) does not wish to hear that his or her own contributions are better, richer, or more profound than those of predecessors? A former therapist who, unlike yourself, was a gullible "recovered memory therapist" or a rejecting "false memory activist" is a handy target for bypassing the hard work of self-examination for both present therapist and client. One cannot combat the negative results for the patient of immersion in dogma by immersion in counterdogma. Again, the therapist must strive for balance, taking care not to take the attractive, but therapeutically dangerous, route of becoming the rescuer, the antithesis of the evil parent or former therapist.

In working with the memory, concentration should be on the patients' experience and their evaluation of internal and external evidence rather than judging the memory as true or false based on the company it formerly kept. If the description of the former therapy and the therapist's judgment of the suggestibility of the patient combine to lead a clinician to believe that the patient adopted the memory as veridical owing to pressure from the former therapist, the new therapist does well to remember that the suggestible patient rarely has lost this characteristic in the time between therapeutic experiences. The greater the possibility that the former therapist has improperly influenced the patient's doubt or certainty, perhaps by claiming privileged knowledge or overreliance on unvalidated checklists, the more important the new therapist's respect for the patient's capacity for independence will come to be. As both patient and therapist succeed in understanding any such processes of influence, those processes can be used to define the boundaries of the existing relationship. Such discussions can and should be quite explicit, recognizing that patient-therapist interactions *are* interactions and may replicate abusive dynamics (Davies & Frawley, 1994), particularly if the therapist does not recognize this possibility and steps into the reality-defining authority role. That is, a well-meaning therapist may replicate abusive dynamics by taking on the burden of deciding what the patients must and must not believe, whom they must or must not love, or what they must or must not do.

The Patient Reporting a Recovered Memory in Present Therapy

A number of compelling reasons can explain or underline why a patient who did not initially remember trauma that has occurred might subsequently recall the trauma in the course of therapy (cf. Dalenberg, 1996). Although belief in the mechanism of repression or repair of dissociation is arguably specific to certain therapeutic orientations, it is more widely understood that discussion of the past may trigger the normal mechanisms relevant to any memory recovery. Therapy may produce renewed motivation to recall, provide associations to long-forgotten events, or reinvoke emotional states reminiscent of such rarely mentioned past events. Hyperamnesia, or memory return, is one normal response to concentration on the details of a past event (cf. Erdelyi, 1993).

The increased discussion of lawsuits by patients, and picketing or ostracism by fellow professionals (Calof, 1998; Pope, 1996), may be affecting more therapists in recent years, leading them to decrease their openness to new victim patients to avoid risk. In the current litigious climate, a therapist may feel pressured to be overly skeptical of client reports to avoid the risk of being sued. But, this skepticism may come at the expense of the client's well-being. The problem is further compounded by the nature of the transference in traumatized persons. In such transference, described as early as 1932 by Sándor Ferenczi (cf. Davies & Frawley, 1994), the client is submissively overcompliant to the signals sent by his or her analyst. While certainly it is within ethical guidelines to avoid patients whose difficulties are beyond one's capacity to help (Principle A and Standard 2.01: "Boundaries of Competence," APA, 2002), it is not acceptable to lead the patient, implicitly or explicitly, to the self-understandings that are in the therapist's best interest rather than those of the patient (Principle A, APA, 2002).

The emergence of a traumatic memory not only leads to predictable increases in existing symptoms (Elliott & Briere, 1995) but also may produce disequilibrium in the therapist-patient relationship. Countertransference disclosure is a reasonable option for a therapist to consider at this point (Dalenberg, 2000; Maroda, 1991), realizing that this period may be a particularly difficult and frustrating time for both participants of the therapeutic dyad.

A second reaction to a recovered memory disclosure that can be counterproductive has been commonly reported in the retraction literature. This reaction involves the therapist's showing intense interest in the recovered material, to the exclusion of other symptom-causing events in the patient's current life (cf. Dalenberg, 2000; Pendergrast, 1995). On the other hand, interest in a patient's memories of trauma may be diminished because of a phenomenon known as *compassion fatigue* (Figley, 1996). In his important theoretical descriptions, Figley defined compassion fatigue as a decreased tendency to respond to trauma with deep empathy because of habituation to the horror of such reports. If patients must "up the ante" to regain the therapist's interest and compassion, it is to be expected that at times they will do so. While dismissing the patient's memory is never recommended, the therapist who continually self-evaluates will address the new memories of trauma while simultaneously increasing empathic attention to other patient issues and known trauma so that the patient does not experience the recovered material as more worthy of attention and sympathy than other memories.

Ethics and Treatment of the "False Memory" Patient

The "Obviously False" Memory

The literature on recovered memory is replete with instances of dismissive comments regarding the gullible therapists who believe in alien abduction, worldwide satanic conspiracies, and cannibalistic cults (cf. Loftus & Ketcham, 1994; Ofshe & Watters, 1994; Pendergrast, 1995). Recovered memory patients may find themselves on the defensive with their new therapists. They may be asked to offer proof for the veracity of their reports and may be seen to be the victims of unscrupulous clinicians; however, even the least-believable forms of recovered memory— alien abduction stories—at times appear to occur independent of any source of implantation. In fact, up to one third of self-labeled abductees claim to have had continuous memories of their abduction experiences (Bryan, 1995).

The ethical issue of how to respond to an improbable memory is thus independent from the reported recovered or continuous nature of that memory. In our own experience, the typical nonpsychotic patient recovering or reporting a highly unlikely memory is quite prepared for the therapist to be less than convinced by the story. Some patients apparently shop for a therapist willing to afford immediate belief or at least to feign such belief. With a patient whose reality testing appears intact, it is most reasonable to disclose one's own biases while (a) not claiming privileged knowledge of the patient's past and (b) not demeaning the patient's belief system. If the therapist can convey an awareness of the plausibility of the belief to the patient (i.e., not give the impression that only a fool would hold belief X), while still admitting their own skepticism, alternatives can be offered as alternatives, not as substitutes necessary to prove the patient's worth or sanity. Such a stance allows change over time without the necessity of losing face.

Therapists facing the "impossible" should also examine their own arrogance in defining the nature of acceptable beliefs. The prominent memory researchers who write of belief in "nonsense," such as past lives or reincarnation, might have been less comfortable writing of nonsense, such as redemption after confession or belief in the Son of God, although as many rational souls may believe in the former as the latter. It is simply not the therapist's job unilaterally to determine that certain of the patient's beliefs are inappropriate per se. Rather, the therapist's ethical interventions might include (a) offering alternative systems; (b) pointing out when existing belief systems appear to be causative of psychic pain; (c) helping clients explore how particular beliefs may serve defensive functions; or (d) teaching modes of hypothesis testing that have been linked to positive client outcomes. No matter what the therapist's moral, political, or scientific view of the patient's beliefs might be, the alternatives offered must be set before the patient as choices to be evaluated on their own merits—with the therapist contributing to the discussion of those merits but not claiming sole authority—rather than presented as requirements for obtaining therapist approval. The exception to this stance is the therapist's clear disapproval of patients engaging in behavior that they acknowledge to be self- or other destructive; disapproval of self-abuse and other abuse is a necessary foundation for any trauma work (cf. Herman, 1992).

Retractors Seeking Their Second Therapist

The issue of false memory may also arise as a person who has recovered memories and later retracted them seeks a second therapist, believing that her first therapist had been consciously or unconsciously promoting the development of the false system. The reader is directed here to the seminal writings of Kenneth Pope on the issue of therapist-patient sex (Pope, 1994; Pope, Sonne, & Holroyd, 1993), in which the therapist must work with a client who has been fundamentally betrayed. The comments made in this chapter about striving not to repeat prior abusive patterns also apply here. Moving the client from an overzealous trauma therapist and a support group of survivors who reward each newly recovered memory, to a champion of false memory syndrome and a support group of retractors who reward each retraction may simply be changing the sergeant to whom the patient is forced to salute rather than turning over control to the individual. This issue is underlined by the researchers who suggest that retractors may be unusually susceptible to social pressure (Reviere, 1997; Singer,

1997), although recovered memory patients are not, as a group, known to be particularly suggestible (Leavitt, 1997).

To date, almost no research attention in the literature has been devoted to the issue that, just as there are true and false recovered memories, there are likely to be retractions of true as well as false memories. The possibility exists that the patient is unwilling or unable to tolerate the pain, symptomatic increase, or disruption in family life that a recovered memory of abuse threatens to cause or has caused. It should not be the second therapist, then, who carves the retraction into stone and distributes blame for the original memory. Again, the present therapist can support the patient's struggle, recognize that recoveries as well as retractions have multiple potential causes, and help the client think through the issues of both veracity and blame. We are aware of therapists on each side of the issue who regularly suggest litigation (even going so far as to hand out attorney cards) against former therapists or childhood abusers. In our opinion, a direct suggestion of this type is always contrary to the therapist's ethical duty to the patient to maintain a clear role (Standard 3.05: "Multiple Relationships," APA, 2002).

The therapist who specializes in recovered memory or false memory owes a special duty of care to the new client, who is likely to know of the therapist's expertise and fear the possibility of being a disappointment. It is helpful to the patient to know that the therapist is aware of the literature suggesting that not all recovered memories or retractions are what they initially appear to be (although many are), and that there is no expectation that a specific patient live out the prototypical scenario of the patient category. Searching for misdeeds of the former therapist is much the same as exaggerating parental mistakes or limitations into malevolent acts against the child. It is more likely to be in the patient's best interest to point out one's own failures and mistakes, taking responsibility for them, praising patient recognition of your (hopefully not frequent) pressure to conform, and noting and affirming his or her independence and self-determination. While the patient learns by example that the former therapy was inadequate, he or she also learns to recognize and resist such pressure in the future, which is often more to the point therapeutically.

Contacting the former therapist is a touchy issue for these patients, particularly if a suit is in progress. When no litigation is involved, special attention should be given to allowing the patient maximal control over the therapist contact; for instance, speaking to the former therapist by telephone only in the presence of the patient and asking for prior approval of any letters sent are reasonable safeguards of patient confidentiality. It is common for patients not to wish for contact between therapists, fearing that the prior therapist will contaminate the present one. However, this fear must be weighed against the loss of information on patient test results, behaviors, and former risk-taking behaviors that might be helpful, or even crucial, to negotiating a new stressful period. Demonizing former therapists allows dismissal of any possible contribution they might provide and is unlikely to be in the patient's best interest. If the patient has reported prior suicidal or destructive behaviors, the failure to attempt to access prior records is a substantial risk that should be specifically addressed in the present therapist's written record.

The Patient Who Retracts in Present Therapy

Many of the issues noted are also relevant to the patient who retracts a belief recovered in present therapy. Litigation fear may push the therapist toward encouraging retraction in the first weeks or toward blocking retraction if the memory has been in place for a period of time. A therapist regularly involved in trauma treatment, however, must model for the patient an acceptance of a process of discovery in which hypotheses about the self are tested, accepted, and rejected in a manner similar to hypotheses about others. Retraction is a danger to the therapy only if the therapist has become overcommitted to the truth of the memory, which is a problem in and of itself. Like traumatic recovery, retraction may produce an increase or decrease in symptoms. With or without such symptom change, the process of retraction can be a substantial life stressor, during which the patient needs a nondefensive and supportive therapist.

Legal Issues Relevant to the Therapist Treating "Recovered Memory" or "False Memory" Survivors

Testifying for the Retractor or Reporter of Trauma

The APA (2002) ethical guidelines allow for the possibility that the therapist may also testify for his or her patient as a fact witness or in an expert role (Standard 3.05c). However, such dual relationships complicate therapy (see Standard 3.05: "Multiple Relationships") since forfeiture of confidentiality through the initiation of a court case may lead to harmful disclosures of private information and may create conflicts of interest (Standard 3.06).

Certainly, the risks and benefits of the decision to enter a forensic arena should be entirely up to the patient. Ready-made packets that allow the patient more easily to sue a parent or therapist with minimum thought or time investment should not be endorsed by professionals. Increased access to this information may necessitate the therapist's intervention to slow an impulsive or angry patient but not to stop the process.

Legal issues in this area are quite complex, thus worth reviewing for the therapist specializing in these areas. A brief historical review of relevant legal issues is presented next.

Third-Party Duty Cases: Adult Patients

Generally, psychotherapists do not owe a "duty to care" to third parties except in a duty-to-warn situation. In various cases around the country, family members who have been accused of sexual abuse by therapy patients have argued for the existence of such a duty. Probably the best-known case of this type is *Ramona v. Isabella* (1994),[5] which arose in Napa County, California, and centered on Holly Ramona, who was then a 19-year-old college student who entered treatment for depression and bulimia. Her therapist, Marche Isabella, asked if she had been sexually abused, citing high rates of abuse among patients with eating disorders. Although Holly initially denied abuse, she recovered memories a year later, after attending a support group. Sodium amytal sessions were then used to investigate the accuracy of those memories. After that, Ms. Ramona confronted her father.

Gary Ramona was an executive with Mondavi Vineyards when he was accused by his daughter of sexual abuse in an action filed in Los Angeles County. He filed a separate action in Napa, California, against Holly's therapist and a hospital, alleging that they had acted negligently and implanted or reinforced her false memories of sexual abuse. His suit constituted one of the first times that these issues were presented to a jury in a case involving an adult patient.

Mr. Ramona obtained a $500,000 verdict. While only appellate court decisions are actual legal precedents, the *Ramona* decision had a profound impact on the debate about repressed memories. A key factor in the trial judge's allowing the matter to go to the jury was a confrontation between Gary Ramona and his daughter that took place on the hospital grounds in the presence of Holly's therapist. Another important factor was that Holly Ramona was administered sodium amytal and questioned under its influence. Mr. Ramona's experts argued that sodium amytal interviews were recognized by the courts to produce unreliable information, a key point in the dismissal of Holly Ramona's suit against her father, after a successful motion by Mr. Ramona's attorneys contending that Holly's memories of abuse after the sodium amytal interviews could not be introduced.

The court of appeal agreed and held that Holly Ramona, the alleged victim, could not be heard regarding her memories of abuse. The trial court in the Ramona case relied on a California Supreme Court decision (*Molien v. Kaiser Foundation Hospitals*, 1980),[6] which held that a medical professional might owe a duty to a nonpatient. In that case, a woman went through a syphilis test at Kaiser Hospital and was erroneously informed that she had syphilis. The physician told her to advise her husband that she had the disease, leading to severe marital problems. The California Supreme Court concluded that the conduct of the physician and hospital were directed against the patient's husband as well as her. While this was seen as a somewhat broad statement of the duty that might be owed to a third party, it has since been limited by the California Supreme Court. In more recent decisions (e.g., *Huggins v. Longs Drug Stores*, 1993), the California Supreme Court held that a precondition to the assertion of any type of direct victim claim is a preexisting relationship between the potential plaintiff and the potential defendant.[7]

In determining whether to find the existence of a third-party duty, some plaintiffs have drawn analogies to the situation in which a patient has a sexual relationship with a therapist and a nonpatient spouse sues. No such cases have found that a duty arises from the therapist to the nonpatient spouse. Thus, this analogy would not seem to support extending any duty to nonpatient family members who are accused of sexual abuse by adult therapy patients.

Several cases outside California have found a duty running from the defendant psychotherapist to nonpatient family members. The first of these was an Illinois federal court case (*Sullivan v. Cheshire*, 1994), in which the parents of a female patient sued her psychologist after she had undergone hypnosis and reported sexual abuse by a sibling. The parents filed suit asserting various theories, including professional negligence, intentional and reckless infliction of emotional distress, and injury to their family relationships. They also contended that the psychologist held himself out as licensed under the Illinois psychology laws when he was not. The U.S. district court hearing the matter specifically concluded that no cause of action could be asserted against the psychologist for malpractice because Illinois law did not allow anyone but the patient to make malpractice claims. The judge further concluded that negligent interference with family relationships would be barred unless the treatment had caused a child to die. The judge concluded that Illinois law would allow an intentional tort suit by the parents for interference with the family relationships.[8] Ultimately, the case went to trial, and the defendant therapist won a defense verdict. In a second Illinois case (*Lindgren v. Moore*, 1995), arising when a father, sister, and brother of a patient sued the patient's therapist for allegedly inducing false memory syndrome, the federal court concluded that, absent a special relationship, no claims could be asserted against the therapist by other family members.[9]

In a Pennsylvania case (*Tuman v. Genesis Associates*, 1995), two parents sued their daughter's mental health counselors after their daughter recovered memories of her parents being involved in sexually assaulting her and participating in satanic rituals. The parents asserted claims for breach of contract, negligent interference with filial relations, intentional infliction of emotional distress, defamation, intentional misrepresentation, and punitive damages. The U.S. district court dismissed the claims for interference with filial relations and emotional distress damages. Because the parents had actually paid for the therapy, the court concluded that their contractual relationship with the defendant therapists gave rise to potential claims if they could meet certain elements. The court held that to maintain a claim for breach of contractual relationship, the parents had to show the following: (a) the therapists had specifically undertaken to treat the daughter for the parents; (b) the parents had specifically relied on the therapists to provide care to their daughter; and (c) the therapists were aware of the parents' reliance on them to provide care to the daughter.[10] Subsequently, the patient filed her own suit against her therapist, alleging that she had not realized that her therapist had been negligent in her treatment of her until she saw her parents' lawsuit and the allegations contained in it.

From these cases, we can deduce certain factors that would lead to a court's allowing a claim to be maintained by third parties, including family members, against a defendant psychotherapist when the patient is an adult. These situations therefore must be taken into account by psychotherapists in treating patients who allege repressed memories of abuse. The circumstances that would appear to give rise to this duty are the following:

1. If there has been a confrontation session at which the patient, the alleged abuser, and the therapist are present, particularly if the alleged abuser does not expect confrontation at the meeting, there is a potential to assert a claim. Mr. Ramona, for example, alleged that the accusation was unexpected and was extremely emotionally disturbing to him. As a general rule, if a parent is going to be confronted, the therapist for the patient should not conduct the confrontation session. It would also be prudent to advise the alleged abuser in writing prior to the meeting that the confrontation is likely to be emotionally distressing, and that issues of sexual abuse will be discussed.
2. When the parents or other family members are paying for the therapy, a contractual obligation may arise to the family members. Thus, psycho-therapists must be careful in deciding whether to allow family members to pay for an adult patient's therapy, particularly when there are allegations of abuse by family members.
3. When the therapist holds collateral sessions with the family members present, some type of quasi-patient relationship may arise.
4. If the therapist uncritically reinforces the patient's memories of abuse, using a position of authority to argue for accuracy rather than allowing for multiple hypotheses to be tested, then it is possible that a court might look to that as a form of negligence.

A comprehensive discussion on the wisdom of having a duty running to third parties in these circumstances is found in Bowman and Mertz (1996), who argued that a number of policy concerns should be considered in allowing third parties to bring suit against therapists. For example, it is reasonable to argue that allowing a family member to bring suit against a therapist would undermine the patient-therapist relationship, thus potentially putting into the hands of abusers a weapon to continue abuse of the patient. Gothard and Ivker (2000) stated that the recent trend in the courts is to support this argument. Citing *Doe v. McKay* (1997), an Illinois case, they recognized that a duty to third parties would be inconsistent with the duty of confidentiality owed to the patient and would require therapists to "divide their loyalty."[11]

Child Patients

The third-party duty issue also exists in regard to patients who were children at the time of treatment and who alleged sexual abuse by parents. There are contradictory decisions around the country on this point. In

Vermont, a U.S. district court held that a father could sue a psychiatrist who treated his son and stepson when the children accused their father of sexually abusing them and being involved in devil worship rituals (*Wilkinson v. Balsam*, 1995).[12] In Colorado, a court concluded that a father who had been accused of sexual abuse by his child could maintain claims against the child's therapist and her supervisor (*Montoya v. Beebensee*, 1988).[13] On the other hand, the supreme court of Texas concluded that a father who was falsely charged with child abuse could not bring an action against the psychologist who had allegedly misdiagnosed the child (*Bird v. WCW*, 1994), stating that "mental health professionals should be allowed to exercise their professional judgment in diagnosing sexual abuse of the child without the judicial imposition of a countervailing duty to third parties."[14]

In a Pennsylvania case (*Althaus v. Cohen*, 1998), a child disclosed to her mother's cancer counselor that her father had molested her. After a report and removal from the home, the child was referred to Dr. Cohen. The child then made increasing numbers of allegations that were dramatic (and at times bizarre). In one analysis of the case, Partlett and Nurcombe (1998) argued that Cohen's liability stemmed from Cohen's decisions to move outside her therapeutic role, becoming involved in criminal proceedings, decisions regarding the child's placement, and the like.[15] Similarly, a therapist who goes beyond the therapeutic role to engage in investigatory activities (regarding the truth or falsity of the allegation) may take on additional liability if the activities are not conducted well (or if the therapist was not trained for such activities). This problem illustrates one reason for the clear distinction between the forensic evaluator (who is ethically obligated to seek outside information) and the therapist (who is not so obligated in most cases).

In approaching these cases, psychotherapists must be clear on what the local state law is with regard to whether a duty to a family member will be found. In any case involving allegations by a child patient of sexual abuse, psychotherapists should be aware that there is a potential for an accused family member to assert a duty to that family member to treat the patient competently and therefore not to reinforce the idea that the patient has been sexually abused. Similarly, however, the child patient, after having attained the age of majority, could assert the duty for the therapist not to automatically *undermine* the idea of sexual abuse (which may be more common, given the likelihood of more salient pressure from the alleged abuser than from the alleged victim).

The problem that the alleged abuser may be a collateral patient is a particular difficulty in child cases since contact with the parent is virtually ensured in cases of therapy with young victims who are still in the home. The potentially greater suggestibility of the child victim, the child's vulnerability to an abuser's threats or requests for secrecy, and the child's lesser knowledge of the gravity of the act of sexual abuse or the gravity of false accusations being made underscore the therapist's responsibility to ensure that the patient's accusations are not being fed to her by an over-interpreting clinician (e.g., symptoms X or Y must mean sexual abuse) or that certain statements (e.g., that abuse did or did not occur) are not being unduly rewarded or punished by the clinician.

Retractor Cases

Suits by retractors have resulted in the largest verdicts of any type of repressed memory cases. As of the date this chapter was written, the three largest damage verdicts in repressed memory cases were recovered by retractors. Two of the verdicts[16,17] were brought by patients against Dr. Humenansky of Minneapolis, alleging implantation of false memories (*Carlson v. Humenansky*, 1996; *Hamanne v. Humenansky*, 1995). The two verdicts combined exceeded $5 million. The largest single verdict to date was $5.8 million awarded to plaintiff Lynn Carl in a suit against Spring Shadows Glen Hospital and psychiatrist Gloria Keraga (*Carl v. Keraga*, 1996).[18] By contrast, other retractor cases have resulted in verdicts as low as $105,000 (*Halbrooks v. Moore*, 1995).[19]

Because the thought processes of jurors are not a part of the court record, it is sometimes difficult to draw accurate conclusions from verdicts. However, some of the jurors in the Lynn Carl case spoke to reporters after the verdict and indicated that they focused on two major areas of concern that are seen in many of the retractor cases: (a) informed consent and (b) the fact that a patient did not improve despite lengthy and expensive treatment over time. The informed consent issue relates to whether a specific recovery technique was used and whether the client was informed (or misinformed) about the likelihood that such techniques would produce accurate memories. Clearly, further discussion among psychologists of the appropriate nature of informed consent is needed (cf. Ebert, 1997).

In addressing the specific instance of repressed memories, a therapist who is utilizing any potentially suggestive techniques such as hypnosis, guided imagery, eye movement desensitization and reprocessing (EMDR), or sodium amytal interviews specifically for the purpose of memory recovery, as opposed to the processing of existing memories, should probably describe the processes more thoroughly. Such communications may include disclosure that memories that arise from using these procedures as recovery aids may or may not be valid. The American Society of Clinical Hypnosis is a resource for sample informed consent forms that psychotherapists may wish to avail themselves of prior to utilizing such techniques. It is better practice to audiotape or videotape each hypnotic session so that the therapist cannot be later accused of using leading questions or implanting memories. In addition, if the therapist is utilizing an unorthodox treatment technique or one not generally accepted, such as past life regression, entity depossession, or alien abduction therapy, the fact that the technique is controversial must be disclosed, and alternative orthodox techniques should be identified.

The other principle that can be inferred from the retractor cases is that, if a jury feels that a patient was falsely led to believe that he or she had been a member of a satanic cult, had murdered children, or had been the victim of vile abuse by family members and that the patient suffered serious emotional distress, the potential for an adverse judgment is quite large. Psychologists are urged in such cases (a) not to overfocus on the bizarre memories; (b) to make clear to the patient that a therapist does not have an investment in the truth or falsity of memories; (c) not to neglect other present-day difficulties of the patient (such as self-mutilation or any other destructive activity); and (d) to address the symptoms allegedly growing out of these events or memories rather than focus on greater and greater detail regarding the memories themselves. Juries also appear to be concerned with the extent to which the therapist played a role in estranging the patient from the patient's family by endorsing cutting off contact with family members or encouraging litigation against family members. Again, the therapist's role would be to explore the likely consequences of varying a decision regarding parent contact, including possible loss of resources and identity or possible gain in self-esteem if abuse is discontinued.

Finally, although the APA (2002) ethical principles are quite clear that a psychologist must keep records (Standard 6.01), many psychologists have the erroneous impression that it is acceptable for them not to take notes or to let the patient dictate whether notes are taken. The obligation to take notes cannot be left to the patient's control. The imperative to take notes is both a practical necessity and an ethical obligation and should include a detailed history taken in the first few sessions. Baseline psychological tests also are extremely helpful. In general, the more unusual or bizarre the memories reported, the more detailed the therapist's notes should be. Psychologists should view with grave suspicion any patient who requests that no notes be taken or who writes descriptions of sessions and then asks that they be returned. An accusation of false memory implantation will be much harder to defend against for the therapist who does not have detailed notes of the process of disclosure.

Summary

As many of the researchers and clinicians cited have argued, the rhetoric of the recovered memory debate has been at times "outlandish, unjustified and needlessly offensive" (Knapp & VandeCreek, 1996, p. 458). However, there is also agreement that part of the emotion is generated by the therapeutic community's inadequate attention to development of a standard of care for these difficult cases. In the face of newly formed consensus statements that recovered memory does exist and must be compassionately included within health care guidelines, more attention to the special needs of these patients should be provided. The guidelines noted are designed to help the professional move toward a balanced and compassionate interaction with clients whose lives have been disrupted by the recovery or retraction of memories of childhood abuse, to encourage further reading to build competence in such treatment, and to give appropriate recognition to the human complexities of trauma treatment.

Notes

1. Poole, Lindsay, Memon, and Bull (1995); Pope and Tabachnick (1995), and Polusny and Follette (1996) reported a rate of 28% in a 1-year time period; Palm and Gibson (1998), who used a longer timeline, suggested a rate of one patient per year on average for a typical clinician.
2. See the personal accounts in Gavigan (1992); Goldstein and Farmer (1992); Gondolf (1992); and Pendergrast (1995).
3. Weiderholt v. Fischer, 160 Wis.2d 524, 485 N.W.2d 442 (1992).
4. James W. v. Superior Court, 17 Cal. App. 4th 246 [21 Cal. Rptr. 2d 169] (1995).
5. Ramona v. Isabella, Case No. 31898 (Cal. Super. 1994).
6. Molien v. Kaiser Foundation Hospitals, 27 Cal. 3d 916 (167 Cal. Rptr. 831, 616 P.3d 813) (1990).
7. Huggins v. Long's Drug Stores California, Inc., 6 Cal. 4th (124, 862 P.2d 148) (1993).
8. Sullivan v. Cheshire, 846 S. Supp. 654 (N.D. Ill 1994).

9. Lindgren v. Moore, 907 F. Supp. 1183 (N.D. Ill 1995).
10. Tuman v. Genesis Associates, 984 F. Supp. 183 (ED PA 1995).
11. Doe v. McKay, 286 Ill. App. 3d 1020, 678 N.E.2d 50 (Ill. App. 2d Dist. 1997).
12. Wilkinson v. Balsam, 885 F. Supp. 651 (D.Vt. 1995).
13. Montoya v. Beebensee, 761 P.2d 285 (Col.App. 1988).
14. Bird v. WCW, 37 Tex.Supp.J. 329, 868 S.W.2d 767 (Tex 1994).
15. Althaus v. Cohen, 710 A.2d. 1147 (Pa. Super. 1998).
16. Carlson v. Humenansky, District Ct., 2nd District, MN, No. CX-93-7260 (1996).
17. Hamanne v. Humenansky, U.S. Dist. Ct., 2nd District, MN, No. C4-94-203 (1995).
18. Carl v. Keraga, U.S. Federal Ct., Southern Dist., TX, Case No. H-95-661 (1997).
19. Halbrooks v. Moore, District Ct., Dallas Co., TX No. 92–11849 (1995).

References

Alpert, J.L., Brown, L. S., Ceci, S. J., Courtois, C. A., Loftus, E. F., & Ornstein, P. A. (1996). *Final report of the American Psychological Association Working Group on the Investigation of Memories of Childhood Abuse*. Washington, DC: American Psychological Association.
American Psychiatric Association. (1993). Statement on memories of sexual abuse. *International Journal of Clinical and Experimental Hypnosis, 42*, 261–264.
American Psychological Association. (2002). Ethical principles of psychologists and code of conduct. *American Psychologist, 57*, 1060–1073.
Beck, A. (1967). *Depression: Clinical, experimental and theoretical aspects*. New York: Harper & Row.
Bower, G. (1981). Mood and memory. *American Psychologist, 36*, 129–148.
Bowman, C., & Mertz. E. (1996). A dangerous direction: Legal intervention in sexual abuse survivor therapy. *Harvard Law Review, 109*, 549–639.
Brown, D., Scheflin, A., & Hammond, C. (1996). *Memory, trauma treatment, and the law*. New York: Norton.
Bryan, C. (1995). *Close encounters of the fourth kind: Alien abduction, UFOs, and the conference at MIT*. New York: Knopf.
Calof, D. (1998). Notes from a practice under siege: Harassment, defamation, and intimidation in the name of science. *Ethics & Behavior, 8*, 161–187.
Ceci, S., Huffman, M., Smith, E., & Loftus, E. (1994). Repeatedly thinking about a non-event: Source misattributions among preschoolers. *Consciousness and Cognition, 3*, 388–407.
Courtois, C. (1996). *Healing the incest wound: Adult survivors in therapy*. New York: Norton.

Courtois, C. (1999). *Recollections of sexual abuse: Treatment principles and guidelines.* New York: Norton.

Coyne, J. (1976). Toward an interactional description of depression. *Psychiatry, 39,* 28–40.

Dalenberg, C. (1994). Finding and making memories: A commentary on the "repressed memory" controversy. *Journal of Child Sexual Abuse, 3,* 109–118.

Dalenberg, C. (1996). Accuracy, timing and circumstances of disclosure in therapy of recovered and continuous memories of abuse. *Journal of Psychiatry & Law, 24*(2), 229–275.

Dalenberg, C. (2000). *Countertransference and the treatment of trauma.* Washington, DC: American Psychological Association.

Dammeyer, M., Nightingale, N., & McCoy, M. (1997). Repressed memory and other controversial origins of sexual abuse allegations: Beliefs among psychologists and clinical social workers. *Child Maltreatment, 2,* 252–263.

Davies, J., & Frawley, M. (1994). *Treating the adult survivor of childhood sexual abuse: A psychoanalytic perspective.* New York: Basic Books.

Ebert, B. (1997). *Informed consent. California Board of Psychology update.* Sacramento: California Board of Psychology.

Elliott, D., & Briere, J. (1995). Posttraumatic stress associated with delayed recall of sexual abuse: A general population study. *Journal of Traumatic Stress, 8,* 629–647.

Erdelyi, M. (1993). Repression, reconstruction, and defense: History and integration of the psychoanalytic and experimental frameworks. In J. Singer (Ed.), *Repression and dissociation* (pp. 1–31). Chicago: University of Chicago Press.

Figley, C. (1996). Compassion fatigue: Toward a new understanding of the costs of caring. In B. Stamm (Ed.), *Secondary traumatic stress: Self-care issues for clinicians, researchers, and educators* (pp. 3–28). Lutherville, MD: Sidran Press.

Gardner, R. (1992). *The parental alienation syndrome.* Cresskill, NJ: Creative Therapeutics.

Gardner, R. (1995). *Protocols for the sex abuse evaluation.* Cresskill, NJ: Creative Therapeutics.

Gavigan, M. (1992). False memories of sexual abuse: A personal account. *Issues in Child Abuse Accusations, 4,* 246–247.

Goldstein, E., & Farmer, K. (1992). *Confabulations: Creating false memories, destroying families.* Boca Raton, FL: SIRS Books.

Gondolf, L. (1992). Traumatic therapy. *Issues in Child Abuse Accusations, 4,* 239–245.

Gothard, S., & Ivker, N. (2000). The evolving law of alleged delayed memories of childhood sexual abuse. *Child Maltreatment, 5,* 176–189.

Herman, J. (1992). *Trauma and recovery.* New York: Basic Books.

Jacobs, W., & Nadel, L. (1998). Neurobiology of reconstructed memory. *Psychology, Public Policy and Law, 4,* 1110–1134.

Joiner, T., & Coyne, J. (1999). On the interpersonal nature of depression: Overview and synthesis. In T. Joiner & J. Coyne (Eds.), *The interactional nature of depression: Advances in interpersonal approaches* (pp. 3–19). Washington, DC: American Psychological Association.

Knapp, S., & VandeCreek, L. (1996). Risk management for psychologists: Treating patients who recover lost memories of childhood abuse. *Professional Psychology: Research and Practice, 27,* 452–459.

Leavitt, F. (1997). False attribution of suggestibility to explain recovered memory of childhood sexual abuse following extended amnesia. *Child Abuse & Neglect, 21,* 265–272.

Loftus, E., Joslyn, S., & Polage, D. (1998). Repression: A mistaken impression? *Development & Psychopathology, 10,* 781–792.

Loftus, E., & Ketcham, K. (1994). *The myth of repressed memory: False memories and allegations of sexual abuse.* New York: St. Martin's Press.

Lynn, S., & Nash, M. (1994). Truth in memory: Ramifications for psychotherapy and hypnotherapy. *American Journal of Clinical Hypnosis, 36,* 194–208.

Maroda, K. (1991). *The power of countertransference: Innovations in analytic technique.* New York: Wiley.

McNally, R. J., Ristuccia, C. S., & Perlman, C. A. (2005). Forgetting trauma cues in adults reporting continuous or recovered memories of childhood sexual abuse. *Psychological Science, 16,* 336–340.

Ofshe, R., & Watters, E. (1994). *Making monsters: False memories, psychotherapy, and sexual hysteria.* New York: Scribner's.

Ofshe, R., & Watters, E. (1999). *Therapy's delusions: The myth of the unconscious and the exploitation of today's walking worried.* New York: Simon & Schuster.

Olio, K., & Cornell, W. (1998). The façade of scientific documentation: A case study of Richard Ofshe's analysis of the Paul Ingram case. *Psychology, Public Policy & Law, 4,* 1182–1197.

Palm, K., & Gibson, P. (1998). Recovered memories of childhood sexual abuse: Clinicians' practices and beliefs. *Professional Psychology: Research and Practice, 29,* 257–261.

Partlett, D., & Nurcombe, B. (1998). Recovered memories of child sexual abuse and liability: Society, science and the law in a comparative setting. *Psychology, Public Policy and Law, 4,* 1253–1306.

Pendergrast, M. (1995). *Victims of memory: Sex abuse accusations and shattered lives.* Hinesburg, VT: Upper Access Books.

Pezdek, K., & Banks, W. (1996). *The recovered memory/false memory debate.* San Diego, CA: Academic Press.

Polusny, M., & Follette, V. (1996). Remembering childhood sexual abuse: A national survey of psychologists' clinical practices, beliefs, and personal experiences. *Professional Psychology: Research and Practice, 27,* 41–52.

Poole, D., Lindsay, D., Memon, A., & Bull, R. (1995). Psychotherapy and the recovery of memories of childhood sexual abuse: U.S. and British practitioners opinions, practices and experiences. *Journal of Consulting and Clinical Psychology, 63,* 426–437.

Pope, K. (1994). *Sexual involvement with therapists: Patient assessment, subsequent therapy, forensics.* Washington, DC: American Psychological Association.

Pope, K. (1996). Memory, abuse, and science: Questioning claims about the false memory syndrome epidemic. *American Psychologist, 51,* 957–974.

Pope, K., & Brown, L. (1996). *Recovered memories of abuse: Assessment, therapy, forensics.* Washington, DC: American Psychological Association.

Pope, K., Sonne, J., & Holroyd, J. (1993). *Sexual feelings in psychotherapy: Explorations for therapists and therapists training.* Washington, DC: American Psychological Association.

Pope, K., & Tabachnick, N. (1995) Recovered memories of abuse among therapy patients: National survey. *Ethics and Behavior, 5,* 237–248.

Reviere, S. (1997). Reflections on false memories, psychotherapy, and the question of "truth." *Psychological Inquiry, 8,* 312–317.

Singer, J. (1997). How recovered memory debates reduce the richness of human identity. *Psychological Inquiry, 8,* 325–329.

Spence, D. (1982). *Narrative truth and historical truth: Meaning and interpretation in psychoanalysis.* New York: Norton.

van der Kolk, B., van der Hart, O., & Marmar, C. (1996). Dissociation and posttraumatic processing in posttraumatic stress disorder. In B. A. van der Kolk, A. C. McFarlane, & L. Weisaeth (Eds.), *Traumatic stress: The effects of overwhelming experience on mind, body, and society* (pp. 303–327). New York: Guilford Press.

12

American Psychological Association and State Ethics Committees

Julia Ramos Grenier and Muriel Golub

American Psychological Association[1]

Ethical behavior within the profession of psychology is governed by ethical principles and a code of conduct. Since the first version of the ethics code adopted in 1952, and published in 1953, through several evolutions leading to the current version (American Psychological Association [APA], 2002), the APA has striven to provide guidance to its members as well as adhere to the association's guiding principle of promoting human welfare. The ethics code, therefore, is designed to protect the public while providing psychologists with aspirational principles and enforceable standards. Enforcement of the code is carried out by the Ethics Committee, which was first formally established by APA in 1947 to develop "guiding principles" (APA Committee on Scientific and Professional Ethics, 1947). The current Ethics Committee has eight members (one is a public member) elected by the APA Council of Representatives and four nonvoting associates who are selected by the Ethics Committee to assist with the work of the committee. When nominating candidates for the Ethics Committee, committee members strive to select individuals who have experience in the ethics process and can provide expertise in particular areas. Also important to this selection process is the need to maintain balance in the female-to-male ratio and to provide cultural diversity.

Since 1996, not only the volume of work of the Ethics Committee but also the complexity of the cases requiring adjudication have increased. While the cause of this increase has not been researched, one can point to such factors as better-educated consumers, the clarity of sanctionable behaviors in the more recent version of the code, and the current code's expansion into such areas of concern as research, teaching, and forensic services. To keep pace with the amount of work, the staff of the APA Ethics Office grew from three in 1985 to 8 in 1990 (APA Ethics Committee, 1991), and then again to 10 plus 2 temporary positions in 1995 (APA Ethics Committee, 1996a). The number of ethics associates (known as fact finders until 1995) also grew from two in 1989 to the current four. Associates participate in the review of cases and attend committee meetings but do not vote on the final committee recommendation. Ethics cases arise from complaints brought by others (complainant cases), from charges lodged by the Ethics Committee (*sua sponte* cases), and from charges following sanctions by other jurisdictions (show cause cases).

Ethics Complaint Procedure

The Ethics Committee's complainant-brought complaint procedure typically begins with an inquiry by an interested party, who may be a client of the psychologist, a family member of a client, or a member of APA. APA members have a time limit of 3 years in which to lodge a complaint, while the public has 5 years. A waiver of this time limit is possible if the allegations are serious and the behavior occurred less than 10 years before filing. Once the Ethics Office receives an inquiry, a check is made to ensure that the psychologist is a member of APA. If a member, a packet is mailed to the prospective complainant, which includes a formal complaint form and information on how to submit a complaint. The complaint form has to be completed, signed, and sent to the Ethics Office before any investigative procedure can be started. Letters of inquiry that are not followed by a completed complaint form are closed. A completed complaint form is reviewed, and supporting materials are requested if they are not already available with the complaint form.

Following review of these materials, the ethics investigator consults with the chair of the committee, recommending either that the matter be closed or that a formal case be opened. If there is insufficient information to determine whether the criteria for opening a case are met, a preliminary investigation may be opened to obtain information from the psychologist against whom the complaint is lodged. The chair may concur with the investigator, or if no agreement is reached between the chair and investigator, the vice-chair of the committee reviews the materials to reach a final determination. If a preliminary investigation is opened, the member psychologist is contacted in writing, is provided the information submitted by the complainant, and is asked to provide information concerning the allegations made by the complainant. On receipt of the information requested during a preliminary investigation, the investigator and chair then decide to close the complaint or to open a formal case. If the complaint is closed, both the member and the complainant are so informed. Rationale for closing the complaint is provided to the complainant only at the specific direction of the committee.

If a formal case is opened, specific charges are lodged and the member is contacted in writing, citing each of the standards at issue and the behaviors alleged to have violated the standards. The member is then required to respond to the charges in writing and can submit any additional information as a defense. Nonresponsiveness to ethics charges is considered an ethical violation. The information submitted by the complainant and the respondent is reviewed by the committee. Committee review of cases is conducted based solely on written information and not on personal appearances by the complainant or the respondent.

The committee meets up to three times per year for 3 days, but the review process actually begins several weeks prior to the meeting. Two committee members are assigned to prepare written summaries of the case and provide preliminary recommendations for sanctions, if any. The other committee members also read the case in detail and participate in any discussion concerning the case. Adjudication of the case takes place at a meeting of the committee, and all of the voting members[2] determine whether the ethics code was violated as charged and decide on any appropriate sanctions, notifications to other entities, and directives (such as cease and desist, tutorial or other educational activities, probation, etc.). Sua sponte cases follow the same procedures as complainant cases.

The procedure for show cause cases follows a different path. Here, the Ethics Committee is usually informed about cases brought against member psychologists by other adjudicating bodies (e.g., licensing boards, courts, etc.). The vice-chair of the committee and an investigator review these cases and decide whether a formal case should be opened. Reasons for not opening formal cases may include such factors as behaviors that do not violate the code, length of time since the infraction, sanctions already fulfilled by the psychologist, and so on. Should the investigator and the vice-chair be in disagreement, the chair is asked to review the case and decide the course of action. As its name implies, a show cause case means that the member has to show cause regarding why he or she should not be expelled from membership in the association for the behavior in question. Therefore, as with complainant cases, the member is asked to provide a written response to the show cause charge, with any supporting information that is available. The committee does not frequently solicit information from any potential witnesses in either complainant or show cause cases but is more likely to do so in sua sponte cases. Show cause cases are reviewed in the same way as the other types of cases, with adjudication by the full, elected committee. Sanctions may range from expulsion from the association to stipulated resignation, resignation while under ethics investigation, or lesser sanctions. Notifications and directives are made as with the other types of cases.

All show cause cases go to the APA Board of Directors, except for those dismissed by the committee. For complainant and sua sponte cases, only the recommendations made by the committee that involve loss of membership go to the Board of Directors, who may accept the recommendation, establish a lesser sanction, or return the case to the Ethics Committee for reconsideration. A case may be stayed by the committee (i.e., action is stopped temporarily) pending the outcome of other processes, such as licensing board reviews and legal proceedings. The Ethics Committee also reviews membership applications when the applicant indicates having had previous legal/ethical violations and when the application is a request for readmission by a member who was previously expelled.

Due Process

Sanctions imposed by the APA frequently have significant impact on the work and even livelihood of members who are found in violation of the ethics code. This is particularly so at this time, when many psychologists must submit such information to review boards, insurance panels, and so on. For this reason, concerns about due process are seriously considered by the Ethics Committee. While the committee considers ethical violations to be a serious matter, it is also concerned that psychologists not be unfairly accused and sanctioned. Due process procedures, therefore, require that the complainant allow the member to respond by signing a waiver of confidentiality, and that the member be provided sufficient time to respond to a complaint. Once the committee makes a recommendation for violation in a case, the member has the right to request review by a three-member independent adjudication panel. The members of the adjudication panel are chosen by the member from a list of six from the full Board of Directors' Standing Hearing Panel. This panel is made up of psychologists throughout the country who are not members of the Ethics Committee and who are appointed by the APA's president. Review of the case is also made with the psychologist being given any supporting information. The decision of this review panel is final.

Another option available when the recommendation is that the member be expelled is a formal hearing before a hearing committee. As with the independent adjudication panel, the hearing committee members are chosen from the Standing Hearing Panel. In this instance, however, the member may be present at the hearing, which is conducted at the APA offices in Washington, D.C. At the time of the hearing, the member is allowed to present any information he or she considers relevant, and the Ethics Committee, represented by the chair, presents the committee's information and opinions. The hearing committee decision is reviewed by the Board of Directors. Neither of these processes is available to complainants, but complainants are allowed to request reopening of a case with the submission of new evidence.

Ethics Committee Data

The Ethics Committee publishes data concerning cases on a yearly basis in an article that appears in the *American Psychologist*. The following information has been summarized from these reports, beginning in 1985.

From 1985 to 2004, the number of inquiries from prospective complainants declined from 288 to 246, although a high of 488 was reached in 1993. It must be noted that not all inquiries lead to a case being opened. In 2004 (APA, 2005), 19 preliminary investigations were opened. In that same year, 20 formal cases were opened in addition to the 55 cases that were carried over from the previous year. This means that a total of 75 cases were active in 2004. As discussed, preliminary investigations and active cases require involvement by the ethics staff and committee members since not only do investigators and the chair and vice-chair review cases but also committee members are assigned as monitors of cases and must communicate regularly with staff. In 2004, 90% of the cases opened were for loss of licensure and 5% for felony conviction, and 50% of the cases included the category of dual relationships in addition to other charges.[3] Dual relationships include sexual misconduct (adult and minor), nonsexual dual relationships, and sexual harassment. Issues involving confidentiality accounted for 5% of the 2004 cases and public statements for 5% of the cases. In 2004, the committee reviewed 6 cases and dealt with 12 actions related to membership, 13 confidential case items, 17 confidential noncase items, and 41 nonconfidential items. One member was expelled, and one member received a stipulated resignation in 2004.

To better understand how the APA's ethics process works, the following fictitious case is followed from the beginning to the end of the review process:

Case Example

Ms. Jones contacts the APA Ethics Office to find out how she may make a complaint against Dr. Doolittle, who she alleges conducted a custody evaluation that led to her losing custody and visitation with her children even though Dr. Doolittle never interviewed her. Following the telephone contact, she sends a letter to the Ethics Office indicating that she is considering filing a complaint against Dr. Doolittle. The Ethics Office sends Ms. Jones the complaint packet, which she completes and sends back promptly. At this point, the office writes to Ms. Jones to let her know that her complaint has been received and is properly filed. An investigator is assigned to the case, and in the case of Ms. Jones's complaint, the investigator determines that based on the documentation provided by the complainant (e.g., reports and transcripts), there appears to be cause for action.

The investigator writes a memo that reviews the pertinent facts of the case and indicates the investigator's opinion to the chair of the committee. In the memo, the investigator cites the ethics code standards that appear to have been violated and describes the behavior that in the investigator's opinion would violate each standard if proven to have occurred. The chair reviews the materials submitted and agrees with the investigator that there is cause for action. A case is opened, citing violations of Standards 9.01 and 9.06, in that Dr. Doolittle allegedly did not personally interview Ms. Jones during a custody evaluation yet formed an opinion regarding her psychological functioning and ability to parent her children; that Dr. Doolittle allegedly did not qualify his opinion concerning the results of the tests he administered to the children based on the fact that the children had been primarily raised in a different country; and that Dr. Doolittle testified during the trial that Ms. Jones is not psychologically fit to parent these children based on her psychological problems, that the children are in need of psychological treatment, and that, "If these children are returned to Ms. Jones's care and live with her in their country of origin, I doubt that there are psychologists who are well trained to provide appropriate psychological treatment in that country." Following this statement, Dr. Doolittle did not acknowledge any possible limitations to this conclusion.

At this point, a charge letter is sent to Dr. Doolittle, with a request for his response within 30 days. Dr. Doolittle writes back 3 weeks later saying that he had been on vacation when the letter from the Ethics Office arrived, and that therefore he needs an extension since he would not be able to prepare an appropriate response in such a short period of time. The investigator writes Dr. Doolittle, granting an extension of an additional 30 days.

In his response to the charge letter from the Ethics Office concerning the charge of having violated Standards 9.01 and 9.06, Dr. Doolittle acknowledges that he never saw Ms. Jones during his custody evaluation because she refused to return from her country of residence to be evaluated. He indicates that he considered this behavior as "diagnostic" of her psychological functioning. In addition, he reviewed several letters that she had written to Mr. Jones and to the children, which he felt revealed significant psychopathology on her part. Based on this information, as well as direct information provided by Mr. Jones concerning Ms. Jones, Dr. Doolittle says that he developed an opinion concerning her psychological difficulties.

Dr. Doolittle states that the children all spoke English, and therefore he did not consider the tests to be biased against them because the tests were normed on English-speaking children. Finally, Dr. Doolittle acknowledges that, as evident in the transcript of the trial, he did make the statement cited, but that he was not asked why he had this opinion about trained professionals in Ms. Jones's country, so he had no opportunity to provide the basis for his opinion or acknowledge the limits of his conclusions.

Since no further information was forthcoming, the monitor assigned to the case and the investigator decided that the case was ready for committee review. Two months prior to the committee meeting, two committee members are assigned as primary and secondary readers of this case. At the time of the committee meeting, the readers present their reviews, and the entire committee discusses the case. Given the information provided by the complainant (e.g., copies of the reports, transcripts of the trial, etc.) and the respondent's response, the committee finds that Dr. Doolittle is in violation of Standards 9.01 and 9.06 since he did not personally assess Ms. Jones to form a diagnostic opinion of her; he did not identify how the results of the tests on the children may have been influenced by their cultural background; and Dr. Doolittle should have provided whatever substantiation he may have had or acknowledged any limitations for his opinion concerning Ms. Jones's psychological functioning, the test results on the children, and his opinion about appropriate treatment for the children in their country.

The Ethics Committee decides to sanction Dr. Doolittle by recommending a censure since his behavior is of "a kind likely to cause harm to another person, but the violation was not of a kind likely to cause substantial harm to another person or to the profession, and was not otherwise of sufficient gravity as to warrant a more severe sanction" (APA, 1996b, p. 14). The harm involved Ms. Jones's loss of custody of the children and being denied visitation rights with them. In addition, the committee issues a cease-and-desist order for Dr. Doolittle not to conduct any other custody evaluations until he has completed (at his own expense) a one-semester graduate course on ethics and a one-semester graduate course on diversity issues and until he has successfully participated in a 20-hour tutorial on custody evaluations. He is to be placed on probation until the completion of all the requirements, and the committee's action is to be reported to the psychology board of his state, the state psychological association, the National Register, the Association of State and Provincial Psychology Boards, and the American Board of Professional Psychology. Dr. Doolittle requests independent adjudication but provides no information that is different from that given to the

Ethics Committee. Thus, the independent panel upholds the Ethics Committee's recommendation.

The Structure and Functioning of a State Ethics Committee

This section discusses the structure and functioning of a state ethics committee and its purpose. Although the discussion is modeled on the Ethics Committee of the California Psychological Association (CPA), some references are made to the ethics committees of other state associations within the United States, especially insofar as ways in which those ethics committees of various state associations differ from one another. The focus of California's ethics committee should be viewed as an example of any state's ethics committee.

One of the hallmarks of a profession, as contrasted to a craft or trade, is the monitoring of the ethical standards of practice of the members of the profession. In addition, professions have written standards for ethical behavior. This is, of course, in addition to the necessity that all members of any profession, as well as members of a trade or craft, follow all applicable laws and legal regulations pertaining to their work. Throughout the United States, the ethics committees of various state psychological associations require that their members adhere to the current (at whatever chronological time) version of the ethics code of the APA. Currently in effect is the 2002 version of the "Ethical Principles of Psychologists and Code of Conduct." These principles and code state and describe the ethical standards of professional psychological practice from the time of the inception of the 2002 version until such time as it is revised. Professional ethical behavior prior to 2002 is measured according to the ethics code that was in effect at the time of the behavior in question. To the present date, there have been six versions of the ethics code of the APA, including the 1989 revision of the 1981 code as required by the Federal Trade Commission. The first code was published in 1953. Other professions, including other mental health professions (psychiatry, social work, marriage and family counseling), each have ethics codes that regulate the ethical practice of their members.

Ethics committees of state psychological associations throughout the United States vary in terms of their field of functioning. Ethics committees have education of members regarding ethical behavior as one of their responsibilities. How this is accomplished varies from state to state and includes such procedures as presentation of workshops, telephone availability for answering questions regarding ethical professional behavior, the writing and dissemination of articles regarding ethical behavior, and so forth. These are not all necessarily done by all state association ethics committees. Many of the determinants of which procedures are used have to do with the size and resources of the state association as well as the willingness of its members to become deeply involved on a pro bono professional level in the development and functioning of its ethics committee.

Some state association ethics committees also investigate complaints about the ethical professional behavior of its members, regardless of whether these complaints are brought by consumers or by colleagues. As long as the ethics committee follows its own written rules and procedures, and those rules and procedures have been approved by at least the state association board of directors and sometimes by the entire association membership, the ethics committee will likely not be held legally liable for its findings, and in some states the ethics committee proceedings will not be available for discovery.

A few states have been investigating the possibility of using mediation as a procedure prior to or instead of the investigation of complaints and the establishment of remedial actions on the part of the respondent in the event that the findings of the ethics committee do reveal unethical behavior on the part of the psychologist. This has not become widespread at the present time and is not being done by the CPA Ethics Committee.

State association ethics committees have, as a bottom line, the threat of expulsion of members from the professional association. This is in direct contrast with recourses and resolutions available to state licensing boards and through civil complaints (such as malpractice suits). However, in these days when society is litigious and malpractice insurance coverage is essential, such insurance coverage may be in jeopardy if there is an unresolved complaint (especially one that ended in expulsion because a member was not cooperative with the ethics committee investigation.) As have earlier APA codes, Section 1.06 ("Cooperating with Ethics Committees") of the "Ethical Principles of Psychologists and Code of Conduct" (APA, 2002) says:

> Psychologists cooperate in ethics investigations, proceedings, and resulting requirements of the APA or any affiliated state psychological association to which they belong. In doing so, they address any confidentiality issues. Failure to cooperate is itself an ethics violation. However, making a request for deferment of adjudication of an ethics complaint pending the outcome of litigation does not alone constitute noncooperation. (p. 1063)

In addition, many managed care companies and hospitals are questioning in their participation agreements whether there is currently, or has ever been, a complaint against the applicant. In the event that there has been one, often a letter of explanation from the applicant is necessary, attesting to the nature of the complaint, the kinds of remediation (if any) required of the applicant, and whether the remediation was completed.

Another function of many ethics committees, including the CPA Ethics Committee, has to do with the screening of all applicants for membership, for possible ethical violations, or for instances of unethical behavior. In addition, all requests for termination or lapse of membership are screened by the CPA Ethics Committee as a CPA member is not permitted to resign from CPA membership while there is an ongoing ethics investigation in progress. Generally, in this situation the member is not required to continue to pay professional membership dues but may not officially terminate membership in the association until such time as the investigation is completed.

The CPA Ethics Committee sends all of the ethics complaints they receive directly to the California Board of Psychology (BOP). The CPA Ethics Committee stopped reviewing complaints in June 2004. Educational efforts are made through the provision and preparation of annual ethical practice workshops in a number of areas, including but not limited to such areas as clinical practice, forensic practice, and managed care interactions and practice. An attempt is always made to include information provided by an attorney regarding the legal responsibilities of a practitioner, as well as some information from a malpractice insurance carrier about current trends in malpractice cases and suggested ways to protect oneself from such a case through legal and ethical practice patterns.

In addition, members of the CPA Ethics Committee constitute and staff a regular ethics hotline, which is available to consumers with questions about the ethical responsibilities of psychologists and is available to member psychologists. For questions that are legal in nature, callers are requested to contact an attorney for legal advice. This service is not available to nonmember psychologists, to whom the suggestion is made to seek consultation from an expert in ethics in professional practice at the expense of the nonmember psychologist. Occasionally, a written request for information and guidance will come to the attention of the CPA Ethics Committee. In this event, such requests from consumers and members receive a response, and nonmembers are again referred to a paid ethical practice consultant of their choice and at their own expense. There has also been a fairly regular stream of articles dealing with matters of ethical concern and interest to member psychologists; these are published regularly by *The California Psychologist,* CPA's regular publication distributed to all members.

The CPA no longer investigates ethics complaints, but in the past when they did there was the consideration of anonymity. Although the CPA has 22 local chapters, these chapters could not provide sufficient anonymity among members of the local chapters for those local chapters to conduct ethics complaint allegation investigations against local members. One of the advantages of being a state association in a state as large as California is that almost always there is a majority of the members of the CPA Ethics Committee who are not even slightly acquainted or involved with either the complainant or the respondent. To process an ethics investigation that guarantees the highest possible degree of due process for both the complainant and the respondent, it is necessary that all those who are involved with the investigation have no knowledge of or acquaintance with either the complainant or the respondent.

In the past, in the event that a member of the CPA Ethics Committee was familiar with either of the parties involved, the members were recused and absent the room when any discussion of the case was. This was also true of the ethics chair, who turned the chair over to the vice-chair in the event that any parties involved were known to the chair. Previously, in the event that a majority of the members of the CPA Ethics Committee did know either the complainant or the respondent, then the complainant was notified of this in writing, and a recommendation was made to the complainant to pursue the complaint with either the BOP or the APA Ethics Committee if the Respondent was indeed an APA member. Now, the CPA sends all of the ethics complaints directly to the BOP.

Prior to 1994, in the event that the respondent was unknown to the members of the CPA Ethics Committee but was neither a member of the CPA or of the APA, a check was made regarding whether the respondent was a member of the respondent's local professional association. If this was the case, the ethics committee of the local chapter may have contracted at no charge with the CPA Ethics Committee to have the CPA Ethics Committee conduct the investigation and make recommendations on behalf of the local chapter's ethics committee. In general, the role of the ethics committees of the local chapters is that of education and of referral of complaints to their appropriate recipients.

The CPA Ethics Committee is considered to be the largest state association ethics committee in the nation. According to the rules and procedures, a total of 33 people may serve as members, although generally membership is up to about 15 members. Committee members are appointed to the CPA Ethics Committee by the CPA Board of Directors on the recommendation and request of the chair of the Ethics Committee. Terms of membership are for 3 years and are renewable by the CPA Board of Directors, with the request and recommendation of the ethics chair.

Ethics chairs serve for a 1-year period and are appointed by the CPA Board of Directors at the request and recommendation of the current CPA president. It is highly recommended that the CPA Ethics Committee chair be someone who has had considerable experience within the field of ethics and has served on the CPA Ethics Committee for a significant period of time. This is especially important since the chair is responsible for the overall flow of work, both educational and investigational, and the work must follow the rules and procedures to protect the committee and the state association from legal jeopardy. In California, the ethics chair serves on a pro bono basis, as do all CPA officers, directors, committee chairs, and members of all CPA committees.

In addition to the members of the CPA Ethics Committee, occasionally pro bono consultants are used in the processing and investigation of a complaint. These are professionals who are recognized as expert in a particular needed area or ethics expert consultants. The CPA Ethics Committee may use such consultants, provided that confidentiality is maintained regarding the identity of the complainant and the respondent.

Membership on an ethics committee needs to be representational of the constituency that it serves. This includes factors such as (a) male/female ratio; (b) geographic diversity; (c) diversity of ethnicity, sexual orientation, religion, and age; (d) urban, suburban, and rural area representation; (e) areas of professional specialization; (f) arenas of practice (e.g., private, governmental or other public or agency service, educational, managed care, and others); (g) graduate schools (accredited/approved, public/private university/training schools, and others); (h) variation in number of years of licensure; and (i) other factors such as political affiliation, socioeconomic level, and others. In addition, consideration must be made for special areas of competence needed by the ethics committee as well as prior experience in ethics. Such experience may include, but is not limited to, ethics experience at the local chapter level, the teaching of courses in ethics, published writings or verbal presentations in ethics areas, as well as other experience that must be evaluated on an individual basis.

CPA Ethics Committee meetings are held no less that six times a year, with each meeting lasting approximately 6 hours. Subcommittees are assigned for various functions; while these are generally three people, major efforts such as convention programming and presentation require larger subcommittee membership. One member of each subcommittee is appointed by the Ethics Committee chair as the person responsible for the monitoring, coordination, and reporting of the progress of the particular subcommittee task. In the past, when the task of the subcommittee involved a complaint investigation, the person responsible for monitoring, coordination, and reporting was referred to as the principal investigator (PI). These subcommittees vary in membership according to specific needs of the particular task, interest, and expertise of the subcommittee members and time availability. An attempt is always made to spread the workload evenly across the membership, with the exception of the workload of the Ethics Committee chair, which is quite different in function and requires greater time commitment than does that of committee membership.

In addition to verbal communication with the members of the CPA Ethics Committee hotline, a large number of written inquiries are received by the Ethics Committee. In 1994, there were 104 written inquiries, and in 1995 there were 159 written inquiries. These inquiries include requests for complaint forms; requests for ethics advice or information, written and public copies of accusations, stipulations, and decisions by the BOP; requests for new membership screenings if the applicant for membership indicated on his or her application for membership that there were (or are) complaints against them of unethical behavior or violations of criminal or civil law; and requests for varied other documents. With the exception of those few written communications that require no response but are simply informational in nature, all written communications receive a response or begin some chain of action.

If the written communication is a complaint form, a case may be opened following various screening measures. The complaint must be against a member of the association for CPA to have valid jurisdiction. The complainant is directed to refer the complaint to the BOP or to the APA Ethics Committee if the respondent is an APA member.

If the complaint is already being investigated by the APA Ethics Committee, the CPA Ethics Committee will not open and pursue an investigation. This is because having the same complaint investigated by two (or more) ethics committees may represent a situation in which the respondent is faced with a kind of "double jeopardy." In the event that the same complaint is or has been reported to the BOP, the CPA Ethics Committee will not initiate or pursue an active investigation until the BOP has advised the complainant, in writing, of the results of the investigation of the complaint by the BOP. In some situations, the BOP's response to the complainant is that there are no apparent legal violations, but that there may be ethical violations. In other situations, the BOP's response may be to ascertain that the complaint is legal in nature, and that they will be investigating and making any necessary mandated recommendations. In still other situations, the complaint may be found to have both legal and ethical components.

In addition to formal completed ethics complaint forms received by the CPA Ethics Committee and to decisions made by the BOP, there is yet another source from which complaints may come. A sua sponte case is one in which a report has come to the attention of the Ethics Committee that a CPA member has been convicted of violating criminal, civil, or administrative laws or regulations or where there is evidence of a possibility of unethical professional behavior on the part of a CPA member as reported through the public media.

Occasionally, a preliminary investigation is done when there does not seem to be enough evidence to warrant the formal opening of a case or in the event that there is confusion about what the complainant is actually alleging as unethical behavior on the part of the respondent. Generally, however, if a complaint has met all of the criteria mentioned, then a formal complaint case is opened. There are approximately 22 complaints filed each year, but only about 10 of them become open cases each year.

Once a case is officially opened, the respondent is apprised of the identification of the complainant and of the exact nature of the complaints that have been set forth, including a list of the principles/standards alleged to have been violated. At that point, the respondent is advised to seek legal counsel, although all responses must come from the respondent personally. Communications from attorneys representing the respondent (or the complainant) will not be answered except with a letter that points out that all communication must come from the respondent (or the complainant) personally.

It is at this point that there is generally for the first time an awareness on the part of the psychologist of the existence of a complaint alleging unethical behavior. The allegation of unethical behavior does not mean that it is certain that unethical professional practice has occurred. Rather, it is the responsibility of the CPA Ethics Committee to investigate any signed complaint as long as the identification and specifics about the nature of the allegations can be presented to the respondent. (If there are anonymous complaints or complainants who request and maintain that there be no notification to the respondent of the identity of the complainant and the exact nature of the allegations, the complaints are destroyed.)

Just as there are with legal cases, there are several statutes of limitations that must be observed. If a complaint is being made by a member of the mental health professions, it must be made within 2 years of the time the alleged behavior occurred, was discovered, or should have been discovered. In the event that the complaint is being made by a consumer of psychological services, then the statute of limitations is increased to 5 years. If the complaint is about a situation involving allegations of serious exploitation of a patient or patients, then the statute of limitations may be lifted on a two-thirds vote of the majority of the members of the CPA Ethics Committee. In this situation, as in all others involving decisions made by vote, the chair votes only to make or break a tie. Beyond this provision, the statutes of limitations used by the CPA Ethics Committee are inflexible.

There are many possible decisions and recommendations that may come about as a result of an investigation into an allegation of unethical professional behavior. These range from a finding of "no violation" to the other extreme of a recommendation to expel from association membership because of a failure to cooperate with the CPA Ethics Committee. Between these extremes are such recommendations as the following, as listed in Section IV.D. of the Rules and Procedures (CPA Ethics Committee, 2008):

1. Respondent be required to modify or stop certain practices;
2. Respondent make restitution or apology to any individual, group of individuals, or organizations affected by the unethical behavior;
3. Respondent be censured or receive some other reprimand by the Committee;
4. Respondent be placed under a period of supervision and/or psychotherapy with fixed terms specified by the Committee and agreed to by the Respondent;
5. Ethics Committee formally recommends to the CPA Board of Directors that the Respondent's CPA membership be suspended for a specific period of time or until certain conditions be met;
6. Ethics Committee formally recommend to the CPA Board of Directors that the Respondent's membership in CPA be terminated through stipulated resignation; or
7. Ethics Committee formally recommend to the CPA Board of Directors that the Respondent's membership in CPA be terminated by expulsion. The Committee may recommend that the expulsion be permanent or that certain conditions, such as the elapse of a specified time period and/or the completion of a course of remedial action be met

before CPA reconsider the Respondent's application for readmission to membership.

In the event that the respondent does not agree with the findings of the CPA Ethics Committee, there are provisions in the rules and procedures for a special hearing to be held. Here, the matter is turned over to a special hearing panel, comprised of three CPA members and one alternate panel member who have been members of the Ethics Committee in the past but are not currently members of the Ethics Committee. There are formal regulations regarding the procedures to be used before, during, and after a special hearing. Again, although an attorney may be present to be available to the respondent (or complainant) for consultation purposes, all participation in the special hearing must be done by the involved individuals themselves. If a respondent refuses to attend such a special hearing, the special hearing will be held nevertheless. If a complainant or witness does not appear at such a special hearing, then all written statements of the complainant (or any absent witnesses) will not be received in evidence. The complainant or witnesses must appear at the special hearing for their written statements to be used, and the respondent is afforded the opportunity to question the complainant and any witnesses regarding their testimony.

The special hearing may result in the findings or recommendations of the CPA Ethics Committee being accepted, rejected, or modified. This is binding on the Ethics Committee unless the Ethics Committee determines that the special hearing panel's findings are not supported by a reasonable standard of evidence, or that the recommendations are clearly disproportionate to the ethical violations found. The right to request a special hearing must be exercised within 30 calendar days following receipt of the CPA Ethics Committee's notification regarding resolution of the case.

All of the previous procedures and responsibilities on the part of the Ethics Committee require strong support staff. All materials received must be identified and logged. Deadlines must be met or noted as having been passed by the respondent (or complainant), accurate minutes must be taken and preserved, and all correspondence regarding cases must be carefully prepared and then sent by certified mail (return receipt requested). A record must be maintained of when each piece of mail is received by its intended recipient. The rules and procedures also specify how and what material is to be preserved and for what periods of time. Accurate tracking, copying, and distribution of confidential case materials are imperative, as is the need to maintain absolute confidentiality in all case matters.

Since the greatest legal vulnerability that any state psychological association faces has to do with accuracy and care in the structure, functioning, and following of established procedures of the ethics committee, one can readily see why high professional demands are made of ethics committee support personnel, ethics committee members, and the ethics committee chair.

The role of the ethics committee is of paramount importance in the maintenance of psychology as a profession, rather than as a trade or a craft. This role must be performed in a manner that provides maximum objectivity and due process, while at the same time providing for a high level of efficiency and a corresponding reduction in the legal vulnerability of the state psychological association.

Conclusion

In conclusion, this chapter discussed the APA and state ethics committees' complaint procedures to demystify the anxiety-provoking process of a formal ethics complaint. It is important to keep in mind that nonresponsiveness to ethics charges is considered an ethical violation by itself. In the description of the due process procedures, the seriousness of these procedures was highlighted because of the tremendous impact that violating the ethics code can have on the work of a mental health professional. Therefore, the committees are also concerned that mental health professionals not be unfairly accused or sanctioned. The need to perform the role of an ethics committee in an objective and efficient manner was highlighted in the description of the structure and functioning of the APA and state ethics committees.

Notes

1. It is not the intent of this chapter to provide a thorough review of all of the procedures followed by the APA Ethics Committee, but rather to provide a general overview of the more common procedures and some recent data. For a complete delineation of the committee's procedures, please refer to the rules and procedures (APA Ethics Committee, 1996b). Note that the rules are frequently revised and may be supplemented by committee policies.

2. Committee members who have prior knowledge of any aspect of a case are recused from discussing and voting on the case.
3. Some overlap results in more than 100%.

References

American Psychological Association. (2002). Ethical principles of psychologists and code of conduct. *American Psychologist, 57,* 1060–1073.

American Psychological Association. (2005). Report of the ethics committee, 2004. *American Psychologist, 60,* 523–528.

American Psychological Association Committee on Scientific and Professional Ethics. (1947). Report of the committee on scientific and professional ethics. *American Psychologist, 2,* 488–490.

American Psychological Association Ethics Committee. (1991). Report of the ethics committee: 1989 and 1990. *American Psychologist, 46,* 750–757.

American Psychological Association Ethics Committee. (1996a). Report of the ethics committee, 1995. *American Psychologist, 51,* 1–8.

American Psychological Association Ethics Committee. (1996b). Rules and procedures. *American Psychologist, 51,* 529–548.

Cslifornia Psychological Association Ethics Committee (2008). Rules and procedures.

Glossary

Bench Trial: A trial in which there is no jury and the judge decides the case.

Civil Lawsuit: A civil action brought before a court in which the party commencing the action, the plaintiff, seeks a legal remedy. Often, one or more defendants are required to answer the plaintiff's complaint. If the plaintiff is successful, judgment will be given in the plaintiff's favor, and a range of court orders may be issued to enforce a right, impose a penalty, award damages, impose an injunction to prevent an act or compel an act, or obtain a declaratory judgment to prevent future legal disputes.

Claim: The making of a demand (asserting a claim) for money due, for property, from damages or for enforcement of a right. If such a demand is not honored, it may result in a lawsuit.

Defendant: The person a lawsuit is brought against.

Demonstrative Evidence: That evidence addressed directly to the senses without intervention of testimony. This evidence may include maps, diagrams, photographs, models, charts, medical illustrations, x-rays.

Deposition: The taking and recording of testimony of a witness under oath before a court reporter in a place away from the courtroom before trial. A deposition is part of permitted pretrial discovery (investigation), set up by an attorney for one of the parties to a lawsuit demanding the sworn testimony of the opposing party (defendant or plaintiff), a witness to an event, or an expert intended to be called at trial by the opposition.

Discovery: The entire efforts of a party to a lawsuit and his, her, or its attorneys to obtain information before trial through demands for production of documents, depositions of parties and potential witnesses, written interrogatories (questions and answers written under oath), written requests for admissions of fact, examination of the scene, and the petitions and motions employed to enforce discovery rights. The theory of broad rights of discovery is that all parties will go to trial with as much knowledge as possible, and that neither party should be able to keep secrets from the other (except for constitutional protection against self-incrimination).

Dual Relationship: A secondary relationship to the therapeutic one that is either contemporaneous or subsequent in time. Dual relationships are not per se unethical. Unethical dual relationships involve either impartment to the therapist judgment or exploitation of the patient.

Expert Witness: A person who is a specialist in a subject, often technical, who may present his or her expert opinion without having been a witness to any occurrence relating to the lawsuit or criminal case. It is an exception to the rule against giving an opinion in trial, provided that the expert is qualified by evidence of his or her expertise, training, and special knowledge. If the expertise is challenged, the attorney for the party calling the "expert" must make a showing of the necessary background through questions in court, and the trial judge has discretion to qualify the witness or rule that he or she is not an expert or is an expert on limited subjects.

"False Memory": A memory of an event that is not true but that a patient may believe to be true.

Forensics: Used for the purposes of the law and therefore provides impartial scientific evidence for use in the courts of law and in a criminal investigation and trial.

Guardian Ad Litem: A person appointed by the court only to take legal action on behalf of a minor or an adult not able to handle his or her own affairs. Duties may include filing a lawsuit for an injured child, defending a lawsuit, or filing a claim against an estate.

Litigation: Lawsuits or administrative actions.

Malpractice: Negligent or unintentional acts by mental health professionals.

Percipient Witness: A mental health professional who has observed facts and circumstances in the case.

Plaintiff: The party who initiates a lawsuit by filing a complaint with the clerk of the court against the defendant(s) demanding damages, performance, or court determination of rights.

Privileged Communication: Conversation that takes places within the context of a protected relationship, such as that between an attorney and client, a husband and wife, a priest and a penitent, and a doctor and patient. The law often protects against forced disclosure of such conversations.

Professional Liability: Coverage designed to protect professionals against liability incurred as a result of errors and omissions that may be negligent or unintentional acts in performing professional services.

Recovered Memory: A purported memory that is suppressed for a period of time and then recalled, usually several years later. The memories may be spontaneously recalled or recalled as part of a course of psychotherapy.

Sexual Misconduct: An act of sexual intercourse, oral sex, genital contact, or sexual harassment with a present or former patient. In some states, the use of sexual innuendo may be seen as sexual misconduct.

Special Master: Mental health professionals who have previous experience in the family court system. Special masters are given decision-making powers that are used when parents are unable to reach resolution on conflicted issues. This hybrid role, which combines mental health, mediation, and legal functions, raises complex ethical issues.

Index

The Contributors

Donald N. Bersoff consults with attorneys and mental health professionals on ethical issues. He received his PhD from New York University in 1965 and his JD from Yale Law School in 1976.

Margaret A. Bogie, MHSA, is a licensed insurance consultant specializing in mental health professional liability issues for the last 25 years. She consults with national professional associations and insurance carriers on professional liability issues.

Eve Carlson, PhD, is a research health science specialist with the National Center for PTSD and the VA Palo Alto Health Care System. She conducts research on the psychological impact of traumatic experiences, with a focus on assessment.

O. Brandt Caudill Jr., JD, has been representing mental health professionals in civil and administrative litigation for over 20 years. He holds a JD from Georgetown University Law Center.

Constance Dalenberg, PhD, is the director of the Trauma Research Institute and a professor in the PhD Clinical Psychology Department at Alliant International University in San Diego, specializing in the treatment and evaluation of trauma survivors.

Russell S. Gold, PhD, specializes in child custody cases and psychotherapy. He maintains an independent practice in San Diego, California, and holds an adjunct position in psychology and family law at Alliant International University, San Diego.

Muriel Golub, PhD, obtained her doctorate degree in clinical psychology in 1975 from United States International University in San Diego, California. Dr. Golub worked at Family Services in Orange County, California, and is currently in independent clinical practice.

S. Margaret Lee, PhD, is a licensed psychologist whose work focus is providing services to divorcing families. Dr. Lee obtained her doctorate in clinical psychology at California School of Professional Psychology in 1978.

Eric C. Marine has been vice president of claims for the American Professional Agency Incorporated since 1991. He directs risk management education efforts for psychiatrists, psychologists, counselors, and social workers for the agency.

Reed M. Mueller, PhD, is a licensed psychologist and vice president of Pacific Research and Evaluation, a program evaluation firm. He earned his doctorate in clinical psychology at Brigham Young University, where he focused on clinical research in psychotherapy outcomes.

Julia Ramos Grenier, PhD, ABPP, is a past member and chair of the APA Ethics Committee and is currently a neuropsychologist with the Tucson Unified School District.

Richard Romanoff, PhD, is an associate clinical professor of psychiatry at UCLA Medical Center and a former member of the California Psychological Association Ethics Committee. He specializes in the area of criminal forensic evaluations.

David D. Stein holds a PhD in psychology (social) from the University of California, Berkeley. He has been in full-time independent practice in clinical and forensic psychology in San Francisco since 1992.

Commissioner Pamela Thatcher hears matters as a judge pro tem for the Riverside, California, Superior Court. With an undergraduate background in history and political science, she is a graduate of the Los Angeles Loyola Law School (JD, 1983).

Arthur N. Wiens holds a doctorate (PhD) and a diplomate (ABPP) in clinical psychology and is professor emeritus in medical psychology at the Oregon Health and Sciences University, where he has taught since 1961.